D0546710

ANCIENT GREECE

ANCIENT
GREECE

AN EXPLORER'S GUIDE

text and photography by

Robert Emmet Meagher & Elizabeth Parker Neave

Interlink Books

An imprint of Interlink Publishing Group, Inc.
Northampton, Massachusetts

First published in 2008 by

INTERLINK TRAVEL
An imprint of Interlink Publishing Group, Inc.
46 Crosby Street, Northampton, Massachusettts 01060
www.interlinkbooks.com

Text copyright © Robert E. Meagher and Elizabeth P. Neave, 2008
Photography and maps provided by Robert Meagher

CONTENTS

PREFACE

This guide, like our earlier volume entitled *Ancient Ireland: An Explorer's Guide*, is meant for the explorer, not the expert. Explorers, no matter how much they may have already seen and experienced, remain driven by the unknown, the unseen. Once the known eclipses the unknown, exploration gives way to exposition. But where to look for the unknown? Deep space? Deep water? The future is largely unknown. But so is the past, for most people today. Besides, the future often repeats the past and proves all too predictable, while the past still holds many surprises.

"Explorers" may seem to be an overly romantic description for the readers, as well as the writers, of this guide. Everywhere we propose to explore is, after all, already on the map, well-marked and well-trodden. We carry no shovels, only books. We have read, many of us widely for many years, about everything we finally set out to see for ourselves. In one sense, then, we have "already been there." The shock in store for us at most every ancient site, however, is that what we have come to know so vividly in our studies, rarely awaits us in our travels. The experience we have is something like finally meeting in person, after a lifetime of awe and emulation, a childhood sports hero, the spark of so many aspirations. How could the bent, exhausted, ninety-four-year-old man or woman before us have once electrified millions and won six Olympic gold medals? Without all that we bring to the encounter—the stories, the voices, the images from old photographs and newsreels, the sheer acknowledged fact of this person's greatness—without all this, we might never even notice the figure in front of us. To one degree or another, the same may be said of most ancient sites. In a word, they are "ruins." They are all far from intact. They are often wildly

Kouremenos Bay from the Peak Sanctuary of Petsofas, Crete.

out of context in their contemporary settings, and their "ghosts"—the great souls who spilled their blood, unleashed their dreams, poured out their poems, or shared their wisdom within these precincts—are gone, long since expired, exorcized, exhausted.

Something, however, survives in these ruins, something that can't be touched elsewhere. Why else would millions of foreign visitors from virtually every corner of the planet make their way annually to the Parthenon or Delphi or Mycenae or Knossos or Delos or Marathon, pause, wonder, pay their respects and then proceed to the beaches, tavernas, shops, all the delights and distractions of contemporary Greece? Some leave unimpressed, empty, wondering why the big fuss, while others leave electrified, ablaze. What accounts for this difference? The simple difference lies in what visitors bring with them to these sites. It is not enough to bring a camera and a bottle of mineral water. The difference between the tourist and the pilgrim lies in the imagination, the mind, and the heart of the traveler. It's a matter of what he or she knows and has learned to love and care about. Ruins, unlike theme parks, leave something, in fact almost everything, up to the imagination. It comes down to stories, big stories, the kind that expand the soul, stir and sometimes break the heart, and change someone forever, make them who they are. These are the tinder that pilgrims carry in their arms. This is why they go up in flames at Delphi while others only sweat.

Explorers stand somewhere between tourists and pilgrims. Tourists won't be interested in this volume, and pilgrims won't need it. Explorers are often short on knowledge and high on curiosity. They want to know and see more, because they know it's a big world out there, and also back there, and they've run out of space, if not air, in the world they inhabit. They want more, and not more of the same. They want to learn, encounter, inhabit something new; and somewhere they've heard or come to be convinced that the past is as good a place as any, and better than most, to find something new, something wonderful. It is this conviction that lies at the root and the core of this book; it is what, from the outset, we share with you, its readers.

In a land as hospitable as Greece, it would require another volume the size of this one to thank by name everyone who has made our journeys as friendly, exciting, and amusing as ours have been. As you travel through Greece, you will quickly compile your own list. Certain friends and colleagues, however, have been especially welcoming and generous to us in this effort; so we extend our special heartfelt thanks to: Stephen Tracy, director, American School of Classical Studies, Athens; Don Evely, curator, British School of Athens, Knossos; Heinrich Hall, director, Irish Institute of Hellenic Studies at Athens; and John Dillon, Regius Professor of Greek, Trinity College Dublin, Emeritus and president, Irish Institute of Hellenic Studies at Athens. We also want to express our admiration and gratitude to Professor J.V. Luce of the Royal Irish Academy and Trinity College Dublin, whose sage reflections on the Minoans and Mycenaeans truly grace this volume. Then we will never forget our long spring sojourn on Santorini, where Triantafyllos Pitsikalis and Erika Moechel-Pitsikali opened their hearts to us as we did ours to them; nor will we ever cease to wonder if there might not be after all a sliver of mischievous, displaced divinity in their ebullient son Apollon, who neglected no opportunity to remind us that he was a "super-hero" if not a god.

Here, on the home front, where ideas become projects, and notes become books, we are once again indebted, more than we can express, to the Olympians of Interlink Books: Michel Moushabeck, Pam Thompson, Juliana Spear, and Moira Megargee. Their warmth, brilliance, trust, patience, and artistry have made Interlink a press nearly without peers and for us, as writers, a treasured home.

Lastly, we thank our readers for entrusting some of the most precious and anticipated hours and days of their year to our suggestions and guidance. Vacations, like honeymoons, have a hard time living up to themselves, but with Greece and not Niagara Falls as your destination, you have already reduced your risk of a let-down.

—*Robert Emmet Meagher and*
Elizabeth Parker Neave

ONE

ENVISIONING AND
PLANNING YOUR TRIP

G reece provokes different images, even fantasies, in different minds. Most have to do with the sun—luminous, revealing, eternal. Some of us picture sun-splashed ruins, while others dream of sun-scorched strands. All of these are strewn with perfect forms—on the one hand, bleached temples, columns, marble gods and goddesses; on the other hand, bronzed bathers, young and old, Olympians all, in their hearts if nowhere else. Everyone speaks of the light in Greece, as if the sun saves itself for Greek skies, but there may also be something about Greece that opens our eyes as nowhere else. All this is to say that most travelers come to Greece with heightened expectations, and it is the aim of this book to do its best to assure that they are not disappointed.

WHY "RUIN" A PERFECTLY GOOD HOLIDAY?

Anyone—even someone drawn to lift this book from the shelf and read this far—might well ask "why ancient Greece?" Why an entire guidebook focused on Greek antiquities? A short question to which there is no short answer. This book, cover to cover, is our best response, but for now, at the outset, it makes sense to point out that Greek sun, surf, natural beauty, nightlife, and cuisine face stiff competition from many corners of the planet, all of which are readily accessible and affordable to anyone considering a Greek adventure or holiday. We love Greece as we love few places on earth, but we must concede at the same time that much of Greece is remarkably stark and barren—all rock and erosion—barely alive it would seem. Other sprawling stretches, especially of its coastlines—are tastelessly overdeveloped. Standing apart from the Greece that is home to Greeks there stands faux Greece, home only to tourists, a land of bars and bedrooms, without schools, churches, neighborhoods, children, old people, family markets, or hospitals. It is not where Greeks live; it is where foreigners play. This Greece, we feel, is best avoided, for the same reason that we do well to avoid fast food. It nourishes nothing in us. Not so with the ancient places of Greece, its deepest and least polluted reservoirs of spirit and beauty.

With some exceptions, you will automatically avoid the worst of Greece when you spend your days among ruins. We call it "ruining" a day, and a day not at least partially "ruined" may just be a day wasted, at least in Greece. This is true for several reasons. Ancient Greek architects—especially when envisioning a sanctuary of some sort, a residence for their most revered clients—gave remarkable attention to the choice of site. They sought out and selected "charged" sites, sites already widely recognized as places of transcendent beauty and power. Mountain peaks, caves, promontories, springs, and headlands were often already places of pilgrimage before any permanent structure was erected to mark the spot. Furthermore, once "marked" with a temple or oracle, such sites were often spared the oblivion and desecration endured by more private and pedestrian spaces. They survived, even if buried, to rise again under the archaeologist's shovel and brush; and, once resurrected, they are uniquely preserved, as the laws protecting Greek antiquities have more teeth than those protecting Greece's other perishable treasures. The simple truth is that archaeologists, like fly fishermen, more often than not find themselves in places of remarkable beauty, as do those enthusiasts who emulate and follow after them.

What is unique and most wondrous about Greece, then, is the richness of its preserved past. Very few other landscapes offer as many open portals to the remote cities and civilizations that have shaped the world we share.

The exciting discoveries and adventures awaiting anyone who prowls and picks among Greece's ruins and ancient remnants are the best reason we know for singling and seeking out Greece for a holiday. These are no reason, of course, for shunning Greece's other delights, and we will endeavor to give each its due in this guide. Our principal focus here, however, is fixed on ancient Greece, not only because it is our obsession but also because the first-time on-site explorer into Greek antiquity needs more guidance than does the first-time beachcomber. The full exploration of ancient Greece requires at least a lifetime, while most travelers to Greece have only a week to ten days at their disposal. There is the rub. Where to begin and how to end? Most general tourist guides give only glancing attention to Greek antiquities, while specifically archaeological guides aim to be exhaustive and thus prove exhausting, even disheartening, to the interest-rich yet time-poor traveler. One strategy, the one we offer here, to meet this dilemma is the detailed itinerary, the blazed trail through what might otherwise prove a bewildering complexity, without practical beginning or end.

ITINERARIES INTO GREEK ANTIQUITY

Blazed trails are admittedly problematic. One or two persons usually do the blazing and everyone else does the following, which often confers undeserved authority upon the blazers' interests and judgment. So long as the blazers are more experienced than the followers, however, this plan still makes more sense than do most alternatives. Any path taken, for whatever reason, always leaves room for wistfulness regarding the numerous other paths not taken. What the path already taken by someone else assures is that the known outweighs the unknown. The pre-tested tends to be more reliable than the untested. Tourists carry guidebooks for the same reason that emperors have always employed tasters—to avoid disaster. The itineraries in this volume make sense and work. What is just as important is that they are non-binding. Think of them as roads, not as rails; and keep in mind that you are an all-terrain vehicle, not a tram. You can and should take the wheel and follow your own instincts and whims, especially on holiday. The point of any adventure is, in the end, to get lost. We offer bearings, initial orientation, a sense of the possible, and sound suggestions. The rest is up to you. Be sure to allow a few extra days to linger when we would have you move on, or to go right when we would have you go left. This is why we ourselves loathe organized holidays and do our best to offer a middle-path between the package tour and the maiden voyage.

We offer four such itineraries here, each roughly 7–10 days in duration, on the ground (or at sea) in Greece. Allowing time for air travel from elsewhere in Europe or abroad, as well as for pre-trip packing and post-trip decompression, each of these itineraries is easily manageable within the span of an average fortnight holiday. The four itineraries together are designed to span Greek antiquity from the early Cycladic and Minoan civilizations of 5000 years ago to the classical period of Athenian preeminence, and at the same time to sample diverse Greek landscapes, from Attika to the Peloponnese to Crete to the Cycladic Islands, with several side-trips. More specifically, three of our itineraries correspond to distinct temporal eras and geographical regions: the Minoan itinerary unfolds on Crete; the Mycenaean itinerary is focused on the Peloponnese; and the Classical itinerary is centered in Athens as a base for exploring local and regional sites. The Classical itinerary makes the fewest demands on its followers. They fly into Athens and remain lodged there for their entire stay. They make their way by foot or public transportation, all within circles wherein English is widely and predictably spoken. The Mycenaean itinerary makes some additional demands, such as navigating the sometimes quite mountainous and remote Peloponnesian landscape in a rental car, negotiating lodging along the way, and quite likely confronting situations wherein mime and a Greek phrase book may have to replace the ready use of English. Neither of these—Classical and Mycenaean—options, however, make particularly strenuous physical demands. Walking, while inevitable and often extensive, is mostly on level, paved or cobbled surfaces. No real climbing or scrambling is called for. The Minoan itinerary, on the other hand, entails some harrowing though not hazardous driving situations, some trekking and climbing on steep, unsure surfaces, and some inevitable moments of linguistic standstill. In short, the Minoan itinerary is for the fit of body and the adventurous of spirit, regardless of age. Before giving up on the Cretan option, however, any hesitant reader should bear in mind that one of the authors is in his sixties, has never considered himself an athlete, and has survived the Cretan option in fine form.

While each of the three above itineraries has its own specific temporal and geographical focus, it is also fair to say that each is in its own way eclectic. Most Greek archaeological sites are layered, spanning thousands of years of occupation and use, despite the evident predominance of finds from one or other period or civilization. The same is true of our itineraries. While focused, they are not exclusive. Each offers a glimpse into the full span of Greek antiquity.

The fourth itinerary offered here is focused on the Cyclades, arguably the most stunning cluster of islands in the Greek archipelago. This itinerary will have special appeal to readers for whom the lure of Greece is inseparable from island-hopping and for whom beaches offer stiff competition to ancient ruins as places to spend a day. After all, Greece—ancient or modern—is unthinkable without the sea, and early Cycladic civilization made some of the first and most enduring contributions to Greek culture and history. This island itinerary offers a glimpse of the full span of Greek antiquity from the late Neolithic and Bronze Age through to the classical period, and takes its readers to two of the most spectacular ancient sites in Greece: the Late Minoan city of Akrotiri, entombed beneath a mountain of volcanic ash in the most catastrophic eruption of the ancient Mediterranean world, and the sacred island of Delos, the mythical birthplace of Apollo and the ancient religious center of the Aegean.

As each of our itineraries begins in Athens and as our readers will arrive in Athens at very different times of day and night, "Day One" will refer in each instance to the first full day in Athens. If you happen to arrive in the early morning and resolve to stand tall against the gravitational pull of jet lag and travel fatigue, then "Day One" could be the day of your arrival. Otherwise, it will be the day following your arrival, your first fully functional and lucid day on the ground in the city of Socrates. For the first three itineraries, "Day One" is assumed here to be Sunday (Saturday for Itinerary #4). This is intentional, as a reminder that not all days are equal for the visiting explorer. Many of the museums and sites featured here are not open every day of the week and have limited hours. For example, most but not all museums and sites administered by the Greek archaeological services, as well as many private or municipal ones, are closed on Mondays throughout the year; and their ordinary hours of opening are often from 8:00 or 9:00AM to only 2:30 or 3:00PM.

These hours can be and sometimes are extended, according to demand, at the height of the summer tourist season, and are amended for national and religious holidays. It's always safest to check such hours on the ground and/or in advance of your trip on the official website of the Greek Ministry of Culture: www.culture.gr, where you will find a comprehensive (though not always current) listing of museums, monuments, and archaeological sites, together with their days and times of opening. Suffice it to say that our itineraries have been designed with these and other limitations and contingencies in mind so as to minimize disappointment. The hours of opening and closing given in this guide were those current in the summer of 2006 and should be taken as no more than suggestions. We have found no guidebook to Greece whose printed hours have proved reliably accurate on the ground. This is because the Greeks change those hours freely, without remorse. Greece, as one local candidly advised us, is the land of suggestions. "Of course," she added, "we have laws and traffic lights like everybody else. They tell you what you should do. But you may have a better idea."

LAUNCHING YOUR EXPEDITION

The next decision to be made—after deciding *whether* to go to Greece—is *when* to go. Just as very few ski areas are at their best in summer, so also Greece is surely not at its best in winter. Even though the "explorers" who follow this guide are not typical tourists, they will be affected by the tourist calendar. Tourism is either "on" or "off" in Greece, which often determines whether something is open or closed; and this applies to ancient sites as well as to hotels and tavernas. Whole towns will all but shut their doors and turn out the lights for much of the year. Once tourism is "on," which is to say once the tourist season has begun, a further distinction must be made between "low season" and "high season." This will determine a range of critical factors such as days and hours of opening and closing, transportation schedules, and pricing. The itinerary least affected by, but not immune from, the turnings of the tourist cycle is the Classical itinerary, since it is based in Athens, which has a full life of its own apart from tourists and so operates on more or less a twelve-month year and a seven-day week regardless of who shows up to see the Parthenon.

So, when does the tourist season begin and end? What are the dates for high and low season? Simple questions to which there are no simple answers. It all depends. On what? On you. And on the millions of other visitors to Greece each year. Modern Greeks watch the annual arrival of tourists in very much the same way as ancient Egyptian farmers monitored the annual rise of the Nile. Both "flows" are unpredictable, calling for responsive ingenuity. Greeks open their doors and turn on the lights when there are enough people standing there wanting a room or a meal to make it worth their while, no sooner and no later. If demand runs high in low season, prices are likely to rise, while if beds are empty in high season, prices tend to fall. If everything were predictable, the Greeks would never have needed the oracles for which they were so famous.

That said, it is possible to make some general statements without too much fear of contradiction. Greece is usually "open" to visitors from late April or early May every year and begins to "close" by late September or early October. July and August are usually the months when tourism reaches flood level in many places. We most highly recommend May, June, and September for the itineraries in this book, because both climate and cost are more moderate during those periods; and sites, while open, are not likely to be overly crowded. Weather is king, however, as the Greeks and their guests live mostly outdoors. Skiers are used to this. They watch the mercury and listen to the weather and plan accordingly. Any explorer planning an expedition to ancient Greece will do well to take a few tips from their brothers and sisters on the slopes. And be sure to watch out for national holidays, when it's best to stay put and celebrate the occasion.

The beach at Vai, Crete.

GREEK NATIONAL HOLIDAYS

New Year Day	January 1
Epiphany	January 6
Greek National Holiday	March 25
Easter*	April/May*
Labor Day	May 1
Ascension Day	May/June
Assumption Day	August 15
War Memorial Day	October 28
Christmas Day	December 25
St. Stephen's Day	December 26

* Exact date varies yearly.

All of the itineraries in this book begin and end in Athens. There are a couple of reasons for this. The first is purely practical. Whether you are traveling to Greece from else-where in Europe or from further afield, it is most likely that you will travel by air and will first touch down in Athens, at the new Elefthérios Venizélos International Airport. The only exception relevant to our four itineraries is Crete, which receives some direct international flights from the United States, Canada, and the UK. There is another reason, however, to begin in Athens. Most first-time visitors to Greece, unless they have only sun and sand on their minds, either want or feel obligated—and well they ought—to set eyes on the acropolis and, in particular, the Parthenon. To your agenda we would add the National Archaeological Museum and the Goulandris Museum of Cycladic Art. After all, most of the sites to be visited in the field have been stripped of their treasures, and these treasures now reside in museums. Every itinerary in this book will be greatly enhanced by time spent in these two world-class Athenian museums.

In this age when the travel agent is all but extinct and the Internet rules, most fliers have their own favorite websites for booking airline tickets, so we will assume that you need no advice or assistance getting the best airline bargains. Apart from international flights to or from Greece, however, you may have further bookings to make, depending on which itinerary you decide to follow. For sea travel to and from Crete and the islands, very little advance booking is usually required, except for the period of greatest demand from mid-July through August. A few days to at most a week advance booking should serve you well. Making changes in ferry bookings can be a complex and unrewarding experience; so it's usually better to wait until your plans are firm before purchasing tickets. Furthermore, we recommend that you book ferry or catamaran tickets personally, face-to-face with a local Greek agent (they're omnipresent), who can and will come to your assistance if rough seas, strikes, or any other unforeseen disruptions require you to revise your itinerary.

This is as good a place as any to say what every visitor to Greece needs to hear and take to heart: relax and let it go.

Greece does not run like any clock you've ever kept. One of the most wise and noble reasons for coming to Greece is to learn another way of looking at life and the world, one that does not place the self at the center and does not collapse when the unexpected happens. The Greeks not only survive but even manage to enjoy days that bear no resemblance to what was envisioned for them. This is a skill worth having; and the Greeks might well charge tuition for teaching it to their guests, as they so often do. So, when you are packing your bags, leave room for your sense of humor and a change of plans; otherwise bring an extra bottle of Valium.

For internal flights, we recommend Aegean Air (www.aegeanair.com) over Olympic Airlines (www.olympic-airways.gr) whenever possible; and for ferries to and from Crete you can turn with assurance to Minoan Lines (www.minoan.gr) or ANEK (www.anek.gr), and Blue Star Line (www.bluestarline.org) for the Cyclades. To sort out and compare your full sea route options, you can go to www.greekislands.gr or www.ferries.gr.

A wider-service, one-stop website to consult in your pre-trip musings and planning is the official site of the Greek National Tourism Organization (www.gnto.gr). In addition to an expected array of information on transport, attractions, lodgings, and so on, they offer a surprising largesse of free downloadable maps—city maps, regional maps, road maps, and trekking maps, many of which are directly relevant to our itineraries. For example, you'll find city maps of Athens and Heraklion, as well as road maps of Attika, Southern Greece, and Crete. In addition to these, we recommend that you seek out, for each of your destinations, an individually focused map from the excellent *Road Editions* series. Especially if you are finding your own way around Crete, the Peloponnese, or the islands, on foot or behind the wheel, you will be grateful for the accuracy and detail provided by *Road Editions* maps (1:250.000 for the mainland, 1:100.000 for Crete, 1:35.000 for Santorini, 1:50.000 for Naxos). They will also prove invaluable in following the nomenclature and directions found in this guide, as we have relied on the *Road Editions* maps at every turn both on the ground and on the page. Road Edition maps are available in Athens at the ROAD Travel Bookstore at 39 Ippokratous Street, but we recommend your securing them in advance of your trip. A Google search for "Road Editions Maps+Greece" will reveal your closest local source.

Rental car agencies are even more numerous than churches in Greece, and they tend to be quite competitive, especially outside of high season. This means that you can and should, if your disposition allows, bargain for the best rate. The best rate, or at least the best posted rate, is assured in advance by Auto Europe (www.autoeurope.com), but their affiliate companies usually require that you sign a contract stating that you may drive only on paved surfaces. This can be a problem in Greece and for the itineraries in this volume, especially on Crete. The same contracts usually make the driver responsible for tires, windshields, and all cosmetic damage to the rental car; and this too is a bad gamble for any driver on Greek roads. What we advise is to shop around and rent a car from an agent who is willing to give you, at a competitive price (easily determined by consulting www.autoeurope.com), "full insurance" with no deductible of any sort. One such small local company, on Crete, is Perla, based in Heraklion. (Ask for Eleni at 28790-42647 or mobile 6946-075563.) We recommend that you hire a compact, air-conditioned, front-wheel-drive car and, in a perfect world, one that does not display the name of the rental company. Keep in mind that you will pay a premium for automatic shift autos, as well as for additional drivers. To economize, decide on a designated driver either already skilled in or willing to practice driving stick shift. Rented cars and their contents are often prime targets for theft. Perla cars, though, look like any other local car and that's reassuring when you leave your car by the side of the road and hike up to an ancient site.

Most readers of this book will need only their passports to gain entry to Greece as tourists and to remain there in that capacity up to three months. Non-EU citizens may or may not have their passports stamped upon entry, while EU citizens walk through Passport Control as they would through the door of their own home. In order to rent a car in Greece you will need a valid drivers license issued in your country of residence.

In addition, you will hear occasionally from a range of sources that foreign drivers are required to carry an International Driver's Permit, but we have encountered no evidence of this requirement on the ground in Greece. Nonetheless, laws and regulations seem to be enforced in Greece on a rotation whose turns are beyond our ken, so for added security and assurance you may wish to acquire an International Drivers Permit before leaving your country of residence. AAs (Automobile Associations) are one convenient source of these permits, though they can also be secured over the internet in a matter of days. If you prefer two-wheeled motor vehicles to the four-wheeled variety, you will need a formal operator's permit or license in order to rent a motorbike or motorcycle in Greece. Many rental agencies will not mention or require such a license when attempting to sell you on moped mania; but their nonchalance does not alter the fact that without a proper license you are in violation of the law and, in the event of an accident, whatever insurance you have will be worth no more than something you found in a cereal box.

The caldera from Chelidonia, Oia, Santorini.

BUDGETING YOUR EXPEDITION

Putting a price tag on a Greek adventure is a daunting challenge. The fluctuating value of the Euro relative to other currencies, combined with the waxing and waning cycles of the Greek tourist seasons, all further complicated by the national sport of negotiation, make for an unpredictable bottom line. With this safety net of provisos beneath us, we offer the following rough set of monetary icons throughout this volume:

Accommodation for two
€ Moderate, 60–90 €
€€ Expensive, over 90 €

Bear in mind that these price ranges take into account the fluctuation from lowest to highest season. Some rooms include breakfast and some do not; and, when included, breakfast can mean anything from a wedge of bread and coffee to a full buffet. Unless otherwise stated, all accommodations recommended in this book are en suite, which is to say they have their own private sink, toilet, shower, and/or bathtub. We have included no budget hotels, "rooms to let," or hostels. These tend to announce themselves and it is up to you to determine the level of comfort and amenities, or lack thereof, that you find acceptable. We recommend, whenever possible, booking your room in advance, whether on line, by phone, or by fax.

Board per meal: cover, main course, salad or vegetable, and carafe of house wine
€ Moderate, 15–40 €
€€ Expensive, over 40 €

Greek fast food is available street-side practically any place you will find yourself. This will include souvlaki, gyros, pizza, and other take-out provisions at a highly affordable price. A solid lunch or light meal of this sort can be had most places for under 5 € and you will find that it hits and fills the spot rather well. The venues we recommend by name represent but a few of the more atmospheric and satisfying sit-down tavernas, for when you are taking your time and not gripping your purse too tightly. We recommend only a few such places, not because they are unique, but because Greeks like to eat out and their streets and seashores are strewn with tavernas. Much of the adventure and pleasure of Greek dining is to stroll and survey menus until you are inspired to settle in somewhere for a meal. One tip in finding a specially authentic meal is to look for a place filled with Greeks. You may not be able to spot Greeks, as they look like many others, but you can hear them, as they will be speaking Greek. Bear in mind that Greeks eat late, not much before 10:30; so you may not find any place full of Greeks before 11PM.

Entrance, travel/tour fees: museums, archaeological sites, boat ferries, tours...
€ Moderate, at or under 5
€€ Expensive, over 5

Most archaeological museums charge an entrance fee of 2 to 4 € , while some exceed this and others are free. Buses and metros are very reasonable, while taxis are for the most part disproportionately expensive. We rely whenever possible on public transport or foot-power, because so many taxi drivers are downright predatory. Not all, but enough to smear them all with bad repute. Greeks make the same complaints, but in words we dare not use here. If you do hail a taxi, make sure to insist that the driver agrees in advance to follow the meter. They are obliged by law to do so, but this is like saying that politicians are supposed to tell the truth. More often than not, if you insist on meter pricing, you will be invited to select a different taxi. If not, buy the driver flowers, and be on your way rejoicing.

Keep in mind that many lodgings and eateries in this guide, much less archaeological sites, museums, public transport, or ferries, do not accept credit cards; and Greeks, like most Europeans, will stare blankly at travelers checks. That said, it is wise to bring at least one credit card with you, keeping in mind that Visa and MasterCard are the most widely accepted. American Express, Discover, and Diner's Club cards are frequently frowned upon or declined. The good news here is that 24-hour ATM machines, like wild herbs, sprout everywhere in Greece; and your bank card, unless it is remarkably odd, will allow you to withdraw Euros as you need them, usually without any fee. Check with your own card-issuing bank regarding fees and how to avoid them when using your card. To determine the current value of the Euro against other world currencies, you can go to www.x-rates.com.

PACKING YOUR BAGS

We know better than to advise anyone on fashion; so we will confine our advice here to practical necessities. Keep in mind, however, that you will have to carry everything you pack. Wheeled suitcases have emboldened many travelers to bring the farm with them; but this is folly in Greece. Greek laneways— often cobbled, terraced, and endowed with donkey droppings— are no place for the latest two-wheeled hard-shell Samsonite. We suggest backpacks—wheeled or wheel-less is up to you.

We will pass over most everything obvious, but we must mention sunscreen with an SPF rating of at least 20. The sun is as dangerous as it is beautiful in Greece; and sunscreen, while available everywhere, is unreasonably pricey in Greek shops. Hats, scarves, and sarongs—with an SPF of 100—are even more effective; so don't leave home without one of each. You will thank us for suggesting rubber swim-shoes too, as protection against hot sand, hard if not sharp rocks, and sea urchins—all of which are often underfoot on Greek shores. Also on our list for the prospective explorer are a flashlight or torch, a compass, and a Swiss Army knife. Remember not to stow the last item in your carry-on cabin luggage. Last but not least—boots. You may think sandals when you think Greece, and that is fine for the beach or the taverna, but much of Greece is uphill and the rest is downhill. You need shoes that you can trust, and that probably means boots. Don't worry about how they look. A quite seasoned Greek archaeologist once told us that the two things likely to bring anyone down in Greece are the sun and loose rocks underfoot. A hat, plenty of water, and common sense will protect you against the former, and a good pair of solid boots are your best defense against the latter. If you are at all unsteady on your feet, a light, collapsible walking stick might be a wise final addition to your luggage.

METRIC CONVERSION

TEMPERATURE

To convert °C to °F multiply by 1.8 and add 32

To convert °F to °C subtract 32 and multiply by .55

LENGTH, DISTANCE & AREA	multiply by
inches to centimetres	2.54
centimetres to inches	0.39
feet to metres	0.30
metres to feet	3.28
yards to metres	0.91
metres to yards	1.09
miles to kilometres	1.61
kilometres to miles	0.62
acres to hectares	0.40
hectares to acres	2.47

WEIGHT	multiply by
ounces to grams	28.35
grams to ounces	0.035
pounds to kilograms	0.45
kilograms to pounds	2.21
British tons to kilograms	1016
US tons to kilograms	907

A British ton is 2240 lbs, a US ton is 2000 lbs

VOLUME	multiply by
imperial gallons to litres	4.55
litres to imperial gallons	0.22
US gallons to litres	3.79
litres to US gallons	0.26

5 imperial gallons equals 6 US gallons

a litre is slightly more than a US quart, slightly less than a British one

TWO

A WALK THROUGH
ANCIENT GREECE

"The Face of Greece," wrote Nikos Kazantzakis, "is a palimpsest bearing twelve successive inscriptions: Contemporary; the period of 1821; the Turkish yoke; the Frankish sway; the Byzantine; the Roman; the Hellenistic epoch; the Classic; the Dorian middle ages; the Mycenaean; the Aegean; and the Stone Age. Pause on a patch of Greek earth and anguish overcomes you. It is a deep, twelve-leveled tomb, from which voices rise up calling to you."

Our walk here is of necessity a forced march through the Greek past, guided by the several itineraries that we have set for ourselves. We will pause to listen to only some of the myriad voices still resonant in the rocks and seas of this most haunted of lands. Even so, our ears will be full and our imaginations set ablaze. Indeed, if we offer our minds as tinder, Greece possesses and provides all the flame we could ever wish for.

IN THE BEGINNING

In the beginning were the land and the sea and the sky. Each time and each place these three converge they come to a unique agreement. Their arrangements precede us. They shape the course of our lives, our stories, our history, no matter where or when we live. Nowhere is this more true than in Greece. And so we will begin with the place.

In Greece, as in our own bodies, we cannot overestimate the importance of water. Who can fathom that we are 98 percent water? The human organism as archipelago—what a thought! It's also a fact of life, and we are the better for it. Greece, admittedly, is rather more solid than we are. Yet over a fifth of the Greek land mass is made up of islands, several thousand of them, if we count every sea-encircled crag. Nowhere in Greece will you ever find yourself more than sixty miles from the sea; and most of the time, with a little lift from a ladder or a hill, you can see it. For 9,000 years the sea has molded the Greek imagination, shaped Greek history, measured the horizon.

Another looming physical fact about Greece is its mountains. They comprise 80 percent of mainland Greece, which may be seen as a massive vertebrate—the Pindos range (the southern extension of the Dinaric Alps)—its spine stretching from north to south and then reaching, like a tail, down through the Peloponnese. The highest of its peaks, twenty of which exceed 6,500 feet, is Mount Olympus, the airy seat of the gods, who oversee their domain from nearly 10,000 feet above sea level.

Greece, in short, is a land of sea and mountains and in this lie some of its deepest challenges and contradictions. Its mountains are formidable barriers to travel, communication, and trade. They divide east from west, creating distinct climates and temperaments, while the north and south are barely connected by a narrow isthmus. It is the land and not the sea that has always threatened to isolate Greeks from one another and their neighbors, while it is the sea that unites them. The Greek people, cut off from one another, often unable to see from one village to the next, face the sea's vast expanse. Like a great door, the sea has long offered to Greeks a way out, just as it has provided others with a way in. Isolation and entanglement are the two sides of the Greek coin. Greece's unique position— on the eastern edge of Europe and the western edge of Asia, fused to the Balkans yet projected into the Mediterranean towards North Africa—has often made its identity difficult to discern and its alliances uncertain.

The third, or perhaps the first, great physical presence in Greece, however, is the sun, which prevails on average for 250 days a year. However shadowed by events or wrapped in smog the Greeks may find themselves, Greece has always been and remains a land of light, a light so unique and indescribable that Lawrence Durrell suggested "one can compare it to nothing except Spirit." This may begin to explain why this land, so profoundly scarred, endures as a place of healing and even of celebration.

WHAT DO WE LISTEN TO? BONES OR BOOKS? POTS OR POETS?

As we walk through ancient Greece, we will encounter two groups of voices vying to tell the stories of the past. The one group belongs to scholars who pour over the myths and legends of early Greece in texts penned, as it were, by the great poets, playwrights, philosophers, and historians of Greek antiquity and preserved in world libraries. The other group of voices belongs to archaeologists who dig up and sift

Minoan Knossos, Crete.

through the material remains of ancient Greece—buildings and burials, sculptures and swords, everything imaginable from decorated pots to discarded olive pits.

Our dilemma is this. When we discover and dig up the Greek past, particularly when it has been undisturbed for millennia, we literally stand in the presence of the past. The past is present to us. We are arguably contemporaneous with it, except for the predictable and measurable effects of time. Material remains neither fabricate nor dissemble; they just are. At the same time, however, they are ineluctably silent. Not so the surviving texts of antiquity. They narrate the past, but are they to be trusted? And even if trusted, how are they to be understood? For centuries, Homer's accounts of Troy, its great war, and its heroes were mostly dismissed as fantasy until the tips of shovels struck the fabled walls of Ilion at Hisarlik in northwest Turkey.

This dilemma is obviously most acute in confronting what we call prehistory, a time and a place either without writing or without texts that we are as yet able to read. "Pre-historic" applies not only to bands of skin-clad hunters and gatherers, but also to imposing urban centers boasting princes and priests, seers and senators. The palaces of Crete and the cities of the Indus Valley—representing two of the great ancient civilizations rediscovered in the last 100 or so years—are mute, however revealed they are to the eye.

This discussion, however, is likely to seem abstractly academic, at least until we take our first stride into Greek prehistory, which conveys us to the island of Crete. In doing so we step clear over the first inhabitants of the Greek mainland who likely arrived in the Lower Paleolithic, 350,000 years ago, as well as Greece's earliest farmers who were tilling the soil by 7000 B.C.E. While these farmers left more of a trace than their hunting and gathering predecessors, examining their remains and accomplishments today is a rarely acquired obsession unlikely to seize the general reader. Not so with Minoan Crete, the power of whose spell is well and widely attested.

THE MINOANS

The story of the Minoans begins and ends at Knossos. Settled in 7000 B.C.E. or perhaps slightly earlier, it represents the earliest known permanent settlement on any island in the Aegean. Where its first settlers hailed from remains a matter of speculation. Anatolia, Asia Minor, is a prime suspect. The language they spoke—as yet undeciphered—was not Greek. The Minoans, then, became Greeks only in retrospect, by association or appropriation. We know of them the way we know of the Trojans—from Greek mythology, not from Minoan or Trojan mythology. It is a truism that history is written by the victors; and, as we shall see, the Minoans, after their long dominant day in the sun, unraveled into near oblivion, until they were rediscovered and celebrated by Arthur Evans only a century ago.

Properly speaking, what we recognize as Minoan civilization emerged in the early Bronze Age. Evans divided its lifespan into three major periods—Early Minoan (EM), Middle Minoan (MM), and Late Minoan (LM)—so as to align Minoan chronology and terminology with those of the other ancient civilizations of the Aegean and East Mediterranean, such as the Early, Middle, and Late Helladic Periods of Mainland Greece, the Old, Middle, and New Kingdoms of Egypt, and the Early, Middle, and Late Cycladic Periods of the southern Aegean. This standard tripartition (complicated still further by subdivisions which we will spare you here) was and is employed more widely and generically to divide the Paleolithic and the Bronze Age. Many of the histories, guides, and plaques that you will read in your research and in your on-site exploring will utilize this terminology, just as they will employ B.C. or B.C.E. and A.D. or C.E. to distinguish between time before and after the Christian Period or Common Era. Having said all that, however, in this guide we are going to use a later, simpler, and more useful, we think, division of the Minoan Age into the following periods: Pre-palatial, Protopalatial, Neopalatial, Final Palatial, and Post-palatial. The defining focus of all of these terms, as you can see, is the Minoan palace. But why?

The "palace" represents the signature architectural structure and material remains bequeathed to us by the Minoans. Having left only material remains to testify to their existence and to tell their stories, the "palace" is the richest Minoan "text" that we possess. Furthermore, it is clear that the "palace" lay at the core of Minoan life and defined its political, commercial, and religious organization. In short, Minoan Crete, at least as we have come to understand it, was a "palace" civilization. We have put quotation marks around "palace" thus far, because even Arthur Evans was uneasy in assigning the word to the monumental, complex Bronze Age centers which he discovered scattered about the island of Crete, the first and incontestably greatest of which was Knossos. He used "palace" for lack of a better word, not because it hit the nail on the head. Also for lack of a better word, others have used and continue to use "temple" to designate sites such as Knossos, Phaistos, and Malia, to name the first and most important three, of these centers.

The fact is that we would have to know and understand a great deal more about Minoan life to find a proper word or description for these structures. Because they combined functions that we would designate as commercial, administrative, residential, social, and cultic, their reach defies simple designation. Our ever-expanding megamalls may eventually serve as illuminating parallels, as soon as we add a chapel and city hall to their all-inclusive menus, though it would be surely premature and misleading at this point to suggest calling Knossos the Great Mall of Crete. Consequently, we will follow tradition in this volume and use the term "palace" as it has been used for a century in writing about the structural epicenters of Minoan Crete.

PROTOPALATIAL CRETE

After centuries of growth and development as an ever more prosperous agricultural society of small farming settlements, a discernible island-wide civilization began to take shape during the Pre-palatial Period. The number, size, and diversity of these settlements increased; and among them a few settlements, particularly in the middle of the island, took advantage of their privileged location and resources, and emerged as focal. First and preeminent among these was Knossos, where around 1950 B.C.E., an ambitious new building project began on Kephala hill, a site already inhabited for perhaps four thousand years. At the same time a similar but not quite comparable structure was underway 35 miles (56km) to the southwest at Phaistos. Both palaces followed— or perhaps more accurately, established—what became a canonical palace structure, one feature of which was a central courtyard oriented on a north/south axis. Each palace faced a sacred mountain—Mount Juktas in the case of Knossos and Mount Ida in the case of Phaistos. Both adjoined rich, fertile valleys from whose soil they derived much of their prosperity. Whether Phaistos was an ally, rival, or satellite of Knossos, is not known; any of these is possible.

During the Protopalatial Period, a number of other palaces were constructed across the island, from Malia and Zakros in the east to Chania in the west, most surrounded by significant towns or settlements. They ranged from "1st order sites" to constructions of lesser scale and importance, which may or may not deserve to be called palaces. What jurisdictional significance these palaces represented is unclear. It is reasonable to speculate that they corresponded to states of some sort, among which there was at least a visible if not functional hierarchy, with Knossos at the top of the ladder.

Minoan Phaistos, Crete.

The palaces represented, among other things, centers of art, craft, trade, and agricultural storage and distribution. They appear also to have been major cult centers, although the peak sanctuaries on nearby sacred mountains were also the foci of religious ritual. Minoan Crete had already by this time realized and begun to exploit its strategic location as a hub for East Mediterranean trade, whose sea lanes connected Egypt, mainland Greece, the Cyclades, Asia Minor, the Syro-Palestinian coast, and Cyprus. While there exists some evidence of Minoan fortifications—some aimed at insiders and others at outsiders—and the development of Minoan armor and weaponry is no secret, the image of at least the early Minoans as singularly peace-loving—in harmony with each other, with foreigners, with nature, and with the gods—forms part of their enduring legacy.

All was well on Crete, it appears, until roughly 1700 B.C.E., when the previously prosperous and peaceful palaces of Crete were destroyed in some form of sweeping catastrophe which left the island strewn with charred ruins. The two usual suspects were, not surprisingly, nature (in the form of earthquakes) and man (in the form of wars). Since the society that emerged from the ruins was an exact replica of the society that had gone down in them, it is not likely that Crete had been invaded and conquered by outsiders. This fact points the finger rather sharply at nature.

After what appears to have been a devastating earthquake or series of earthquakes, destroying virtually every palace on Crete, the Minoans began at once to rebuild, and on a more grand scale than before. Natural disaster had only temporarily broken the Minoan momentum which had been building speed for millennia. With barely a pause for grief and loss, Minoan Crete arose reborn in the Neopalatial (New Palace) Period.

NEOPALATIAL CRETE

On a scale never before seen in the Aegean, nor on the Greek mainland for that matter, the Minoans created a flourishing, palace-centered civilization whose artistic, commercial, and perhaps political and military influence expanded greatly from the time of its full recovery in the early 17th century to at least the mid 15th century B.C.E. The palaces, peak sanctuaries, shrines, regional centers, and villas or country houses were never more numerous, elaborate, and affluent than in this the apogee of Minoan civilization. Key islands in the Cyclades became "Minoanized" during this period, which may reflect colonization but just as likely reflects profound cultural and commercial influence. The latter was clearly the case in the emerging Mycenaean centers of the Peloponnese. Minoan products and craftsmen were in strong demand throughout the East Mediterranean and made their way even beyond that sphere. The Minoan artifacts of this period are so distinctive and engaging that over 3,500 years later they are immediately recognized and revered in museum cases throughout the world.

If there was ever a time in the history of Minoan Crete that matched the account given by the classical Athenian historian Thucydides over a thousand years later, it was the period of Neopalatial (or Late Minoan 1B) Crete. He writes: "And the first person known to us by tradition as having established a navy is Minos. He made himself master of what is now called the Hellenic sea, and ruled over the Cyclades, into most of which he sent the first colonies, expelling the Carians and appointing his own sons governors; and thus did his best to put down piracy in those waters, a necessary step to secure revenues for his own use... as soon as Minos had formed his navy, communication by sea became easier, as he colonized most of the islands, and thus expelled the evildoers" (*Peloponnesian War*, tr. Richard Crawley, I.4.1; 1.8.2–3). Despite this tradition relayed to us by Thucydides, it remains a matter of doubt and dispute whether such a king named Minos ever truly existed, much less presided over all of Crete and the southern Aegean. Regardless of his reality or stature, however, it was his name that Arthur Evans gave to the entire civilization of Bronze Age Crete.

The facts on and in the ground, however, do seem to corroborate at least portions of the tradition preserved by Thucydides and underlying the more familiar and fantasied Minoan legends of the Minotaur, Ariadne, Theseus, the labyrinth, Europa, Daedalos, Ikaros, and so on. The pre-eminence of Knossos from the earliest palatial period is clear from the archaeological record, as is its prevailing cultural influence on the island, east to west, north to south. The political system in place, however, remains elusive. Was Knossos the first among equals, or the center of power? Regrettably, we have no grounds for resolving such questions. What we can say is that whether or not Minoan Crete was ever an acknowledged "thalassocracy"—a maritime empire— as Thucydides suggests, it was undeniably a brilliant, flourishing civilization which reached the peak of its power and prosperity in the period of the new palaces, until island-wide disaster once again struck to bring the Minoan golden age to an abrupt and appalling end.

This time it seems clear that man, not nature, was the agent of destruction. More specifically, in the mid 15th century B.C.E., Crete sustained a devastating series of destructions that left most significant Minoan sites—palaces, villas, shrines, towns—in ruin. Among the palaces, only Knossos survived, indeed all but intact, which is a rather telltale fact, which of itself could suggest one of several possibilities: that Knossos, as a result of island-wide insurrection had vanquished all of its island rivals or threats; that Knossos, due to its superior forces, had alone survived a Minoan civil war; or perhaps that the island had been invaded from beyond its shores and that the conquerors had preserved Knossos as their seat of power on the island. What is known is that at the end of the day, Knossos was the sole seat of power left standing and it was increasingly "Mycenaeanized" from that point on. Most notably, its records began to be kept in Linear B, an early written form of Greek, rather than in Linear A, a distinctively Minoan script. This could mean that the island had self-destructed in civil war and the Mycenaeans had stepped in either during the conflict to assist Knossos or after the conflict when Knossos was too weak to resist its hegemony.

THE ENDGAME OF MINOAN CRETE

During the Final Palatial Period, Minoan civilization, limping along on one palace, went nowhere. Even the one remaining palace—Knossos—was questionably Minoan by this point. Mycenaean influence and presence spread throughout the island, as witnessed by pottery finds and characteristically Mycenaean "warrior graves" and chamber tombs. Finally, in the latter part of the 14th century B.C.E., Knossos too was sacked and burned to the ground, never to be rebuilt until Arthur Evans restored a few of its walls and staircases in the 20th century of our era. Meanwhile, most of the other palaced centers had revived, minus their palaces, and Chania could be said to be flourishing. Even this partial recovery, however, was undone in the notorious upheaval of the 12th century, when not only Crete but the entirety of the East Mediterr-anean witnessed widespread devastation, most probably at the hands of both man and nature, partners this time in wreaking widespread havoc. The Minoan remnants fled to what have been unearthed and named "refugee settlements" in the mountainous inland of the island. There they disappeared from sight, forever.

THE MYCENAEANS

Crete was, in the early Bronze Age, the unrivaled prodigy of the Aegean. The mainland of Greece lagged far behind. True enough, the Argolid, late in the Early Helladic Period, in the late 3rd millennium B.C.E., had once been able to boast of Lerna. With its massive stone and mud brick fortification walls and its relatively sophisticated House of Tiles, Lerna had anticipated the advanced organization and architecture of the Minoan and later the Mycenaean centers; but Lerna already lay in ruins well before the first Minoan palaces appeared on the scene. Latecomers, however, often make up for lost time.

There is convincing evidence that, even before the introduction of settled agriculture, the inhabitants of southern Greece were traveling by sea. It comes as no surprise, then, to find that the Mycenaeans—thousands of years later in the second millennium—were accomplished seamen and traders. Furthermore, since the Mycenaeans' roots may with some confidence be traced to Anatolia, the likely homeland of the Minoans, it is also no surprise to find them in close commercial and cultural contact with the palace civilizations of Crete.

MYCENAE AND CRETE

Contact between the prosperous Minoan civilization and the impoverished Mycenaeans came early and played a singularly formative role in the development of the Peloponnese. The island of Kythera, just off the southeast tip of the Peloponnese, whether a Minoan colony or not, had been rather thoroughly Minoanized by the beginning of the Protopalatial Period and served as a stepping-stone for Minoan trade with mainland Greece. Aegina, in the Saronic Gulf, was another such staging point for Minoan goods and influence. Clearly, the balance of

Storage jar (pithos), Palace of Malia.

trade between the ascendant Minoans and the backward Mycenaeans leaned precipitously in favor of the former. The Mycenaeans were mostly a market for Minoan resources and wares. It has been suggested that the few early Mycenaean exports to Crete may have included slaves and mercenaries. Suitable slaves were easier to locate and acquire than were able warriors, and the Mycenaeans proved themselves more than able warriors over the ensuing centuries. From the outset, the Mycenaeans, whether out of disposition or necessity, revealed a marked inclination and gift for warfare, while the Minoans did not. Commerce, even without conquest, has always required muscle. For one thing, the Minoan thalassocracy was never without threat from pirates and rivals, and it may be that the early Mycenaeans assisted the Minoans in securing their sea lanes and defending their interests.

In the Minoan Protopalatial Period, then, the contact between Mycenaeans and Minoans grew steadily. In the beginning this resulted in what might be called a Minoanization of the Peloponnese, as the Mycenaeans absorbed Minoan goods, technology, and aspirations. Whether they were responding to the Minoan challenge or simply following their own cultural clock, the Mycenaeans soon began, however, to develop a complex civilization of their own. Ranked societies, organized around a central authority, are more likely to create a surplus of products, which promotes trade and eventually multiplies wealth, equating to power. The Argolid, and Mycenae in particular—the Knossos of the mainland—emerged as the center of many of these developments. In the Middle Helladic Period, an unfamiliar prosperity emerged in the Peloponnese, and this new wealth was increasingly concentrated in the hands of a few privileged chiefs, themselves mostly transplants or "blow-ins" from Asia Minor or beyond, who divided the Greek mainland into proprietary regions for their own aggrandizement. The liaisons of these warlords with the Minoan leaders, their possession of high status Minoan weapons, jewelry, and consumer goods, and their accumulating wealth gave the Mycenaeans their first kings, who would sooner rather than later begin to build their own palace complexes to demonstrate their stature and to protect their possessions.

THE RISE OF THE MYCENAEANS

As the 15th century approached its midpoint, the Mycenaeans were rapidly closing the power gap between themselves and their Minoan mentors. As the Mycenaeans were developing their own distinctive culture, Knossos was showing signs of Mycenaeanization. The protégés were gaining ground on their patrons. Mycenaean trade mimicked Minoan trade and began to secure a place for itself in the Aegean. We can only wonder when the Minoans came to realize that these formidable rivals were somehow their own creation. Then came the widespread destruction of the Minoan palaces. Whether or not this occurred at the hands of the Mycenaeans, it unquestionably played into them. The fact that the Mycenaeans controlled Knossos, the last palace left standing, after the dust settled and the last fires were out casts a long shadow of suspicion on them. Their karmic opportunity to suffer systemic collapse would come, but not for several centuries. For now they were in their ascendancy. The Mycenaens, whether by design or by default, stepped into the shoes and onto the decks of the Minoans and became the unchallenged lords of the Aegean.

The first mainland palaces provided monumental testimony to the distinct Mycenaean character, so markedly different from that of the Minoans. The Minoans sited their major palaces in reverent recognition of an enclosing holy landscape and oriented them towards sacred mountains, so that the natural and constructed environments might form a ritual unity. Furthermore, it may be argued that cultic space and practice lay at the center of Minoan palace life, perhaps presided over by a sacral king or queen. Whence the lingering uncertainty over whether "palace" or "temple" best serves to name these structures. No one, on the other hand, would be tempted to call their Mycenaean counterparts "temples." With the exception of Pylos, they are unmistakably citadels, all about clout, not piety. Self-contained, secure enclosures, eventually girded by cyclopean circuit walls, the major Mycenaean citadels have at their core the great megaron, the pillared throne room of the *wanax* (king).

The remarkable administrative prowess and military might of the Mycenaeans soon became fully manifest. From their original strongholds in the Argolid and the southern Peloponnese, the Mycenaeans extended their imperium into central Greece and the islands. Mycenae, Tiryns, Pylos, Thebes, Goulás, Midea, Asine, Orchomenos, Gla, Thebes, Iolkos, and Athens are among the known Mycenaean centers, most likely forming a federation of autonomous states presided over by independent kings, possibly bonded by blood, bound by some form of political-military pact, and sharing a common language, religion, and culture. An elaborate road system linked the major centers to one another. Indeed, the Mycenaean genius extended to engineering, so that their roads, bridges, and waterworks even today startle the imagination.

THE MYCENAEAN EMPIRE

We know that the commercial and cultural connections of the Mycenaeans were vast in scope and diversity, even by today's standards. It may be said without exaggeration that the East Mediterranean world—encompassing mainland Greece, the Aegean Islands including the Cyclades, Crete, Asia Minor, Egypt, Cyprus, Palestine, Phoenicia (Lebanon), and Syria—comprised a broad commercial and cultural consortium at the height of the Mycenaean Period. One preliminary hint of this is suggested by the fact that among the grave goods unearthed in Grave Circle A at Mycenae were objects from Mesopotamia, Syria, Egypt, Nubia, Anatolia, Northern Europe, and Afghanistan.

Eventually, from their fortified bases in mainland Greece, the Mycenaeans partially colonized the Aegean coast of Anatolia, including Rhodes, and eventually controlled Crete. Inspired and mentored by the Minoans, the Mycenaeans took an early interest in the Levant; and, once they presided over the Aegean, the Mycenaeans established for themselves what may have been colonies, or perhaps only trading posts, in the Near East, most notably in Syria, Palestine, and Cyprus. In turn, from the seaboard cities of the East Mediterranean, the Mycenaeans gained unquestionable access to the preeminent cultures of Mesopotamia, partly through the Hurrian-Mitanni-Hittite links with northern and central Mesopotamia. The seaboard cities gave the Mycenaeans still another link with Egypt.

Mycenaean finds have been uncovered in numerous sites from Lower to Upper Egypt, as far south as Nubia; and the influence of Minoan-Mycenaean art on the artistic revolution of the Amarnian era of Akhenaten is evident to some scholars. In fact, Mycenaeans, who are thought to have fought with the Egyptians in the early sixteenth century against the Hyksos, appear to have returned among the "Sea Peoples" to invade Egypt and the Levant in the late thirteenth century, completing the collapse of what had been a prosperous and relatively stable period for the entire region. The general crisis that followed the decline of the Egyptian and Hittite empires and the extensive raids of the "Sea Peoples" plunged the East Mediterranean and the Near East into a long period of chaos and absolute decline. The Trojan War seems to represent but one notorious moment in the ferocity that marked the end of the Mediterranean Bronze Age.

Finally, the reach of the Mycenaeans north and west into Europe is startling to consider. They reached Sicily and the Lipari Islands as early as the sixteenth century, and Ischia soon afterwards. Their trade connections, whether direct or indirect, reached as far as Britain, Scandinavia, and Central and Eastern Europe. Indeed, it would be well to pause here to consider further, briefly, the implications of Mycenaean travel and trade. Their direct contacts with Crete, Anatolia, Egypt, and cities along the Syro-Palestinian coast gave to the Mycenaeans at least indirect access not only to the cities and peoples of Mesopotamia but also to all of the other cities and peoples who were or had been trading partners with Mesopotamia and the Near East. With this realization, the sphere of possible Mycenaean contact, direct or indirect, widens well beyond the Aegean and the Mediterranean to the Arabian Sea and crosses the vast reaches of Iran to India.

THE DECLINE AND FALL OF THE MYCENAEANS

The world of the Late Bronze Age in the Aegean and East Mediterranean was a turbulent and high stakes arena, in which today's rival could easily become tomorrow's ruler. The Mycenaeans had played this game well against the Minoans and for two centuries they survived and flourished, holding their own amongst the East Mediterranean's superpowers, most notably the Egyptians and the Hittites, who shared the diplomatic title "brother," a name reserved for equals. In the mid-13th century the Mycenaeans were at the top of their game and at the peak of their power. This was most probably the period of the Trojan War (or perhaps Trojan Wars, as Homer may well have conflated a number of conflicts into a single tale). Recent archaeological discoveries at the site of Troy at Hisarlik, confirming that the Troy of the Late Bronze Age was fifteen times the size attributed to it by earlier excavations, combined with the translation of revealing Hittite imperial records from Hattusas, point to the fact that Helen's war was no slight skirmish, but rather a major Mycenaean conquest of one of the most prosperous and strategically pivotal properties in the ancient world.

The 13th century, however, brought new challenges and threats to the Mycenaean empire. The battlements of Mycenae and Tiryns were dramatically expanded at this time. Mycenae, perhaps anticipating a long siege, also dug a deep under-ground passage leading to a secret cistern, all enclosed by the new north-east extension of the citadel's fortifications. Before systemic catastrophe struck, however, the empire began to lose its grip and unravel. New dynasties took over chief centers of Mycenaean civilization and went their own way. Mycenae lost major trade routes and partners and its prosperity rapidly declined. Upheaval, like lightening, struck one site after another. The end was approaching. By the end of the 13th century, most of the major Mycenaen sites had been destroyed. The Athenian citadel atop the acropolis was the one fortunate exception. Like the devastation that had swept across Minoan Crete more than two centuries earlier, from which the Mycenaeans had greatly benefited and likely participated, this ruin of the Mycenaean centers resembles an unresolved crime scene. Earthquakes, internecine strife, marauding Sea Peoples, Dorian invaders, even plague have all been suggested as possible perpetrators, either acting alone or in concert. In fact, the Mycenaean debacle was but one part of the general collapse of advanced Bronze Age civilizations in the East Mediterranean, which only Egypt survived. Despite a brief revival in the mid 12th century, the Mycenaeans never recovered as a homogeneous civilization nor a recognizable power. Instead of rebuilding their citadels they abandoned them. Many fled to the coasts, the islands, and to Asia Minor, but at this period of chaotic upheaval, one refuge was only slightly better than another. Mostly, however, the Mycenaeans went back to the countrysides where they had started, and dug in, contributing their labor, genes, and genius to the survival of their families and to the eventual rise of archaic and classical Greece, when they would be seen as the forebears of a glorious new Greek ascendancy.

FROM DARKNESS TO LIGHT

Long labeled the Greek "Dark Ages," the centuries between the Mycenaean unraveling and the archaic revival are perhaps better seen as a time of determined struggle and recovery. This is not to say that the survivors did not go through dark times. The collapse of the Mycenaean centers had scattered most Greeks back onto the land, into farms and villages. Without the centripetal force created by the palaces, Greek life on the mainland was again quite local and lowly. For the most part, they didn't go out to the wider world and the wider world didn't come to them. Literacy was lost; but it had always been the prerogative of professional scribes. To most everyone else it was no more than scribbling and its disappearance could not have been deeply felt. The prosperous were now impoverished, a leveling that brought with it important lessons for the future. Not surprisingly, the population declined and survival made more daily sense than kleos or fame. This was the age of iron, which Hesiod lamented as the lowest and meanest of times, a time defined by toil.

Poseidon or Zeus? Scholars disagree. National Archaeological Museum.

Toil, however, if blessed by the gods, is not without its fruit. By the 8th century the Greek revival was well underway. To be sure this was not the revival of Mycenaean clout and magnificence, but something else altogether. The new cohesiveness that crossed from village to village and region to region, giving Greeks a growing conviction of unity, despite their internal differences and conflicts, was rooted in a shared language, religion, and cultural legacy. The 8th century witnessed the first Olympic games, the first Greek colonies in Italy, the appearance of pan-Hellenic holy sites such as the oracle of Apollo at Delphi, and the sung splendor of Hesiod and Homer.

Politically, the Greeks made their way through a series of experiments and reforms whose direction was towards greater and greater equality and inclusiveness. Sketched in simple, broad strokes—from monarchy to oligarchy to aristocracy to timocracy to tyranny to democracy—the few relinquished their privileges and the many asserted their rights. The Spartans, admittedly, marched to their own drummer and developed an idiosyncratic system of government all their own, eventually providing a fatal counterweight to the rise of the polis, and to the most preeminent polis of all—Athens, our focus for the classical age.

THE POLIS

The Greek polis (city-state) was neither unique nor miraculous in its development, though it surely marked a great achievement. Over two thousand years before the Greek city-states began to take shape, the Sumerians of southern Iraq had developed a similar, though hardly identical, polity. The early Sumerian city-state comprised an urban center, with a sacred, cultic *temenos* (precinct) on elevated ground at its center, abutted by commercial and administrative complexes, and surrounded by a bustling town. This urban center, in turn, was encircled by extensive land cultivated to provide not only the city-state's own needs but also an ample surplus for trade with other cities of Mesopotamia and beyond. At least for a while, these cities appear to have been governed by an equal among peers, answerable to a bicameral assembly. In time, however, as military threat and adventurism became more a matter of course, hereditary kings assumed all but absolute power, which describes a similar eventuality on the Greek scene as well in the age of Alexander. The purpose of this brief diversion is to suggest that clichéd references to the "Greek Miracle" are neither accurate nor flattering. The Greeks were the world's most avid students before they became the West's most revered teachers. The Greek polis, like all of the other achievements of ancient Greece, was not cut without pattern from whole cloth, but rather woven from countless diverse strands gathered far and wide. Genius is largely a matter of keeping eyes and ears wide open, of learning from everything and everyone, and then releasing upon the collection a fresh, keen, unfettered imagination.

Like the Sumerian city-states, the Greek city-state was made up of a large territory or state (*khora*) and an urban center (*asty*). In the case of the city-state of Athens, the city was called "Athens" and its surrounding state was called "Attika." To clarify and complicate matters just a bit more, the city-state as a whole was simply Athens and all of its citizens, whether they lived in the city or the countryside, were Athenians, just as citizens of New York State are New Yorkers, whether or not they reside in Manhattan. Reasonably prosperous and politically engaged Athenians seem to have had both a city house and a villa in the country. It was traditionally important, even critical, for a citizen to own land, to be rooted in the soil he pledged himself to defend, and so to be self-sufficient enough to speak and act freely, not from need or self-interest.

Every polis, besides ample land, an urban center, and of course, a sizeable population required several essential elements: a temple, a theater, and an agora. In former Mycenaean centers, like Athens, the temple of the city's patron deity occupied the acropolis, the elevated citadel where the king's *megaron* had once stood. When the kings were dethroned the gods took their place. Only the gods' authority was absolute now; all authority belonged to the people, who presented and debated and voted on their laws and motions below in the administrative buildings of the agora or in open assembly. Here it was one citizen one vote, which was not at all the same as one person one vote, because free-born women, slaves, and resident aliens or guest workers were not citizens. The acropolis, then, with its temple or most often temples, was sacred space, where the mutual affairs of mortals and immortals were addressed; the agora was secular space where the commercial, legal, and administrative affairs of state and the citizenry were addressed. The theater, curiously, was physically and metaphysically midway between the acropolis and the agora, between the sacred and the secular. The theater itself lay within a sacred *temenos* and its dramas represented a ritual celebration of the god Dionysos; at the same time it was here that the citizens of Athens often confronted the darkest, most violent and unspeakable desires and acts that poison lives and threaten cities: blasphemy, incest, matricide, infanticide, rape, suicide, wartime atrocities, and so on. In addition to providing entertainment and diversion, the theater was a place of communal self-disclosure, purgation, enlightenment, and healing.

THE SAVIOR CITY

The Athenians were proud of many things. Among them was their claim to be autochthonous, to be sprung from the very land that they inhabited. And that land, a roughly drawn peninsular triangle with the sea on two sides, was quite vast, compared to that of other city-states. Comprising nearly 1,000 square miles or 2,500 square kilometers, Attika was the size of contemporary Luxembourg and a little larger than Rhode Island. Athens was an open, ambitious, restless city and became a magnet for artists, poets, intellectuals, fine craftsmen, merchants, and anyone craving the energy of a vital city. At its peak in 431 B.C.E., its population is estimated to have reached between 300,000 and 350,000, while no more that 50,000 of these were citizens, i.e., freeborn Athenian males. The rest were either women or imports (slaves, resident aliens, or immigrants).

It was the Persian Wars that launched Athens onto the mainstage if not the world stage. To the east, in Asia Minor and beyond, the Persian Empire had replaced the Hittites and the Great King of the Persians, Darius, was increasingly annoyed at Greek claims to what he saw as his holdings along the eastern Aegean coastline. This land had been a source of contention between Greeks and West Asians since Mycenaean times. One old and recurring flashpoint was the city of Miletus, most recently seized and razed by the Persians in 494 B.C.E. The time had come for the Persians to subjugate the insolent, meddlesome Greeks once and for all. When the Greeks defied Darius' demand for ritual submission, he launched, in 490 B.C.E., what he assumed would be an unstoppable expeditionary force and invaded the Greek mainland. Crossing the Aegean and landing in northeast Attika, the Persian force prepared to march on Athens, never imagining the Greeks would initiate their confrontation. Though vastly outnumbered, the Greek force—urged and led by the Athenian Miltiades—did just that, charging the Persians and routing them at Marathon. The Persians fled to their ships without any souvenirs, much less spoils. The Greek mouse had roared, and the Persian behemoth had run.

After the humiliating Persian defeat at Marathon, no one in the Mediterranean world, and certainly no Greek, harbored any doubts that the Persians would be back. But it took ten years. In the meantime, the Athenians had struck gold, or rather silver. Coming upon an extraordinarily rich vein of silver on state land in Laureion, the city-state of Athens suddenly possessed immense disposable wealth. Rather than disperse this windfall among her citizens, Athens, persuaded by Themistokles, decided to build a fleet of warships (triremes) surpassing that of any state in Greece. By 480 B.C.E., just in time for the second Persian invasion, the Athenian fleet boasted 200 ships.

It was Xerxes, the son of Darius, who resolved to avenge his now deceased father's humiliation and crush the Greeks once and for all. In 480 B.C.E., he led a truly vast multi-national force drawn from every corner of the Persian empire. Thirty-one Greek states—outnumbered as never before—stood united against the Persian land and sea forces and inflicted devastating defeats on them at Salamis and Plateia. After Salamis, Xerxes himself went home and left the conduct of the ill-fated war to his son-in-law.

Both at Marathon and at Salamis the Athenians had played the key hand in saving the Greek states, the free world as they saw themselves, from tyranny. More than any other of the Greek states, Athens claimed credit for twice repelling the Persian barbarians and declared itself the champion of freedom and democracy, the unrivalled leader of the free states of Greece. They saw their city as the military, cultural, commercial, and moral capital of Hellas, a beacon of light and a bastion against darkness. They fortified their own city as never before, and to fortify all of Greece created the Delian League, an originally voluntary consortium of city-states and islands, who would remain on alert against future threats to Greece. It was, as it were, a 5th century Greek N.A.T.O. Each member contributed ships or funds or both to maintain a standing defense force and a war chest in anticipation of all-but-certain future Persian invasions—all under the leadership of Athens.

For a relatively brief period, Athens shone as never before and never since, defining once and for all the Greek classical age. Mid-5th century Athens may be said to be the original "city on a hill." This was surely as Perikles saw or at least envisioned it. With funds partly pirated from the Delian Treasury, Perikles presided over an ambitious civic building program that gave to his and our world a cut gem—the Parthenon—and much more. He and his city were clearly engaged in doing nothing less than giving Greece a capital, as stunning to see as it was formidable to oppose. The poets and playwrights, sculptors and historians, philosophers and potters all collaborated in the ephemeral creation of a timeless legacy.

THE TYRANT CITY

Athens, however, was already steering a deviant course. Emboldened by their new prosperity, prestige, and power, they began to pursue empire. Despite their protestations to the contrary, they began to treat their allies as their subjects. Ideologically committed to their own form of radical democracy, they saw it as their mission and their right to foster, or if necessary to force, this democracy on their sister states. Neutrality or dissent were no longer options. You either supported Athens or you braced yourself to be her enemy. Sparta, the oddest man out in this crusade, rightfully saw Athens as a threat and came to realize that the two of them—Athens and Sparta— were on a sure collision course. Sparta, Korinth, and other either likeminded or fearful states banded together to form the Peloponnesian League to counter Athens' Delian League. Both sides saw war as all but inevitable, and so it proved to be.

The ensuing Peloponnesian war lasted nearly thirty years and was by far the most savage conflict ever yet fought on Greek soil. When you consider the modest geographical footprint of the war and the scale of the casualties and destruction endured,

	Crete	Mainland	Cyclades
3000–2000	Early Minoan	Early Helladic	Early Cycladic
2000–1600	Middle Minoan	Middle Helladic	Middle Cycladic
1600–1100	Late Minoan	Late Helladic	Late Cycladic

there is little to do but groan at such an unthinkable concentration of atrocity and agony. What is more ferocious and disfiguring than a civil war, except perhaps a war fought over ideology or religion? The Peloponnesian War was both. Traditional warfare in Greece was brutal but brief. A battle might last only hours or even minutes. When one side yielded the field, the other side declared victory, erected a trophy, and collected its dead. The practical aim of war was to bring the enemy to submission, whereas in the Peloponnesian War the aim—practically senseless but ideologically pure—became to annihilate the enemy. Any line between warriors and innocents, between young and old, was ignored. War became indistinguishable from atrocity.

In the end Athens lost everything. Her prosperity and democracy, her people and her principles had all been fed to the consuming ache for empire, to *pleonexia*, the quest for the boundless. Her decisive defeat and ensuing decline brought the classical age to an effective end. The future of Greece, such as it was, lay in the north. The torch of empire, which eventually consumes every hand that grasps it, was passed to a young boy named Alexander, tutored by Aristotle, who is said to have slept with the *Iliad* under his head.

TIMELINE

All dates below are B.C.E. Some are confidently exact, others rough approximations, and one or two are little more than wild guesses.

1900	The first Minoan palaces
1700	Destruction of Minoan palaces followed at once by rebuilding
1600–1400	Peak of Minoan prosperity and power
1500	First Mycenaean palaces
1500	Catastrophic eruption of Thera
1450	Destruction of Minoan palaces (except Knossos)
1400	Collapse of Knossos' naval supremacy
1375	Destruction of Knossos
1300–1200	Height of Mycenaean power Mycenaean Sack of Troy
1200–1100	Widespread destruction in the East Mediterannean
1100–1000	Ionian colonies in Asia Minor; Dorians in Peloponnese and Crete
800	1st Spartan settlements in Lakonia
700	Poetry of Hesiod and Homer
490	1st Persian invasion of Greece, under Darius; Persian defeat at Marathon
480	2nd Persian invasion of Greece, under Xerxes; Persian defeat at Salamis
479	Persian defeat at Plataea
478	Formation of the Delian League
431–404	Peloponnesian War
429	Death of Perikles in the plague
404	Surrender and occupation of Athens
399	Death of Sokrates
356	Birth of Alexander
336	Accession of Alexander to the throne
323	Death of Alexander

THREE

GETTING ACQUAINTED
WITH GREECE

I n this chapter, we make no pretense to either compre-
hensiveness or depth. Far from an encyclopedia of Greece,
ancient and contemporary, it is instead a miscellany of bits,
an explorer's taster's menu, as it were, of Greece, intended only
to whet the appetite and open the imagination. Everyone, when
entering unfamiliar places, needs to have a few bearings, a few
things to look for, a few things to keep in mind and think about,
a few initial questions answered; and here we offer some suggestions.

ENCOUNTERING ANCIENT GREECE

We begin with ancient Greece, which is not the Greece that
you will first encounter, at the airport or on the flight over, but
simply because it came first and inspires this volume. You will
arrive in Athens, the greatest of the Greek cities of antiquity;
so we may well begin with some thoughts about what it was
that made a city like Athens a city at all.

GREEK CIVIC ARCHITECTURE

The essential architectural structures of any classical Greek
city were the temple, the agora, and the theater. Without these
public spaces, a city could not conduct its public life; and
without public life, there was no such thing as a Greek city.

Just as every Mycenaean citadel had its presiding king,
so every Greek polis had its patron deity. The temple precinct
was for the god what the *megaron* had been for the king—a
place to hold court, to receive dignitaries, suppliants, priests,
and civil servants. Ancient cities, not surprisingly, hosted
many gods and goddesses; and so the acropolis and
surrounding city was strewn with temples, shrines, and sacred
sites within and without its walls. The Greek temple, it should
be noted, was a "great house" for a deity (embodied in a cult
sculpture), not a place of assembly for believers, like a
Christian *ekklêsia*, a Jewish synagogue, or a Muslim mosque.

The agora, originally a market, was the city commons where the city conducted its business in every sense of that word—commercial, administrative, and social. This is where laws were made and enforced, where goods were sold, where proclamations were posted, and originally where citizens convened in assembly.

The theater, literally the "seeing-place" (*theatron*) was where the city convened for its dramatic festivals. In Athens, the great theatrical festival of the year was the City Dionysia, at which previously selected tragic and comic playwrights would stage their original entries before an audience numbering well over ten thousand.

Public life—sacred and secular, religious, political, judicial, commercial, and cultural—called for the erection of monumental architecture, as grand as the city's aspirations would demand and as its means could provide. Private life, of course, also required built structures, but these were typically modest and ephemeral, constructed mostly of wooden beams and mud-baked brick. Where these structures have left any trace at all, it is barely more than a foundational footprint. Private life was of little significance against public life, and this discrepancy was reflected for all to see in their respective venues. Cut stones, from the beginning, were reserved mainly for palaces, citadels, temples, civic buildings, and fortifications. Private citizens would come and go, one generation at a time, but the city would endure, like the natural landscape which surrounded and supported it. It was not until the 5th century B.C.E. that Athens built entire temples from marble, mostly quarried from their own local sources on Mts. Hymettos and Pentelikon. Sculptors, on the other hand, mostly coveted and employed the finer, translucent marble from the island of Paros.

The three principal "orders" of classical Greek architecture were the Doric, the Ionian, and the Corinthian as illustrated below. The Doric order, widely considered to be the purest and highest embodiment of Greek architectural genius, belongs mostly to the 5th century B.C.E., though it was occasionally combined thereafter with the Ionian and Corinthian orders. The source of the upward tapering Doric column and its capital may lie in the fact that the earliest columns were inspired by and fashioned from felled trees. Their early ornamentation, consequently, was carved in wood, not stone. The Ionian order was developed on the islands of the Aegean and in Asia Minor, while the Corinthian order was said to have been invented by 5th-century sculptor-architect Callimachus. The Corinthian order differs from the Ionian only in its use of the ornate acanthus capital.

The perfection of the **Doric** order is to be found in the Athenian Parthenon. Other examples include: the temple of Hephaistos in the Athenian agora, the temple of Apollo at Corinth, and the temple of Hera at Olympia.

The temple of Artemis at Ephesus and the Heraion of Samos bear witness to the roots of the **Ionian** order in Asia Minor and the Aegean Islands, respectively. Two of the most famed examples of Ionian temples on the Greek mainland are the temple of Athena Nike and the Erechtheion, both situated on the Athenian acropolis.

The first known employment of an acanthus capital, which marks the **Corinthian** order, was in the interior colonnade of the cella of the temple of Apollo at Bassai in the Peloponnese, dated c.430 B.C.E. Some later exemplary instances of this order are the Tegean temple of Athena Alea and the *tholos* (rotunda) at Epidauros. The Romans were fond of the Corinthian order and often employed it for their monumental structures. One of their gems was the temple of Olympian Zeus in Athens.

The diagrams below show some of the essential elements of Greek temple architecture.

1: Capital   2: Architrave
3: Frieze   4: Metopes
5: Triglyphs   6: Cornice
7: Entablature (elements above the capital)
8 • Pediment (below)

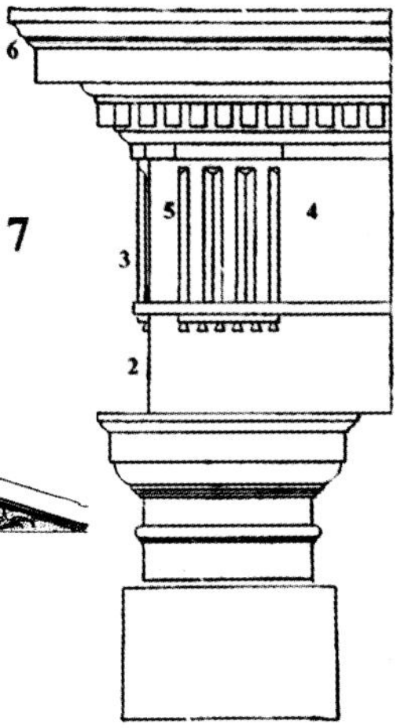

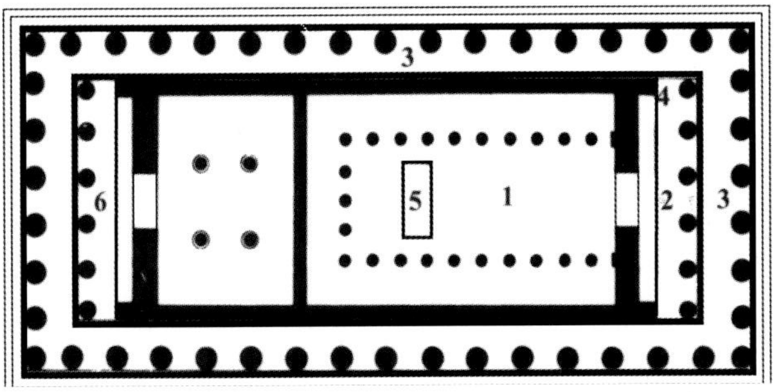

1: Cella 2: Pronaos 3: Colonnade 4: Anta 5: Cult statue 6: Opisthodomos

MOVERS AND SHAKERS OF ANCIENT GREECE

No line is more critical in life than the one separating what is within from what is beyond our power to influence or control. Wisdom and piety begin and end with the proper drawing of that line, and the ancients were generally no better at drawing it than we are. For that which they thought to be beyond them they looked to and relied upon the gods, whom they mostly envisioned as at least more powerful than themselves; for the gods could ward off death. This is finally what made them gods (*athanatoi*, "deathless"), while men (*thnetoi*, "deathful") stood powerless against the approach of death. "Even the children of the gods," wrote Euripides, referring to the half-divine offspring resulting from divine dalliances among mortals, "go dark in death." Otherwise they were all too human: male and female, young and old, beautiful and deformed, gracious and vengeful, lustful and chaste, sweet and fierce, distant and meddling. Their lives were, like ours, the stuff of soap operas—often tawdry and pathetic, occasionally exciting, yet always entertaining.

THE IMMORTALS

AMALTHEA
Cretan Sea nymph, daughter of the Ocean and nurse to the infant Zeus in the Diktaian Cave. In gratitude, Zeus launched her among the stars as Capricorn.

APHRODITE (VENUS)
Daughter of Zeus, born off the coast of Cyprus from the sea's gleaming froth, she is the goddess of love, sexuality, and delirious desire. With deep roots in the Middle East and Crete, she remains a multivalent goddess whose bright side brings passion and pleasure and whose dark side brings war and death.

APOLLO (PHOEBUS)
Son of Zeus and Leto, born on the island of Delos, patron deity of music, divination, prophecy, the arts, and the light of day. He is most often portrayed in youthful tranquility, holding a lyre or a bow.

ARES (MARS)
Son of Zeus and Hera, god of war and strife, sometime consort of Aphrodite. The most hated of the gods, he is rarely portrayed or revered.

ARTEMIS (DIANA)
Daughter of Zeus and Leto, twin sister of Apollo, goddess of the wild, mistress of animals and the hunt. She is the guardian of young girls as they approach marriage and childbirth. She is often portrayed carrying a bow.

ASKLEPIOS

The god of health and healing. His cult symbol, the snake, survives today in the caduceus, the emblem of the medical profession.

ATHENA (MINERVA)

Daughter of Zeus and Metis, born in full panoply from the pate of her father. Patron goddess of Athens, she is the goddess of wisdom, household arts, and of war-craft.

DEMETER (CERES)

Goddess of grain and fertility, daughter of Kronos, sister of Zeus and Rhea, and mother of Persephone. Her roots lie in East Asia and Crete, and her secret rites, mostly likely imported from Crete—the Eleusinian Mysteries—were among the most important pan-Hellenic mystery religions of antiquity.

DIKTYNNA

The goddess of Mount Dikte, a huntress-goddess of mountains and the remote wild. Specially venerated in Western Crete, she was also worshipped at cult centers in Sparta and Athens.

DIONYSOS (BACCHUS)

Dionysus, son of Zeus and Semele, god of wine, ecstasy, revelation, and theater. Rescued as a fetus from his mother's incinerated womb and inserted into the thigh of his father, he was born of Zeus, as was his half-sister Athena.

HEPHAISTOS (VULCAN)

Son of Hera, the product of divine parthenogenesis, lord of fire and volcanoes. A smith by trade, he is the patron of all those craftsmen employing fire in their handiwork (potters and metal-workers). He is lame and is often depicted carrying a smith's tongs.

HERA (JUNO)

Daughter of Kronos and Rhea, sister and wife of Zeus. Queen

of the sky, goddess of fertility, and patroness of marriage. Frequently at odds with her husband over infidelities, she took fierce revenge on certain of his lovers and their offspring.

HERMES (MERCURY)
Son of Zeus and an Arcadian mountain nymph, he is the guardian of the agora, of the household, of thresholds and crossroads. Patron of commerce, he is the herald of the gods, patron of commerce, and escort of the souls of the dead on their journey to the netherworld. He is portrayed with winged sandals and bearing a messenger's staff.

HESTIA (VESTA)
Daughter of Kronos and Rhea, sister of Hera and Zeus. Goddess-guardian of the home and the household hearth, she is often portrayed enveloped in a cloak.

ZEUS (JUPITER)
Son of Kronos and Rhea, brother of Hestia, Demeter, Hera, Hades, and Poseidon, and king of the Olympians, the reigning divine dynasty throughout Greek antiquity. Nicknamed *Kretagenes* (Cretan-born), his mother Rhea gave birth to him in the sacred Diktaian Cave and he was then hidden by his grandmother Gaia from his infanticidal father. Cretan legends also have him dying on Crete and being entombed on Mount Juktas. This belief that Zeus was subject to death brought down on all Cretans the widespread slur that they were the most incorrigible liars in Greece.

THE MORTALS

ACHILLES
Peerless all-but-immortal warrior hero of the Trojan War, the focus of the *Iliad*. Presented with the all-defining choice of a short life with undying fame or a long life in obscurity, he at first chose the former. Later, he thought better of his decision, but it was too late. The momentum of war and passion for

revenge over the slaying of his beloved companion Patroklos, drove him back to battle and to his culminating duel with Hektor, prince of Troy.

ARIADNE
Daughter of King Minos and Pasiphae and once a vegetation goddess emanating from the Great Mother. She helped Theseus, the slayer of the Minotaur, escape from Knossos and fled with him to Naxos, where Theseus abandoned her.

AGAMEMNON
Late Bronze Age King of Mycenae and commander-in-chief of the Greek armada to Troy to retrieve his brother's wife, Helen, and to repay the Trojans for their violation of Greek hospitality. His reign marks the highpoint of Mycenaean Greek unity and power and also highlights the ambition and violence that characterized that age.

ALEXANDER
The son of King Philip of Macedon, who unified Greece under his rule. All of the previous Greek empires—the thalassocracies of Minos and Agamemnon and the Athenian empire of Perikles—pale into insignificance when measured against the conquests of this virtual boy who would be god. After avenging the earlier Persian invasions of Greece his armies conquered everything in their path as far east as the Punjab. (Also, another name for Paris, Prince of Troy.)

CLYTAEMNESTRA
Queen of Mycenae, wife of Agamemnon, mother of Iphigenia, Elecktra, and Orestes. When her husband slew their daughter as a sacrifice to Artemis for fair winds to Troy, she vowed the revenge that she finally brought down on him the night of his return, hacking him to pieces in their bath and so fueling a further round of revenge, in which Orestes and Elektra collaborated in slaying her and her lover.

DAIDALOS (DAEDALUS)

Legendary Cretan inventor and engineer in the service of King Minos. His most notorious creation was the hollow likeness of a cow that allowed Queen Pasiphae, cursed with a deviant lust by Poseidon, to mate with a white bull, whose resulting offspring was the Minotaur. To flee from a less than grateful patron, he fashioned wings for himself and his son Ikaros, who plummeted to the earth when he flew so close to the sun that his wings melted.

HELEN

Daughter of Zeus and Leda, wife of Menelaos, queen of Sparta, the radiant *causa belli* of the Trojan War. A child sprung from god-sized lust and violence, her life was forever a fusion of the two. She was at the same time the promise of bliss and the assurance of doom, as destructive as she was irresistible. Whether she ran away with or was abducted by Paris, the ensuing devastation was the same.

HERAKLES (HERCULES)

Son of Zeus, the most beloved of all the Greek heroes and demigods. His labors epitomized the struggles and achievements of the turbulent, violent, and great-hearted Greeks who revered him. Cloaked in a lion's skin and wielding a club or a bow, he was the archetypal hunter, warrior, and lover and thus embodied the central preoccupations of ancient Greek myth and poetry.

IDOMENEUS

King of Knossos, son of Deukalion and grandson of Minos. His illustrious name enters the Greek record in the *Iliad* when he leads the Cretan contingent—numbering eighty ships and representing seven Minoan towns—to Troy, in support of Menelaos and the Greek cause.

IPHIGENEIA

Daughter of Agamemnon and Clytaemnestra, princess of Troy, first blood of the Trojan war. Lured to the Greek camp by the promise of marriage to Achilles, she stood alone there with her mother against an army led by her father and accepted her savage fate with a bravado and courage that inspired the poets and playwrights of antiquity.

Minos

Legendary king of Knossos, son of Zeus and Europa, brother of Sarpedon and Rhadamanthys. Minos created a great maritime empire, Sarpedon died at Troy, and Rhadamanthys married the mother of Herakles. Minos and Rhadamanthys were appointed by Zeus as two of the three judges of the dead.

Oedipus

Legendary king of Thebes, son and husband to his mother Jocasta. Exposed in the wild as an infant by his royal parents and left to die, he finds his way back to his rightful throne but not before he unwittingly murdered his father. His royal marriage to his mother and its offspring horrified and captivated the Greek imagination.

Odysseus (Ulysses)

King of Ithaka, husband of Penelope, and Trojan war hero. The invention of the Trojan horse, the ruse that ruined Troy, has been attributed to him. The story of his return from Troy, preserved in the *Odyssey*, is the sole surviving "return" narrative from that period.

Perikles

Preeminent Athenian political leader in the mid-5th century B.C.E. Nicknamed the "Olympian," Perikles led the citizens of Athens on the path to radical democracy, empire, and civil war. A victim of the plague that struck Athens early in their conflict with Sparta, Perikles never lived to witness or endure the disastrous outcome of the empire he had envisioned and fostered.

Theseus

Son of Aegeus and King of Athens, he is credited with the unification of Attika. When the Athenians were subjected to King Minos and annually required to send off seven young girls and boys as human victims for the Cretan Minotaur, Theseus sailed to Crete and slew the Minotaur. On his return, however, he failed to change his sails from black to white, a signal prearranged with his father to indicate that he was alive not dead. In despair at the black sails, his father Aegeus plunged off a cliff giving his life and his name to the waters below.

SACRED SITES IN ANCIENT GREECE

Sacred space is neither at first nor in the end a matter of architecture. It is, rather, a matter of place. Sacred space, like water, must be discovered, whether it resides high on mountain peaks or deep within the earth. All true temples or shrines are first charged with the power of the sacred before they take shape in stone or wood. The word temple (*templum* in Latin, *hiera* in Greek) has as its first and truest meaning not a human construction but a sacred place or object, to which any construction is a fitting after-the-fact response. Buildings only mark or point to temples. And so we would be deeply mistaken to conclude from the dearth of temple buildings on Minoan Crete that they were without temples; for their temples, their sacred places or precincts, were the surrounding mountain tops and caves, in alignment with which they sited their palaces.

Sacred space, then, is a place apart from other places, where we encounter or risk encountering a power that we never truly comprehend. It is never a place where we are in control. The Greek word for sacred place or precinct (*temenos*) preserves within itself this root sense of separation; for it comes from the verb *temnein*, to cut. The sacred place, then, is cut from the cloth, as it were, of common space, removed from common use, and marked for some higher purpose.

The ancient Greeks encountered and communed with the sacred in many different spaces, each of which became a point of daily, seasonal, annual, or occasional intersection between their lives and their gods or other powerful forces and spirits beyond their comprehension. Here are a few of the spaces that you will see as you explore their landscape, sacred and secular. Not all, but most of these have long since lost their "charge";

for the sacred, like radiation, seems to have a limited half-life. One stunning exception is Delphi. While its once magnificent buildings lie mostly in ruin, it remains and will remain a true *templum*.

Caves

Caves have always excited curiosity, wonder, and apprehension. As if diving into the sea's depth, we invariably take a deep breath before entering a cave, even though there is no shortage of air within. It is one way in which we mark the passage into another realm. They are among the world's first sacred places, it's first sanctuaries. Often associated with both birth and death, they represented the deepest inner recesses of the Mother Gaia, Mother Earth, the mysterious, benign abyss from which all life comes and to which it returns. Caves are natural *temenoi*, precincts already cut off and set apart from the everyday rounds of life. They are, as it were, "found" temples, indescribably older than the skills, tools, and leisure required for the first humanly constructed temples of which we find no evidence until the Neolithic period. Of Crete's nearly two thousand caves, some became focal cult sites. Among the most sacred were Miamou near Phaistos, Arkalochori and Skoteino near Heraklion, Eileithyia at Amnisos, the Idaian cave and the cave of Kamares on Mount Ida, the Diktaian Cave in eastern Crete, and the Psychro in western Crete.

Peak Sanctuaries

There was, as early as the paleolithic period, when human beings virtually indistinguishable from ourselves first walked the earth, only one recognized life-principle, clearly envisioned as feminine, whose body was the earth, a body that could be entered in awe, wonder, and excitement through the mouths of caves. Mounds and mountain-tops, gentle rises in the earth as well as towering conical or pyramidal peaks, often clefted softly like breasts and containing, further down their slopes, deep, mysterious caves—all of these high and hollow places of the earth were sacred to the Mother of All. They were her bodily presence and were alive with her power. The Minoans often oriented their palaces, and the later Greeks their temples, in alignment with sacred mountains as if to dwell in the Great Mother's embrace. By the Middle Minoan Period several Cretan Peaks were places of cult, where offerings were made and bonfires lit on certain days of the year. Some of these sanctuaries were eventually marked with precinct walls and permanent shrines. Among the most famous peak sanctuaries on Crete are those on Mount Ida and Mount Juktas, Petsophas near Palaikastro, Prinias near Siteia, and Traostalos north of Zakros.

PALACE AND DOMESTIC SHRINES

Ensconced within the palaces, villas, and homes of Crete and later the mainland there have been found rooms or crypts set aside for cult activity, often of the Household or Snake Goddess. These shrines are rarely of any significant architectural importance and may consist of a small room or space set aside with a low bench or ledge along one wall to hold cult images, ritual paraphernalia, and votives. These spaces sometimes have a central pillar. Notable Cretan examples may be seen at Knossos (the shrine of the Double Axe and in the House of the Chancel Screen), and a later Mycenaean example at Mycenae. The city of Athens, in the classical period, was known for its innumerable shrines and sanctuaries, quite apart from its magnificent monumental temples. This remains true today throughout modern Christian Greece, as many families have their own chapels which they maintain and dedicate to one or other aspect of Christ, his Holy Mother, or to one of the saints. On the island of Patmos it is said that there are more churches or chapels than people, which can only be a slight exaggeration.

Temples

There are those who have argued that temples (i.e., built structures, dedicated to and equipped for public ritual) were once common if not universal in the towns and settlements of Minoan Crete and the Mycenaean mainland. This argument

Temple of Zeus, Olympia

becomes stronger as more examples of these are discovered and identified as such sites as Malia (or Mallia), Gournia, Ayia Triada, Mycenae, Tiryns, Keos, and Phylokapi.

These free-standing temples, surrounded by open space, were understood as the dwellings of a god or gods, embodied in an iconic or aniconic idol. Whether the Minoan palaces themselves may be seen as temples or temple complexes and as the dwellings of divine or sacred rulers, is still a matter of discussion and dispute. In contrast, the Mycenaean palaces or citadels, while they contained shrines, were clearly the privileged and fortified residences of kings, warlords, their families, and close comrades. The plan of the first monumental Greek temples was that of the *megaron*, the central throne room of Mycenaean kings; once the kings were cast off, it was the gods who occupied the high places of Greece, dwelling and holding court, as it were, in spaces altogether reminiscent of their profane predecessors.

Oracles

Human life, individual or collective, all but incessantly requires that we make decisions, that we choose wisely between multiple alternatives. Meanwhile everything hangs on making the right choice, taking the right path, doing the right thing, at the right moment. War, marriage, commerce, travel, agriculture—every aspect of our lives—is fraught with uncertainty and risk. We mostly act in the dark, because we never know what the outcome of our actions and choices will be. We know only the past and the present, and we know them only partly and poorly. The gods, however, see all; and they would be our surest guides if only they would tell us a little of what they know. In oracles, the curtain is not lifted but the gods can be coaxed to speak through it and reveal what we cannot see, particularly in response to specific questions put to them. The oldest known Greek oracles was at Dodona in northern Greece, while its most eminent and widely consulted oracle was at Delphi in central Greece.

There were and are countless other marked or charged sites dotting the ancient landscape in Greece from Minoan times to the present: sacred enclosures around holy trees, rocks, or springs; crossroad and threshold shrines; tombs and cemeteries; hero or relic shrines; lustral basins and spring sanctuaries; and theater precincts dedicated to Dionysos.

THE ANCIENT GREEK TABLE

Of all of the achievements of ancient Greece, the Mediterranean diet is among the most widely admired if not imitated today. All the same, it is still on offer today in any local taverna in Greece. Three of its stellar staples, ancient and modern, are olives, wine, and honey. Today, as thousands of years ago, Greece is a landscape of olive groves and vineyards, as well as low-lying meadows and steep hillsides carpeted in herbs and wildflowers. Here it is indeed possible and recommended to eat and drink the scenery.

Olives

The olive tree is an astonishing plant. An evergreen even in punishing heat, it endures without much water or tending, and grows to be extremely old. Some olive trees are thought to be over 2,000 years old. Its fruit has sustained and pleased multiple civilizations since prehistoric times. Virtually every part of the tree was found useful. The fruit provided food, while the oil was used for cooking, burned for fuel and in lamps, blended with fragrances for scent, and used for making soap and medicines. Olive pits were burned in potters' kilns and pulp laid down as fertilizer. Olive branches served as construction materials, and olive wood was prized then as now for carving bowls and spoons. Athletes after their contests and warriors after their battles restored themselves by pouring the oil of the olive from head to foot and scraping it away, taking sweat and dust, grime and gore with it to leave the body smooth and glistening.

In ancient times, as now in many places, olives were harvested by shaking or striking the branches, gathering the fallen fruit by hand or in cloths spread on the ground beneath the tree, sifting the olives to separate them from the leaves and twigs, and finally sorting those olives best for curing and eating from others suitable for pressing. The latter were first

doused with hot water, crushed in a press, and put into a large vessel with water to settle and separate. Later the water would be drained out and the oil was ready.

Olive trees are depicted in miniature engravings on seals, on friezes decorating temples and palaces, and on pottery. Images of a goddess with an olive tree can be found on Minoan seal rings. Olives were found in a pot during the excavations at Zakros on Crete, preserved by being submerged in water. Apparently, when found, they were still plump as though just picked, but shriveled as soon as they were exposed to the air. The enormous pithoi, filled with olive oil and stored throughout the palace of Knosses, must have contributed to the fierceness of the flames that destroyed the palace.

In ancient Greece the olive tree was sacred and protected. It was identified with earth goddesses, with Athena, goddess of war and peace, and was worshipped in tree cults. In Classical Greece the olive tree of Athena on the Acropolis was venerated in her name. The Minoans of Crete are first credited with making the olive a successful commercial export, trading the oil with neighbors in the Cyclades, the Northern Aegean, and the Near East. Olive oil was, in the later classical world, a principal product and export of Attika. In the mid-5th century B.C.E., it is estimated that the state of Attika alone possessed between five and ten million olive trees. Even today Greece is one of the world's major exporters of olives and olive oil.

Wine

Wine—a gift of the gods and a comfort to man—was seen by the ancient Greeks as easing the way into both love and war, offering brief respite from sorrow and loss, and inducing sleep when all else fails. In Greek mythology it is Dionysos who is the god of all the fluid forces of nature and so the god of the grape and wine. He is, among other things a "hippie god" whose revelers—high on his mysteries and his brew—often leave a wake of ecstatic chaos behind them. Dionysos is frequently

Olive tree and leaves

depicted on pots and drinking cups holding his signature *thyrsos* (a fennel staff tipped with a pine cone) in one hand and a long-handled drinking cup (*kantharos*) in the other, surrounded by vines and clusters of grapes. Wine was an important element in countless cults and rituals, private and civic.

Winemaking is as old as the vine in Greece. In ancient times wine was always mixed with water. Grapes, both white and red, were dried for raisins and pressed for wine with the feet or with a press. The excavated villa at Valthypetro on Crete is the site of a fine, well-preserved press complete with spout and vat. Wine also provided vinegar, the strongest acid available in the ancient world, with many everyday medicinal and culinary uses.

Today you can still see innumerable vineyards, some very large and some very small, across Crete, the mainland, and the islands, soon to become wine for the family, the village, the cities, and for export. The wines of Greece are varied and seriously underrated. Greek wineries, especially the smaller ones, make some of the finest wine in Europe, which is a rather well kept secret. The signature table wine of Greece—retsina—is, however, hardly a fine wine and may best be described as an acquired taste. And it happens to be a taste which they have had a long time to acquire, as Greeks were drinking retsina or resinated wine as early as the Mycenaean

period. One of the special delights of traveling through Greece used to be to compare the retsinas of each village and taverna, whereas all too often today the menus offer only one or two nationally distributed and quite innocuous brands.

A number of regions and islands of Greece are especially known for their wines: Crete, the Peloponnese, Samos, and Santorini among them. Two very local specialities are the "sun wine" of Santorini, the "black wine" of Samos, and a unique lemony liqueur made on Naxos called "citron."

Honey

Honey is one of the truly ancient comestibles of Greece and one of the sweetest offerings of nature to the human table. Long ago the honey from wild bees was sought out in forests and in rocky cliff-side fissures. In time, however, bees were domesticated and their honey more simply harvested. In ancient Greece it was the mythical Kouretes—the nine youthful sons of Earth assigned to save the baby Zeus—who were said to have tamed the bees and developed a way to extract their golden gift. They protected him from his baby-swallowing father Kronos with powerful songs and martial dances to mask the wailings of the baby god.

Bees not only provided the main source of sweetener in the ancient world but also wax. Honey and wax were used for medicinal, cosmetic, culinary, and commercial purposes. Honey was fermented to create alcoholic brews in Egypt, Greece, and Babylonia. It was also used for embalming, as corpses, especially children, were inserted into giant pots and suspended in honey. To "fall into the honey" was an expression roughly equivalent to "kicking the bucket" except that the latter has no accompanying connotation of preservation or rebirth. Honey, a food of the gods, was often used in ritual contexts. Like wine and olive oil, it was often poured out in libations to the gods and the dead.

One very striking cultic representation of bees in ancient Crete is the golden Minoan bee pendant from Malia, dating from the 17th century B.C.E., on which two bees delicately twine around a disc of pollen.

ENCOUNTERING MODERN GREECE

Our aim in this brief section is to provide you with some tips, cautions, reassurances, know-how, and "survival skills" likely to be helpful more than once during your trip. We will attempt to avoid the obvious, keeping in mind that one person's obvious is often another's brainstorm.

It's Suddenly All Greek to Me

The first, most forceful reminder of where you have just landed is likely to be the fact that suddenly what you see and hear is in Greek—signs, announcements, conversations. It is one of the great triumphs of Greek culture and spirit that the Greeks have managed to retain their native tongue and alphabet across at least four thousand years, despite so many centuries of conquest and occupation by foreign powers—Romans, Venetians, Turks, Germans, and Italians. Greek is a gloriously rich and adaptive language. It is the language of Homer, Plato, Euripides, the Christian Scriptures, Kazantzakis, and many more. So why not make it your language as well? It will do you no harm to learn a few words and phrases of modern Greek, if for no other reason than to toast and honor its beauty and sheer survival. Besides, knowing a bit of Greek will allow you, at the least, to amuse your Greek listeners and may even endear you to them. Making the effort to say something, perhaps only a greeting, to your hosts in their own language acknowledges that you are the foreigner and that it is you, not they, who don't speak "the language." Beyond this, rest assured that most Greeks today know some English, and many are fluent English speakers. But even these may have difficulty comprehending certain regional accents; so speak slowly and repeat yourself patiently when necessary, as you would wish and expect if they were speaking Greek to you.

Here is not the place for a tutorial in modern Greek. There are many excellent teach-yourself texts, CDs, and cassettes available in bookstores and on the Internet. Go to www.smartphrase.com/Greek for a helpful listing and assessment of self-inflicted Greek language courses, dictionaries, grammars, and phrasebooks. Committing one half-hour a day to learning some Greek for a month or two before you travel and then carrying with you a traveler's English-to-Greek phrasebook will surely enhance your explorations and interpersonal exchanges in Greece. The truth is that most travelers making their own way through Greece will find themselves at least once in a situation in which English is not an option, and it is surprising how much of a difference it will make if they can read the Greek alphabet and know a few words and phrases. Sign language, mime, inventive pictograms, and a sense of humor can make up any gaps that remain.

At the very least, we urge you to learn the Greek alphabet. Road signs, bus and boat destinations, and other crucial signage are usually in Greek and English, but there are always those times when only Greek appears and you have to make a consequential decision all the same. An additional complication is that there is in Greece no official nor uniform method of transliteration from Greek to Roman characters. This is because there is no direct phonetic correspondence between many Greek characters and character-clusters and their English counterparts; so the Greeks on every level— from government publications to road signs to taverna menus—invent their own, without any rules and with barely any attention to consistency. The result is that most Greek words or names may be and are spelled in a dizzying variety of different ways when transliterated into English. Uniformity in this regard is an idle dream. You will just have to be flexible and creative, not only as you make your way through Greece but also as you make your way through this text. In writing this guide, we are often caught between the following: the familiar form of a name, the form according to any one consistent transliteration scheme, and the name as you may actually see it written on a road sign or on the front of a bus. Everyone knows, for example, "Athens" or "Delphi" or "Crete", but you may also see these written, for example, as "Athina, Delfi, or Kriti" or still other variants of the same. To get you started on your career as a Greek code-breaker we offer the following:

Greek Characters: (upper/lower case)	May be written* as:	Sounds like: (as in…)
A / α	A/a	h**a**rm
B / β	V/v	**v**ine
Γ / γ	G/g GH/gh H/h Y/y	(before e/i): **y**es (before a/o/u): **gh**etto
Δ / δ	D/d Dh/Dh Th/th	**th**is
E / ε	E/e EH/eh	**e**gg
Z / ζ	Z/z Ts/ts Dz/dz	**z**oom
H / η	E/e I/i	b**ee**t
Θ / θ	Th/th	**th**ought
I / ι	EEee	b**ee**t
K / κ	K k Cc	**k**ite
Λ / λ	L/l LL/ll	**l**ive***
M / μ	M/m	**m**eet
N / ν	N/n	**n**eat
Ξ / ξ	X/x CHS/chs	ta**x**i
O / o	O/o	s**o**cks
Π / π	P/p	**p**et
P / ρ	R/r Rh/rh	**r**iver
Σ / σ	S/s SS/ss	**s**it (except σμ = mz)*
T / τ	T/t	**t**op
Y / υ	U/u I/i EE/ee Y/y	b**ee**t
Φ / φ	PH/Ph F/f	**f**ood
χ / χ	CH/ch KH/kh H/h	lo**ch** (except before a/e/i: **h**e)
Ψ / ψ	PS/ps	wra**ps**
Ω / ω	O/o	s**o**cks
EI / ει	EI/ei E/e I/I	b**ee**t
OI / οι	OI/oi I/I	b**ee**t
AI / αι	AI/ai A/a	g**e**t
OY / ου	OU/ou	s**ou**p
AY / αυ	AF/af AV/av	either **ahf** or **ahv****
EY / ευ	EF/ef EV/ev	either **eff**ort or be**v**erage**
HY / ηυ	IF/if IV/iv	either b**eef** or **Eve****
ΜΠ / μπ	B/b MB/mb	**b**ob*** (except mid-word = m me**m**ber)

NT / ντ	NT/nt ND/nd	**d**og (except mid-word = un**d**er)
ΓΚ / γκ	GK/gk G/g NG/ng	**g**ot except mid-word = bi**ng**o)
ΓΞ / γξ	NX/nx X/X	a**nxi**ety
ΤΖ / τζ	TZ/tz	ban**ds**
ΤΖ / τζ	TS/ts	gli**tz**
ΓΓ / γγ	GG/gg G/g NG/ng	bi**ng**o

* By "may be written as" we mean that you may actually see these written as one or other of the forms cited here. For example, you will frequently find the Greek snack or sandwich wrap called a "γυρω" written in Roman characters as: gyro, giro, or hero. Greeks, in practice, sometimes try to follow a more or less uniform method of transliteration, but more often than not they attempt to render in Roman characters what they think it sounds like (but to whom is the question). As mentioned above, there is no standard phonetic system used to transliterate Greek. Therefore, you have to be as free and inventive in deciphering these transliterations as their authors were in creating them.

** AU, EU, NU are pronounced "AHF," "EF" and "EEF," respectively, when they occur before voiceless consonants (Θ, Κ, Ξ, Π, Σ, Τ, Φ, Χ, Ψ); otherwise they are pronounced "AHV," "EV," and "EEV".

*** ΒΒ ββ, ΣΣ σσ, ΛΛ λλ are pronounced as if they were single consonants, though they may be transliterated with either a single or a double consonant.

THE POLITICS OF HOSPITALITY

In ancient Greece, the rites of hospitality stood among the most sacred of all observances, and adherence to them was enforced under the watch and arm of Zeus. Times have changed in this regard. Today the tourist police (24-hour emergency helpline 171) do duty for Zeus, protecting the rights of all foreign visitors; and, although mere mortals, they generally do their job well. What's more, whereas the ancient rituals of hospitality called for the host to provide any guest-stranger with two night's bed and board *gratis*, as well as a bath and fresh robe upon arrival, today's guests are expected to produce their credit cards at reception. Another poignant and powerful aspect of ancient hospitality was that guests were to remain anonymous until after the friendly bond of fellowship had been sealed with a shared meal, lest the level of welcome be contingent upon the stranger's particulars, such as nationality, blood line, etc. The welcoming of a guest was to represent the life-affirmation of one human being by another, expressive of the fundamental friendship and goodwill that was held to be the natural relationship between human beings. Time has taken its toll too on these convictions and observances.

While Greeks remain as warm and welcoming as most any hosts you are likely to encounter in your travels, they do have their likes and dislikes, and some of these are strongly influenced by recent political history. In this context, it needs to be noted here that there is rather wide and deeply felt resentment and hostility towards the United States' foreign policy, stretching back at least as far as the close of the Second World War. The truth is that the United States has been no friend to Greece for the past half-century and more. The Greek Civil War, the fascist military junta or infamous Reign of the Colonels, and the perennial enmity between Greece and Turkey are three of the political realities which have left their scars on every older Greek you will meet, while younger Greeks regularly take to the streets over U.S. Middle East policies and practices. In all of these times and events the United States has deeply betrayed or disappointed Greece, and the Greeks do not forget this fact. One of the oldest mottos and marks of the Greek hero was "to do good to one's friends and to do evil to one's enemies," and by this measure the Greeks have had no choice but to regard the United States as an enemy for all that they have suffered at the latter's hands. This said, the Greeks have never forgotten the open doors that so many of their grandparents, aunts, uncles, cousins, sons, and daughters have found in America over many decades, particularly after World War II. Talk to any Greek long enough—it usually doesn't take long—and he or she will tell you about their relative in Chicago or Boston or wherever else. For this and many even better reasons, they are perfectly able and ready to distinguish between governments and their peoples. They know that governments everywhere lie and do wrong, including in Greece, and only rarely will they hold that against the individual citizen of goodwill.

The bottom line here is that we would advise citizens of the United States to keep a low political profile. Greece is not the place to wave the stars and stripes. Greece is not a dangerous place for Americans, but it is also not a cozy place for those who boldly or loudly assert American hegemony, as if they were at a rally. The Greeks will accept their differences with others, so long as those differences are respected on both sides; and silence or discretion is often the best way to demonstrate that respect.

NAVIGATING & NEGOTIATING GREEK ROADS

Finding your way along Greek roads can be a maddening endeavor unless you embrace it as an intellectual challenge or perhaps a battle of wits. Once you are out of major towns or cities, Greek roads rarely have numbers or names or at least rarely reveal them to the motorist. For the most part, what road signs there are indicate directions or rather destinations. The destination on any given sign, however, will only occasionally represent your actual goal. What you need to do is to determine whether the destination indicated lies in the direction that you wish to take. We have yet to discern any clear logic or prejudice at work to account for which specific destination along a given route will be featured on a road sign at any given point. This means that the route you are traversing may change names many times as you make your way along it. Your best counterstrategy will be to study your map in advance, tracing your route and noting the towns or cities that lie either short of or beyond your chosen destination. Any one of these may hold the key to finding your way and holding your course. Keep in mind that signs may change from Greek to English at will and that the spelling on the English signs may prove inventively variable. To reduce the likelihood of losing your way, you may wish to consult in advance a very useful route-planning tool provided on the internet at www.viamichelin.com

A further caution and complaint. You will notice, as we have, that Greek signage, particularly to archaeological sites and museums, is often largest and loudest at a considerable remove from the signed destination. Even minor sites are often awarded a major sign fifty or sixty kilometers out from the site itself, and followed by quite clear and helpful signs for most of the way. Then, on the close approach to the site, something very strangely inhospitable and unhelpful happens. The signs thin out and often disappear altogether. You are suddenly left to your own devices and intuitions. It is as if you are being told that if you've made it this far you can find your own way from here. The truth is, of course, that maps suffice to keep the explorer on course until it's a matter of minor roads or town streets, when only locals know their way for sure. And that's when you will often experience nothing less than total abandonment. In some cases, not even the site itself will be given a placard. It is important, Albert Camus once wrote, that there be mysteries, and it is for us only to ponder them. On a less profound level, it's a matter of scent, and so it's up to you to develop a nose for the ancient.

One last bit of advice. Unless you race cars for a living, you are sure to find the Greek roads a harrowing experience. If Dionysos presides anywhere in Greece to this day, it is behind the wheel. Greek drivers, or the vast majority of them, are possessed by a force to which most of our readers are unlikely to have any ability or desire to tap. It is not only a question of speed, but also a matter of that third eye which most visitors simply do not possess and so are unable to see, as Greeks seem to, around blind turns on mountain passes. I say this not to discourage anyone from driving in Greece, but rather to say that if you have well-established or even simmering anger management issues, you may consider offering the wheel to someone else. The brake, not the accelerator, is the key to serene longevity in Greece.

CAUTIONS AND CONCERNS

Most accidents and mishaps, people say, occur at home or very nearby; but not all. Greece is not a dangerous place, but it does present some hazards that are best held in mind, not so that they might keep you awake at night, but so that they might keep you aware and safe in your travels. Anyway, here is our own favorite list of cautions and concerns for your consideration.

The Greek police, sometimes highly visible and at other times seemingly absent, are in fact ready at hand to keep you safe and secure; and they are also there to enforce the laws. Some of those laws, not surprisingly, concern illegal drugs. Greek drug laws are among the most fierce in Europe, and any violation of them is all but certain to land the violator in a Greek prison. These sites are not on our itineraries and we do not recommend them. Another danger-ridden infraction, one that might be more tempting to those guided by this book, is the illegal purchase or acquisition of antiquities. Any "ancient" (dated prior to 1830 C.E.) object or partial object, down to the least sherd or pottery fragment, requires an export permit. Keep in mind that such objects, apart from being available on the black market, are also occasionally underfoot in ancient sites. If they are found in your luggage, they and you are likely to be confiscated.

The most formidable hazards in Greece, however, lie directly overhead and underfoot. The sun and loose stones bring more tourists down than does anything else. If you wear a hat, sunscreen, and reliable footwear, carry lots of water and look where you are going, you can improve your odds dramatically. Furthermore, if and when you trek in remote and rocky places, carrying a cell phone or letting someone know where you're going and when you expect to return are surely wise precautions to take.

There are not many dangerous critters lurking in the Greek landscape. There is the rare viper or scorpion, but they dwell mostly in the imagination of the fearful. Bees and wasps sometimes swarm the countryside, but their brief attention spans tend to make them only a passing problem. Lyme ticks are present in Greece, but the incidence of Lyme disease is still very low. In your rambles, you are likely to come across local dogs. Most of these will only wag their tails, perhaps adding a barrage of dutiful barks to prove that they are indeed gainfully employed. Among working dogs, sheep dogs are likely to be the most territorial and aggressive. In such encounters, common sense argues neither to confront nor to run from them. "All things in moderation" remains a useful maxim in Greece; and so a steady, confident retreat is often

best. If dogs present a menace, we've been advised to reach
for a sizeable stick or a few large stones, which gesture alone
apparently conveys that our species mean business. It also
won't hurt to shout "Feé-gay" in as low, loud, and
authoritative a voice as you can produce. This is not a word
to be used idly to dispel unwanted humans whom you
encounter. Far more common and annoying than any hostile
fauna, however, are the innumerable varieties of sharp thorny
hedges and dry underbrush bristling with tiny spikes or
needles. Next, regarding more apparently amiable and
enticing vegetation, unless you are well versed in Greek herbs,
fruits, and vegetables, it's best not to eat what you find on
Greek hillsides. The Greeks often spray their fields with toxic
chemicals, and many plants which look more or less familiar
and harmless can be quite poisonous. In short, it's far safer
though less romantic to bring your food with you on walks
rather than to nibble the flora as you go.

Next, an odd sort of caution. Walkers may occasionally
come across military outposts or bases in the most unexpected
and remote places. Warning signs for these sites are often only
in Greek. So, if in your rambles you see anything or anyone
that looks markedly military, it's important not to let your
curiosity get the better of you. Simply proceed on your way,
at once. Most importantly, do not take any snapshots.
Photographing Greek military sites is simply not tolerated.

Lastly, we come to some travelers' worst nightmare—
earthquakes. The fact is that Greece lies in a zone with an
impressive history and vulnerability to earthquakes. This is
reason, however, neither to avoid Greece nor to lose sleep
once you arrive. It may be reason, though, for you to inform
yourself regarding what to do in the event of a tremor or a
quake. For example, contrary to common lore, we have been
instructed, by sources in whom we place great trust, not to
seek out a door jamb or stairwell, but rather to "stop, drop,
and hold," that is, to stop in our tracks (making no attempt to
exit a building), to drop to the ground, to crawl under some
substantial object, such as a table, bed, or desk, and to hold
onto it until the quake subsides. Only then, as we have been
told, should any attempt be made to exit a building, avoiding

all elevators, power lines, fires, gas leaks, and compromised structural elements. Readers for whom this is an area of concern should seek out their own most trusted advice on assessing the risk and responding to the event of an earthquake, whether they plan to visit Crete or San Francisco or Boston, all of which lie on major fault lines.

ITINERARY ONE

MINOAN CIVILIZATION:
CRETE 1900–1400 B.C.E.

PRINCIPAL SITES

"Essential Athens"
Temple of Olympian Zeus, Acropolis Museum,
Theater of Dionysos, Odeion of Herodes Atticus,
Acropolis, Agora, National Archaeological Museum,
Goulandris Museum of Cycladic Art

Iraklio....*archaeological museum*

Knossos....*focal palace of Minoan civilization*

Malia....*Minoan coastal palace and town*

Gourniá....*Minoan Acropolis and town*

Mokhlos....*Minoan harbor settlement*

Khamaízi....*Minoan villa*

Palaikastro....*Minoan harbor town*

Petsofas....*Minoan peak sanctuary*

Sitía....*archaeological museum*

Zakros....*Minoan coastal palace and town*

Gorge of the Dead....*Minoan burial caves*

Aghios Nikolaos....*archaeological museum*

Diktaion Cave....*sacred cave, birthplace of Zeus*

Vathypetro....*Minoan villa*

Phaistos....*Minoan palace*

Aghia Triada....*Minoan palace-villa*

Kommos....*Minoan port*

Armeni....*Minoan cemetery*

Khania....*archaeological museum*

ARRIVAL IN ATHENS

This itinerary, like the three others in this guide, begins in Athens, with arrival in Athens' new Eleftherios Venezelos International Airport. Unlike its predecessor, "Venezilos" or "Spata" (as it is commonly known) is well designed, easily negotiated, and linked directly to the city center by both Metro and rail lines, as well as by taxi and bus. Before leaving the airport, you will do well to stop by the EOT (Greek National Tourist Organization) office in the arrivals hall and pick up free copies of their Athens map, cultural events guide, and other free hand-outs, such as up-to-date lists (for Athens and Greece) of current openings and closings at every state archaeological site and museum. Also ask for a free "Athens Public Transport Pocket Map"; and, if they don't have one for you, try the ticket counter at the Syntagma Metro station. If you miss or take a pass on the airport tourist organization office, there is another very helpful EOT office, several minutes' walk from Syntagma, at 26a Amalias (30-210-331-0392) open Mon–Fri 09:00–19:00, Sat–Sun 10:00–16:00.

Since all of the Athenian hotels recommended here are located in or near the traditional, in fact ancient, district known as the Plaka, we will assume that you will be seeking a bus or Metro to Syntagma or Constitution Square, which adjoins the Plaka. The airport bus to Syntagma runs roughly every twenty minutes, takes about an hour, and costs just over €3 per person, while the Metro leaves every thirty minutes, takes a half hour, and costs €10 for two persons. In general we avoid Athenian taxis whenever possible and we are not alone in this. They have a dire and mostly well-deserved reputation for unarmed theft. I have heard the view expressed more than once that Athenian taxi drivers ought to be required to wear masks to alert the unsuspecting visitor to the true nature of their profession.

DAYS ONE AND TWO

Days One and Two in this itinerary correspond directly to the first two days in "Itinerary Three: Classical Civilization" found on pages 223 through 258. In case you are already familiar with Athens and its treasures or for some other reason prefer to skip or reduce your time in Athens, simply make your way to Crete and proceed to Day Three. Depending on which form of transport you choose for your journey to Crete, you may need to cut short your second day in Athens and visit the sites you missed when you return from Crete.

BED AND BOARD

Our recommendations for lodging and eateries in Athens may be found in "Itinerary Three" on pages 212 through 215. At this point you will be spending between one and three nights here, as determined by the particulars of your arrival in Athens and departure for Crete.

TRAVEL TO CRETE

As Crete is an island, there are only two ways to reach it—in the air or across the sea. The latter, of course, will consume more of your time and the former more of your money. The choice is yours; but for our purposes, keeping count of the days in this itinerary, we will assume that you have reached Iraklio and checked into your hotel there by either the night of Day Two or the morning of Day Three. Either the overnight ferry from Piraeus or a 40-minute flight from Athens will keep you on this schedule. The air carriers of choice are Olympic and Aegean, while Minoan Lines and ANEK lines offer reliable overnight ferries year round.

DAY THREE

Whether you settled in the night before or you've just arrived by boat and dropped off your baggage at your hotel, this day of exploring officially begins at the Archaeological Museum of Iraklio, the world's premier museum of Minoan civilization and ends at the site of ancient Knossos, once the center of the Minoan world.

PRINCIPAL SITES

Iraklio Archaeological Museum

While there is nothing grand or splendid about this museum's buildings, its holdings are both extraordinary and exhausting. Be warned that you might easily expend several days rather than several hours here exploring its collection. The twenty numbered display rooms contain artifacts from the Neolithic to the Roman Period, but the overwhelming focus of its collection is Minoan. We recommend that you ration your energy and concentrate on objects from the Bronze Age, which are to be found on the ground floor in rooms I–X and upstairs in rooms XIII–XVI and currently room XVIII.

If you wish to be guided through the museum, room by room, case by case, you might attach yourself to a tour, if one is at hand, or purchase a guidebook at the front desk. The *Blue Guide: Crete* offers a learned and illuminating sequential commentary on the collection. Another less scholarly and more intuitive approach is to proceed slowly, scanning the offerings in every room and spending time with whatever catches your eye and excites your imagination. What you can't and won't miss is the fine skill and exquisite taste of the Minoan artists, much of whose work is as easy to covet today as it was presumably four thousand years ago. The freedom of line, the celebration of nature, the reveling in color, and the reverence for life are all contagious, timelessly so.

Though we leave you to your instincts and devices to find your own way through the museum, we must interfere to the extent of urging you not to miss the following: the wildly exuberant collection of Kamares pottery in room II; the Phaistos disc and the countless finely carved sealings (if your eyes are up to such minute detail) in room III; the bull's head rhyton and the snake goddess figurines from Knossos in room IV; the golden bee pendant from Malia in room VII; the carved stone vases from Ayia Triada in room VII; the rock-crystal rhyton from Zakros in room VIII; and of course the fresco fragments and the Ayia Triada sarcophagus in room

XIV upstairs. Lastly don't miss the special collection of Minoan gold signet rings, most specially the so-called "Ring of Minos" in room XVIII. Bear in mind that the museum was in the process of re-organizing its collection when we last visited; so you may find that some items have changed rooms since then.

Perhaps first among the triumphs of Minoan art were their fresco paintings, which were without precedent or peer in the ancient Mediterranean and Middle East. What you will see of them here in the "Hall of the Frescoes" (room XIV) are the disappointingly bare remnants of once glorious masterworks. The wonder is that anything remains of them. From these fragments, however, it has been possible—not without keen and generous imagination—for artists to reconstruct at least some of the lost wall paintings that once adorned the ancient Minoan palaces of Crete. Nothing has so vividly preserved the lives, the faces, the spirit of the Minoan peoples as have these fresco fragments, so like snapshots or memories too old and tattered to do much more than survive.

As you make your way through this startling store of treasures lifted from a host of Minoan sites across Crete, remember to fill the pockets of your memory with as many as you can carry with you, so that you might bring them back in the next several days to some of the sites bereaved of them. There they will infuse with life and color and sound zones of dirt and stone otherwise silent and lifeless.

To extend and deepen your study of Minoan art and culture, the museum offers a modest but worthy selection of books at its front desk; and, to address more immediate appetites, there is a terrace café, where you might consider having a bite of something before setting out for the bus station and making your way to Knossos.

Located at 1 Xanthoudidou at the northeast corner of Plateia Eleftherias (30-2810-280370). Open Mondays 13:00–19:30 and Tues–Sun 08:00–19:30. €€ Currently closed to the public; contact museum for details.

The Palace of Knossos

However inconvenient, it is only fair to begin this brief introduction on a note of unknowing. Knossos was undoubtedly the epicenter of Minoan civilization, but whether the complex bearing that name should be called a "palace" remains fully open to question. It seems to have served many functions as: a cult center architecturally aligned and ritually connected with the nearby peak sanctuary on Mt. Juktas; a commercial hub for the collection, storing, and distribution of produce and wares, as well as the creation and sale of various arts and crafts; an administrative center presiding over at least a large portion of north-central Crete and possibly at one point over all of Crete; and, lastly, a luxurious, high-status residence. "Palace" is a convenient but also inadequate shorthand designation for what we know was at least much more and possibly quite other than a palace. "Palace" after all connotes a royal residence, and it is simply unknown whether Knossos was ruled by a king, a queen, a priest, a priestess, or some other authority. King Minos sits enthroned in myth and in the writings of antiquity, but archaeologists are less ready to yield him the throne based on their findings. All the same, the tradition established by Arthur Evans and more or less honored in the breach has been to call Knossos and other cognate structures on Crete "palaces" and we shall do the same here.

Knossos was the first of the Minoan palaces and seems to have provided the template for future palaces across the island. Each arose amidst a flourishing settlement or town and followed a similar plan. At the palace core was a large central court, usually aligned on a North-South axis, and surrounded by a labyrinthine complex of other rooms designed and designated for a variety of functions. A second court was laid out on the western edge of the palace. The palaces at Phaistos and Malia,

Palace of Knossos, Crete

begun roughly at the same time, were the first after the erection of Knossos and followed its plan. Some of the later and lesser palaces lacked certain canonical features of their predecessors. The nearly complete absence of fortifications at Knossos and across the island remains one of the more striking characteristics of the Minoan settlements, for which there is no obvious or convincing explanation. The Minoans were powerful and wealthy and can hardly be said to have kept to themselves. Neither lazy nor lacking in the necessary skills, the fact seems to have been that even though they lived in a dangerous world they only rarely and then quite minimally chose to fortify themselves.

The history of the palace or rather palaces at Knossos was a long and turbulent one. After the destruction of the first palace, most likely by earthquake in approximately 1700 B.C.E., rebuilding began at once at Knossos and elsewhere. While incorporating surviving elements of the earlier palace, the second palace at Knossos took on an enhanced scale and well surpassed any of the other palaces on Crete. Not including the West Court, the more or less square palace comprised over 20,000 square meters or about 5 acres. The central court alone measured over 1,200 square meters. The New Palace at Knossos then flourished for centuries and somehow survived the otherwise thorough devastation of the mid-15th century B.C.E., perhaps serving as the military and administrative center for a Mycenaean regime on the island. Soon afterwards, however, Knossos began its irreversible decline and was finally laid to waste around 1375 B.C.E.

What you see today is this last palace, or as much of it as has survived a long series of destructive forces, inflicted by both man and nature. Some would count among these the inventive reconstructions wrought upon the site by its first and most notorious excavator, Arthur Evans. Archaeology is inevitably part science and part imagination, in admittedly unregulated proportions. Most archaeologists today, however, seated in the academy, acknowledge the primacy of science in the field as well as in the classroom. A common assessment of Evans, notwithstanding his great stature, is that he may have let his imagination run loose over the ruins of Knossos, inventing and to an extent setting into concrete an image of the palace and its people as close to fantasy as to fact. One caution to take from this is to chew rather than immediately swallow the names given to various areas and rooms in the palace. The unknown still surpasses the known at Knossos and the site is surely not diminished by its presence.

There is no need to supply a site plan or walk-through instructions to the partially restored excavation because Knossos today comes equipped with ramps, walkways, viewing points, and interpretive placards at every turn, enabling visitors to make their own way through the site and to know at any point what they are seeing, its history, and its significance. All you have to do is to find your way to the beginning of the self-guided tour along the right or south side of the West Court, where you will walk towards the West Entrance to the palace, joining there the new system of elevated timber walkways. As you make your way through the site, however, take frequent occasion to look out and beyond the ruins to the surrounding countryside, whose contours will not have changed dramatically in the past four thousand years. Built on the Hill of Kephála, a place of residence since 7000 B.C.E., the palace of Knossos controlled and enjoyed the rich natural resources of the Kaíratos River valley, its initial source of prosperity. The immediate surrounds of the palace once comprised a town of well over 10,000 inhabitants, some living in spacious villas. The sea lies less than six kilometers to the north; and it was on the sea that Knossos extended its reach and wealth, creating what was for the time a vast commercial empire.

In myth, Knossos is the palace of the great King Minos and Queen Pasiphae, the home of their passionate, wayward daughter Ariadne, the workshop of the ingenious Daidalos, the lair of the murderous Minotaur, and the battleground of Theseus where he slew the bull-headed monster, lifted a curse from his people, and lost his heart to a princess. It is also the site of Herakles' seventh labor, and the point of lift-off for the fateful first flight of Daidalos and his son Ikaros.

Located on Knossos Road, 5km south of Iraklio (30-2810-231940). Open daily 08:00–19:30. €€ Frequent buses from KTEL bus station A (ask at hotel for directions).

IMPRESSIONS OF MINOAN CRETE

There is a land called Crete in the middle of the
wine-blue water,
a handsome country and fertile, seagirt, and
there are many
peoples in it, innumerable; there are ninety cities.
Language with language mix there together.
There are Achaians, there are great-hearted
Eteokretans, there are Kydonians,
and Dorians in three divisions, and noble Pelasgians;
and there is Knossos, the great city, the place
where Minos
was king for nine-year periods,
and conversed with great Zeus.
>   —*Homer,* Odyssey, *tr. Richmond Lattimore,*
>   *xix.172–179*

Idomeneus the spear-famed was leader of the Kretans,
those who held Knosos and Gortyna of the great
walls,
Lyktos and Miletos and silver-shining Lykastos,
and Phaistos and Rhytion, all towns well established,
and others who dwelt beside them in Krete
of the hundred cities.
>   —*Homer,* Iliad, *tr. Richmond Lattimore,*
>   *ii. 645–648*

And the renowned smith of the strong arms
made elaborate on it
a dancing floor, like that which once in the wide
spaces of Knosos
Daidalos built for Ariadne of the lovely tresses.
>   —*Homer,* Iliad, *tr. Richmond Lattimore, xviii.*
>   *590–592*

The people of Crete unfortunately make more
history than they can consume locally.
>   —*Saki (H.H. Munro)*

BED AND BOARD

In central Iraklio, we can recommend with confidence these affordable hotels all of which are within convenient walking distance of the city's museums and restaurants: the very basic Hotel Lena, 10 Lahana St. (30-281-022-3280) www.lena-hotel.gr €; the stylish Atrion Hotel, 9 Chronaki St. (30-281-024-6000) www.atrion.gr €€; and the Kastro Hotel, 22 Theotokopoulou St. (30-281-028-5020) www.kastro-hotel.com €€ with its helpful staff and reliable car rental connections. They are all in the neighborhood between El Greco Park and the waterfront street of Venizelou, east of the Historical Museum. We can also suggest several more upscale choices. Located in central Eleftherias Square, across from the Archeological Museum, the Astoria Capsis Hotel (30-281-034-3080) www.capsishotel.gr €€ offers a refreshing rooftop pool and balconies. For a Venetian harbor-side view in elegant surroundings consider the GDM Megaron Luxury Hotel 9 D. Beaufort (30-281-030-5300) www.gdmmegaron.gr €€ or the chic Lato Boutique Hotel 15 Epimenidou St. (30-281-022-8103) www.lato.gr €€.

DAY FOUR

Today is a day full of kilometers to traverse and sights to see. The end of the day will find you in the small seaside village of Mokhlos, roughly 100km east of Iraklio. In the meantime, you will visit two major Minoan sites, Malia and Gournia. While the archaeological site at Malia offers a small café with snacks and light fare, you may prefer to secure provisions in Iraklio for a midday picnic at some scenic coastal spot of your choosing. The first order of the day, however, is to pack up your belongings, check out of your hotel, get behind the wheel of your rental car, and find the new national highway east in the direction of Aghios Nikolaos and Sitia. Your first scheduled stop, as it were, will be at the archaeological site of Malia, roughly 35km east of Iraklio.

PRINCIPAL SITES

The Palace and Town of Malia

Human habitation on this site can be traced to 8,000 years ago, but like the other major Minoan sites, Malia's first palatial structure was constructed around 1900 B.C.E. (in this case incorporating elements of an earlier pre-palatial settlement), and was destroyed two centuries later. Malia's second, or new, palace represented a close reconstruction of the first and suffered the same fate as all of the other Minoan palaces (with the exception Knossos) around 1450 B.C.E. Like other Minoan palaces, Malia is thought to have been linked with a pre-existing peak sanctuary, in this case on nearby Mt. Profitis Ilias.

Entrance to the palace today is through the west court, whereas in prehistory principal access would have been through entrances at the north and south of the palace. As no significant reconstruction has occurred here it is difficult at first glance to appreciate much beyond the general layout and vast scale of the site. Fortunately, however, Malia offers a small but very informative interpretive center, complete with an excellent reconstructed model of the palace whose ruins lay strewn just outside. We recommend that you visit this on-site center and study its scale model of the second palace of Malia before finding your own way through the remains.

The palace at Malia, occupying 7,500 square meters or 3.5 acres, was third in size on Crete and was in all likelihood the cultic and administrative center of a Minoan state or province extending across much of eastern Crete. Its status as sovereign or satellite, independent or subject, is uncertain

Aghia Varvara Bay

Khrysolakkos

Malia

Quartier Mu

Agora

Palace

Hypostyle
Crypt

Quartier Z

Quartier E

and may have changed at various points across the Minoan centuries. It has been proposed and argued that the king of this palace was once Sarpedon, the youngest brother of Minos.

The excavated palace was surrounded by a large city and had its own harbor. The focal point of this palace, like its other Minoan counterparts, is the central court, lying on an approximate North-South axis, with porticoes on its northern and eastern sides and a square altar in its center. The myriad rooms, chambers, and crypts comprising most of the remaining complex have been identified as serving the diverse cultic, commercial, administrative, and residential functions the typical Minoan palace. Despite its canonical design, the fact that Malia was constructed mostly from the local red sandstone gives it a different feel and look from Knossos.

Surrounding the palace complex lie a number of excavated portions of the once flourishing Minoan city. Those of greatest interest are the open square or agora; the enigmatic structure, perhaps a council chamber, now known as the Hypostyle Crypt (under a protective roof); and a complex of buildings bearing in the designation Quartier Mu, all of which went out of use at the close of the First Palatial Period. A number of on-site explanatory panels will help you find your way and make sense out of what you see. It is conjectured that the various political, cultic, commercial, and craft activities once centered in these extra-palatial areas were, during the Second Palatial Period, arguably a period of increased centralization, brought within the walls and control of the palace. Interestingly, there exists some parallel evidence that Phaistos also had a council chamber or political center outside its palace walls.

Set apart, to the north of the palace, lies the Minoan funerary complex known as Khrysolakkos, or "gold pit," whose finds include the famed golden bee pendant displayed in the Iraklio Museum. At this point, if you then walk east towards the sea, you will discover a line of defensive walls dating from the period of the new palace. These and similar defensive walls elsewhere, though exceptional, indicate that the Minoans occasionally recognized and responded to the need to fortify their communities. Only five minutes on foot from the sea, the palace and town of Malia were unusually vulnerable to sudden attack, which may explain why these modest defensive walls were thrown up between them and the sea.

Located 2km beyond (east of) the modern resort town of Malia and signposted from the national highway (30-28970-31597). Open Tues–Sun 08:00–17:00. €

The Acropolis and Town of Gournia

Gournia is perched on a hill (or a low mountain, if you live in flatlands) facing Mirambelo Bay, near the Isthmus of Ierapetra. Its attractiveness begins with its sea-scape setting. Human habitation on this site is traced to the late Early Minoan Period, around 2300 B.C.E. During its 1,100 years of settlement, Gournia suffered and survived the familiar Minoan cycle of destruction and rebuilding. Its central structure, which may or may not be designated properly a palace, was erected around 1600 B.C.E., in the century after the principal early palaces on Crete had been destroyed and rebuilt. When it too was destroyed in the mid-15th century, it was never rebuilt, and the entire site, after several hundred years of partial reoccupation, was abandoned altogether.

Compared with other Minoan ruins, Gournia is remarkably well preserved. The remaining lanes, partial walls, and thresholds provide the imagination with all that is needed to walk its streets and explore its houses, shop, shrines, and public buildings with some real remission of the millennia that have passed since this town last flourished. The well-planned integrity of this once prosperous and peaceful Minoan settlement, with all of the components of a complete Minoan community—houses, craft shops, agora, central shrine, mini-palace, public court or theatral area, and nearby cemetery—conveys a surprisingly timeless glimpse into everyday life in a Minoan town.

You will receive a site plan with your entrance ticket to the site, and with this you can find your own way through the town's neighborhoods and to the key public areas such as the town court or agora and the so-called palace. It is advisable, however, also to wander randomly through the town at your own pace and whim; for only in this way will you find the intriguing bits of the city that have been unearthed and await your discovery, like ingenious drainage systems, altars, and shrine areas.

Located roughly 16km southeast of Aghios Nikolaos, sign-posted from the national highway. Open Tues–Sun 08:00–15:00. €

Departing Gournia, your day's scheduled explorations are behind you, and all you have to do is to find your way to Mokhlos, where we strongly recommend you spend the night. Getting back on the national highway east in the direction of Sitia, you will eventually have to choose between two different side-roads to Mokhlos. The first will appear on your left after roughly 15km. This is the more direct route. If you miss this turn, or if you are feeling a bit more adventurous, your next and last chance to turn off to Mokhlos will appear again on the left after another 7km on the eastern edge of the town of Sfaka. Both turns are signposted and, with the help of your *Road Editions* map, you should have no difficulty finding the small, sometimes quite sleepy village of Mokhlos, on water's edge and surrounded by mountains. Here you can have a swim, check in to your room, and have a drink or a meal. Mokhlos, within the modest scope of a weary explorer, has it all. One additional possibility, either at the end of the day or first thing in the morning, you might consider exploring is the minor yet interesting Minoan site of Mokhlos, for you are, after all, spending the night in an ancient Minoan settlement.

The Minoan Harbor Settlement of Mokhlos

Despite all contemporary appearance, Mokhlos was once an important harbor settlement. The harbor would have been far more protective in those days, because what you now see before you as an island was once, it was thought, attached to the mainland, providing welcome shelter from the prevailing winds from the northwest. While there are some

Late Minoan remains on the current mainland just behind the village, the principal excavations have focused on what is now the island, the heart of the pre-palatial settlement at Mokhlos. Unless you swim there (not recommended) you will need to be ferried to the island, and this can happen without much effort. In the summer there is a dedicated boat making multiple trips to the island, and off-season a private trip can be arranged with a local fisherman by your host at Hotel Sofia (see below). Depending on when you arrive in Mokhlos, you may be able to find a boat the same day or else reserve one for the following morning.

Some of the burial gifts unearthed in the island cemetery are quite splendidly precious, suggesting that at least some ancient locals possessed great wealth. These finds are divided between the museums at Sitia and Aghios Nikolaos. The excavated remains on the island today include Minoan houses and a cemetery. The island's fort and obviously its white chapel are post-Minoan. The island is hardly a must-see site, but you may well find it alluring, as many just-out-of-reach unknowns tend to be.

BED AND BOARD

While Mokhlos boasts a number of attractive lodgings, we recommend this one in particular, especially for its perfect location and friendly, helpful host, Georgios Petrakis: Hotel Sofia (30-284-309-4554, fax 30-284-309-4238) € Rooms 3 and 4 are extra-spacious and come with their own private balconies facing Mokhlos Island and overlooking the tavernas and sea below. Ensconced herein the sound of the waves will gently lull you to sleep. The hotel ("hotel" is perhaps a misnomer, as there are only five rooms) also offers a number of studio apartments on the hill at the top of the village at a price not much higher than a room in the hotel. In the studios, ask for one on the west side with a sea view. If you wish to trade amenities for charm, you will find nearby, on the shore road but outside the village, the resort Hotel Club Paladien Mokhlos (30-284-309-4211, fax 30-284-309-4688) which has rooms and studios, and a pool.

For your evening meal, we suggest that you take advantage of the memorable ambience and traditional fare offered by any of several enticing tavernas clustered in the harbor, facing the island. We were very pleased with our meal at the Hotel Sofia and recommend it warmly, but you will likely want to take a pre-dinner stroll, conduct your own survey of menus, and follow your own inner genius.

DAY FIVE

Tonight will find you settled in the port city of Sitia, where you will spend two nights. Once you trace your way back to the national highway at Sfaka, Sitia lies a mere 45 km away to the east. In between, however, we recommend that you explore the site at Khamaizi, which will delay your arrival in Sitia until midday. After checking into your room there, it's then off to Palaikastro and Petsofas before returning to Sitia for the night.

PRINCIPAL SITES

The Minoan Villa of Khamaizi

Khamaizi is all about location. If you've ever entertained a doubt whether the Minoans had an eye for stunning real estate, Khamaizi will knock that doubt right out of you.

This late 3rd millennium, pre-palatial Minoan villa, whose rooms enclose a central court, enjoys an idyllic rural setting and offers, on every side, grand views of a timeless Cretan landscape of terraced mountaintops, olive groves, and vineyards, all vibrant with the sounds of birds, seen and unseen.

When first excavated in 1903, some thought that this was a peak sanctuary, but further discoveries in 1971 dispelled that notion and confirmed it to be the remote villa of some obviously fortunate and wealthy Middle Minoan family. Its unusual oval shape, whether deliberate or suggested by the shape of the crest on which it is perched, is testimony to the versatility of its architect. While there is not much to explore within the ruins, this will be of no consequence as you gaze full circle at the serene panorama of the Piskokephalo Valley.

Located 16km east of Sfaka, a right turn-off signposted from the national highway. Follow signs to the site. As the road narrows and climbs, you will have to decide for yourself how far to go by car and when to park and make the rest of the way on foot. This will depend largely on the turning radius of your car and your own comfort level. Nothing hazardous. It is a quite scenic and modest trek to the hilltop villa, which will become visible before you as you ascend. Open site, no closing hours or fee.

The Minoan Harbor Town of Palaikastro

This site on the northern extremity of the east coast of Crete, occupied from the Neolithic through the Roman Period, once represented a thriving Late Minoan port, surpassing the town of Gournia in scale (over 50,000 square miles, or 12.4 acres) and design. Missing, however, is any sign of a great house or palatial structure. The surface ruins today are uninspiring to the naked eye, doing little more than suggesting the layout of the Minoan town, spreading out on either side of a paved "Main Street" and harbor road. Finds from the site are housed in the Sitia Museum, and most notable among these is the chryselephantine (gold and ivory) statuette of a young male known as the Palaikastro Kouros, perhaps associated with the cult of Diktaion Zeus, known to have been practiced here in later Greek and Roman times, more specifically from the Geometric Period through the 4th century C.E.

For our purposes here, however, this brief glance at Palaikastro is but a prelude to a far more exciting expedition to the nearby and not-to-be-missed peak sanctuary of Petsofas.

Palaikastro is located on the northeast shore of Crete, 20km from Sitia. Leaving Sitia on the shore road along Sitia Bay, proceed roughly 10.5km, until you nearly reach the mammoth abandoned resort at Dionissos Village. Following signs to Palaikastro, turn right and go roughly 7km to reach the modern town of that name.

Finding the archaeological site, commonly called by its Roman name Roussolakos, from this point can be a challenge, requiring some instinct and possibly a willingness to ask directions. From the town plateia or central square, drive in the direction of Zakros and almost immediately turn left at a sign for Hotel Marina Village, which will take you most of the way to the site. When we were last there, in 2005, the site was signposted on signs which looked as if they might just last another winter. Hopefully they have been replaced with more helpful and enduring signage. Regardless, if you head towards the sea and more specifically the salt flats that have usurped the ancient harbor, you will surely see the site.

Open Tues–Sun 08:30–15:00. No fee.

The Minoan Peak Sanctuary of Petsofas

The climb to the summit of Petsofas and its important Minoan peak sanctuary (alt. 215m) is well worn, clearly marked, steep and exhilarating. For thousands of years, devotees, pilgrims, goats, sheep, and explorers like us have been wearing smooth the stones underfoot. It is a rigorous climb (nothing dangerous); so bring a good supply of water. The views along the way and from the top are drop-dead

Kouremenos Bay from the Peak Sanctuary of Petsofas, Crete

spectacular. If the weather is kind and visibility high, this climb will surely be one of the most memorable of your Cretan adventures.

Little remains of the ancient walled precinct and shrine complex which once crowned the summit. The countless votive offerings (including diverse figurines, plaster horns of consecration, bronze daggers, lamps, and stone libation vessels bearing Linear A inscriptions) left by pious Minoans have long since perished or been removed to the museums at Sitia and Aghia Nikolaos. It is well to remember, however, that this peak, like most sacred sites of Greek antiquity, was surely a sanctuary long before any formal stone structures were erected here. Precinct walls, altars, offering tables, and all of the accoutrements of permanent cult places mark a sacred site but do not themselves make it sacred. Whatever inspired the cult on this peak surely preceded, and we might argue survived, the sanctuary structures of which only random stones remain.

The ascent to Petsofas lies behind (south of) the archaeological site of Palaikastro (or Roussolakos). You can walk the entire way or, better, drive part way and park the car as close to the base of the hill as possible. The oft-invoked and reassuring landmark for finding your way in the hinterlands behind the site is a tin roof covering a roadside well. From there you will likely find a series of somewhat makeshift signs pointing the way to the south slope of the hill of Petsofas. At the base of the trail you will find a farm fence, a goat pen, and the trail leading up and off to the left. It is blazed all the way to the top. Open site, no closing hours or fee.

After the day's driving and two significant climbs, you may be looking for a beach before retracing your path to Sitia. If so, we can make a couple of suggestions. You will notice on your map that just north and east of modern Palaikastro there extends a long beach (marked as a thick blue line) facing Kouremenos Bay. This is excellent for swimming and windsurfing. Another prime beach site lies about 8km north along the coast at the beach resort of Vai, famed for its palm tree forest and for the tourist crush in July and August. From Vai, the return to Sitia is 24km.

BED AND BOARD

We recommend that you base yourself in Sitia for two nights. It's a pleasant, lively port with everything you'll need and is conveniently located for exploring the Minoan sites on the eastern edge of Crete. The Itanos Hotel (30-284-302-2900) www.itanoshotel.com € is a beacon of yellow and blue on the harbor off the main plateia, or square, of Sitea. The hotel offers a substantial breakfast buffet and the well-kept, sea-facing third-floor rooms have particularly good views from their balconies. A little further down the harbor from the Itanos is the Hotel Flisvos (30-284-302-7135, fax 30284-302-7137) € with clean, functional rooms, some with sea views, and private parking. The Itanos has its own taverna € on the water, and a stroll along the harbor will reveal other appealing harbor side restaurants such as Zorba's. Two more exceptional eateries are the Gato Negro taverna € at the north end of the harbor and the Taverna O Michos € one street in from the harbor at 117 Kornarou. Both are known for their fresh, authentic Cretan cooking.

THE MINOANS

After a long Neolithic gestation, Bronze Age Minoans achieved brilliant successes in art, architecture, and the orderly development of their palace-centered civilization. Their culture remained distinctive and homogeneous for at least 1,500 years. For the last 500 years, before they were overwhelmed by natural disasters and submerged by Mycenaean Greek militarism, one could apply to them the words of the Hebrew psalmist, and say that there was "peace within their walls and plenteousness within their palaces." The durable and peaceable nature of their palace period culture stands in marked contrast to the militarism seen in contemporary Anatolia (Hittites) and New Kingdom Egypt.

There must be lessons for us if only we could retrieve them. I don't deny there must have been a "downside," in serfdom and superstition, but this seems to have been more than counter-balanced by the bright gaiety and life-enhancing quality of their better selves. Contemporary Egypt strikes me as heavy, gloomy, and death-obsessed by comparison.

We obviously cannot return to the structure of belief and ritual that sustained Minoan culture; but we should, I think, try to emulate them in our response to the beauty and utility of the world of Nature. The root of religion is reverence, and I am sure the Minoans combined a happy piety with a sense of respect verging on awe as they viewed their flowery plains and snow-covered peaks. Undoubtedly we desperately need to set about conserving our world in the same spirit. We must try to mitigate our aggressions against the animal and vegetable kingdoms. We must try to foster, not dominate and subdue. And if we are to take this path, we must recapture a sense of the sacredness inherent in created life. Christians have been schooled to revere the Heavenly Father; they must learn also to follow the Minoan lead and show more respect for Mother Earth.

I should like to end with a remarkable phrase from Cicero, a great exponent of natural religion. Three words only: TERRA SACRA DEORUM. "THE EARTH IS A SACRED PLACE TO THE GODS." This puts the concept of the "sacred" in a somewhat unusual perspective. When we consecrate a place or an object or an action, we tend to look upwards, dedicating it to a higher power. It would be salutary, I suggest, for a change, to follow Cicero, and Milton too, who pictured the pendant Earth suspended from Heaven by a golden chain, and to think of the gods as looking down on Planet Earth, and saying to themselves: What a beautiful, what a marvelous, what a sacred place!

—*J.V. Luce*

DAY SIX

After a predictably brief visit to Sitia's archaeological museum, the day's destination lies 37km south and west along the east coast of Crete at the modern seaside village of Kato Zakros. Situated here are the ancient Minoan palace and port town of Zakros as well as the Gorge of the Dead, lined with ancient but largely inaccessible Minoan cave tombs. Blessedly close at hand, as welcome antidotes to the heat of the sun-baked gorge and ancient city, you will find an alluring lineup of seaside tavernas adjacent to the archaeological area, serving excellent fresh grilled fish, seafood, and other regional specialties. (We can testify with enthusiasm to the red mullet coming off the grill at Taverna Nikos Platanakis.) There's also an attractive pebble beach mercifully shaded by a long row of pine trees. You will not want to leave this spot, but the return to Sitia is inevitable. We recommend that you visit the archaeological site first and then, perhaps after lunch, explore as much of the gorge as time and energy reserves permit.

PRINCIPAL SITES

Sitia Archaeological Museum

This relatively small, well-designed museum deserves a stop, as it contains many of the most important finds from the region's extraordinary number of excavated archaeological sites, including Mokhlos, Khamaizi, Palaikastro, Petsofas, and Zakros. Aerial photographs of these and other sites, as well as panel presentations, provide a very helpful introduction to, or reminder of, the archaeological riches within an easy drive of this hub.

The apple of this museum's eye is the Palaikastro Kouros, a .5m high composite statuette, most probably of a deity, perhaps the young Cretan Zeus, made from hippopotamus ivory and gold. There is also an extensive collection of huge burial pots (*pithoi*) and clay sarcophagi.

Located on the left side of the road out of town in the direction of Ierapetra (30-284-302-3917). Open Tues–Sun 08:30–15:00. €

Minoan coastal palace and town of Zakros

The Minoan palace of Zakros, whose situation on the eastern edge of Crete is both strategic and protected, was once the administrative center of Minoan maritime trade with the Middle East—Egypt, Cyprus, and Lebanon. Of the four known great palatial structures on the island, Zakros was the smallest, measuring approximately 80m by 80m, with a central court comprising only 360 square meters, less than a third of

the size of the central court at Knossos. It was also the last to be discovered and unearthed. Until its final catastrophe in the mid-15th century, Zakros flourished, not because its surrounds were fertile but because its reach across the seas was long and lucrative. It was the only one of the great palaces not to be plundered at the time of its destruction. Its treasure chests, intact until they were unearthed in the early 1960's, have yielded invaluable evidence and examples of the wealth and wares of this once pivotal commercial port. Many of the extraordinary finds from Zakros may be seen in the Sitia and Iraklio (room VIII) museums.

Here at Kato Zakros, rather than the town's growing up around the palace, the reverse may have been the case; for the palace whose ruins are visible today dates from the New Palace Period, when the adjacent town was already prosperous. The town's protected harbor, besides sheltering and receiving trading ships from the Eastern Mediterranean, was presumably a key base for the Minoan fleet whose charge it was to guarantee the security of the island from external attack.

The palace plan that comes with entrance to the site will prove crucial in locating the identified sectors and rooms of the palace complex. Note that the town excavations, to the north of the palace, are off this plan but of course are quite visible and prominent on site. The site entrance, at the east wing of the palace, is not actually where we would recommend that you initiate your visit; so, after entering as you must through the appointed gate, proceed northeast not more than 50m to the site exit, which will place you on the ancient harbor road into town from the sea, with the principal original entrance to the palace (no more than a limestone threshold today) to your left and the town ruins mostly up and off to your right. Rather than enter the palace at this point, we suggest that you take advantage of the height available to your right and ascend into the town. The spot we have in mind can be located by looking for a roped-off stone and terra cotta bench. This is, as it were, the best seat in the house, but no longer available for sitting. Instead, any equivalent nearby vantage point will do. From there you will be facing southeast looking down on the palace below, with the sea on your left and mountains on the other three sides. From this height you can survey the entire palace, locate the main points of interest on your site plan, and then descend to investigate the site as you wish, at your own pace. As in other canonical Minoan palaces, the central court lies at the core here. The west wing is focused on cultic activities, while the east wing comprises the royal or state apartments and administrative center. The south wing contains a mix of workshops, and the north wing includes storage areas, a bath, kitchen, and dining facility. The nearest major peak sanctuary, with which Zakros is thought to have been ritually connected lies several kilometers to the north at Traostalos (alt. 515m).

Even the most direct route involves a great many turns and squiggles, but may still be traced without difficulty on your map, taking you through Mitato, Karydi, and modern Zakros. One rather daunting option is to leave your car at the western end of the Gorge of the Dead and walk the full length (8km) of the gorge to the ancient Minoan town; but we recommend driving all the way to the modern village of Kato Zakros, parking along the beach, and exploring as much of the gorge as you wish starting from and returning to its eastern entrance. Anyone initially attracted by the first option should keep in mind that it will require an 8km return through the gorge at the end of the day, unless an alternative means of transport can be found to one's car.

Located 37km southeast of Sitia on the eastern coast of Crete adjacent to the modern village of Kato Zakros. Open daily 08:00–17:00. €

The Gorge of the Dead

This torrent-carved gorge is a natural wonder. Its myriad natural caves have been utilized for burial from at least the Early Palatial Period. Access to them can be hazardous depending on which one you choose to explore. If you decide to venture up the gorge wall and into one of the caves you will need at the very least a solidly supportive pair of shoes, preferably boots, and a flashlight. To reach most of the caves, however, you must have formal rock-climbing gear, as well as the properly accompanying skill and experience. Unless you are a trained and experienced climber or a blood relation to Spiderman, we recommend that you merely gaze up in wonder at the caves from below as you make your way through the gorge.

Located just west of the Zakros archaeological site. Open site, no closing hours or fee.

Day Seven

At this point we have an optional adventure to suggest. Depending on your timetable, however, you may wish to waive this excursion to the birthplace of Zeus and, instead, proceed directly to the Minoan palaces of Phaestos and Aghia Triada and the ancient port of Kommos (see Day Eight). So as not to retrace familiar ground, you can drive southwest from Sitia to Irapetra and from there proceed west along the national highway to the turn-off (between Mires and Tymbaki) to these sites, a total journey of roughly 170km.

Otherwise, today will take you on a steep and spectacular mountain journey to the Lasithi Plateau and across to the Diktaion Cave, a focal cult site of the Cretan Zeus, and finally to the quiet, remote village of Aghios Georgios. The journey from Sitia to Psychro, the nearest town to the natal cave, measures under 120km; but the your progress will be slowed considerably by the pitch of the road and its countless curves, as well as by the predictably incessant urge to pull over and drink in the panoramic vistas. You will see on your map that there are two competing routes to Mesa Lasithi, their point of convergence located only 5km from Psychro. One takes you from Sitia to Aghios Nikolaos, where you take a left turn south and west in the direction of Mardati and Kritsa, joining an unsurfaced road north at Andeliakos. The other also takes you on the national road; but this time you pass Aghios Nikolaos, exiting at Neapoli, where you turn south in the direction of Vryses and proceed all the way to Mesa Lasithi. Both roads promise stunning scenery as well as harrowing hairpin turns. As you can see on your map, the second route, less than 10km longer than the first, offers a major surfaced road, which will likely be decisive for many motorists. Either way, it is only another several kilometers from Mesa Lasithi, through Ahios Giorgos, to Psychro and the cave of Zeus.

First, a note on the Lasithi Plain. Cultivated since Minoan times, this richly fertile alluvial plain—measuring 30 square kilometers—is one of the most productive agricultural areas of Crete. Among its major crops are apples, potatoes, almonds, and some grains. The rugged, year-round inhabitants here, whose remote, often unspoiled villages lie scattered around the edges of the plain, have the unique distinction of living beyond 800m above sea level. The rest of their fellow Cretans choose lower, less challenging climes. The oval Lasithi Plateau, encircled by mountains, resembles, and has often served as, a natural fortress with seven natural gates or passes through its battlements. Besides its abundant harvests and strategic potential, however, the plateau is a beautiful sight in any season and especially when its orchards are in bloom.

PRINCIPAL SITES

The Diktaion Cave

A place of cult and pilgrimage from at least the Early Minoan Period through the Roman era, this cave was one of the most sacred precincts on Crete. As a focal site for the worship of Zeus, this is said to be the site not only of his secret birth but also of his ravishing of Europa, the consequent mother of King Minos. It was here that Zeus was raised by the Kouretes, the nine bee-keeping sons of Gaia or Earth. Votive objects discovered in the cave include figurines of gods, animals, and humans, doubles axes, and Kamares potsherds. Many of these finds are exhibited in the museum of Iraklio. The upper cave offers evidence of an ancient precinct wall and altar, while the dark pool in the lower cave has yielded a large number of offerings from the Late Minoan Period and later. Mount Dikte is also the haunt and cult site of Diktynna, the huntress and mistress of the animals on its wild slopes.

The first sight of the cave mouth can take your breath away. It is a great, mysterious maw. It also reminds us of the impenetrable inward depth from which Earth first brought forth Starry Heaven and into which he soon plunged himself in the blind invention of sex. This too was where the youngest son of Heaven lay in wait with a flint blade to castrate his father in the act and usurp his throne. This cave must have evoked these and other stories of the beginnings of the world and its gods, which eventually focused on Zeus. It seems to lead to the womb of the earth and seems the safest of all seclusions, whether as a place to hide from a murderous father

or to have your way with an abducted princess. Zeus, of course, did both here, we are told.

Perched 200m above the village of Psychro and 1025m above sea level, the Diktaion cave is both a demanding and a rewarding climb, as the views from its height are spectacular. The ascent can be made less arduous, however, if you follow our advice here. You will notice that the marked approach to the cave is up a steep, rock-paved incline worn very smooth and thus slippery. It is, in fact, a true hazard when wet. To ease the ascent and to lessen the weight in your wallet, donkey rides are available for a price only slightly less steep than the path. What you learn only after reaching the top, however, is that there is a comfortably graded, paved ramp from the cave to the base of the hill which is marked and provided for your return. It was not visible, of course, from the entrance below. The obvious fact is that what can be descended can be ascended as well; so we recommended that you use this convenient walkway both to reach the cave from below and to return. To find it, walk to the left side of the parking lot as you face the marked path of ascent until you approach the "Taverna Cafe Bar Chalavro" and at that point look to your right where you will see the walkway described above. This way you avoid the donkey hawkers as well as the rigors and risks involved in taking the official route. Ignore all of this, naturally, if you've always wanted to climb 200m on the back of a donkey. Regardless, the above-mentioned taverna will provide welcome refreshment and grand vistas after your pilgrimage to the Bethlehem of Minoan Crete.

Located just beyond and above the village of Psychro, which lies less than 2km west of Aghios Georgios. Signposted as "Spileon." Open 08:00–19:00. € (Hours are seasonal and often unpredictable.)

BED AND BOARD
The village of Agios Georgios is a window into old Crete with men dressed in traditional Cretan garb, dogs sleeping in the street, and few tourists. Greek hospitality can be enjoyed at the well-polished Hotel Maria (phone and fax 30-284-403-1774) € designed with traditional Cretan architecture in mind and lovingly decorated with bright folk textiles. Request a front-facing room and enjoy your own ivy-covered balcony. The Hotel Rea, € on the main street of the village, is run by the same owners and has simple rooms above the ground floor taverna where Kyria (Mrs.) Spanakis prepares tasty local dishes for your evening meal.

DAY EIGHT
It is best to rise early today, as every hour will count, whether behind the wheel driving or on the ground exploring. The journey from Aghios Georgios via Vathypetro to Phaestos will cover roughly 135km. This route will take you north from Aghios Georgios through Tzermiado, Gonies, and Kato Horio to intersect the national highway, which you will then take west in the direction of Iraklio. At Iraklio take the road south towards Knossos, Peza, and Pyrgos, but before reaching Pyrgos, turn right onto the road west towards Asimi, Aghia Deka, Mires, Tymbaki, etc. Halfway between these last two, however, or just over 6km west of Mires, you will see a road on your left heading

south and signposted "Phaestos." After exploring the palace at Phaestos, you may either visit the lesser palace at Aghia Triada or proceed directly to the Minoan port of Kommos, where there is an inviting beach with which to reward yourself at the end of an admittedly exhausting day of clocking kilometers and examining ruins.

En route to Phaestos there are a number of sites that you may or may not choose to visit. We will do little more than mention all but one of them here, both because of the unlikelihood of your gaining access to them and because Phaestos is at this point still far off. The sites I have in mind are all in or near Archanes. This is, indeed, arguably one of the premier archaeological areas of Crete; for situated within several kilometers of the small town 15km south of Iraklio are: the peak sanctuary of Mt. Juktas; the Minoan palace site of Tourkoyeitonia; the Minoan cemetery of Phourni; the notorious human sacrificial shrine of Anemospilia; the lovely Minoan country villa of Vathypetro, and a small but informative one-room archaeological museum (30-2810-231940, open Wed–Mon 08:30–15:00, no fee) whose exhibits provide an illuminating introduction to the surrounding sites. This rich concentration of Minoan remains would be a prime destination if only these sites were predictably open to the public, which they are not, with the exception being Vathypetro, which we will describe below. If, however, there occurs within the next several years a major injection of support and funding to reopen these sites and you learn of this, then we definitely recommend that you spend at least a few hours here touring Archanes' extraordinary archaeological offerings, and we recommend too that you begin your tour in the town museum. Regardless, if you are passing through Archanes at lunchtime, the town's central plateia is most inviting and is encircled by a number of excellent tavernas.

At the least, however, as your drive past Archanes, you will want to gaze up at Mt. Juktas (alt. 811), with which the palace of Knossos was architecturally aligned and ritually associated. This was said to be the burial place of Zeus, remembering that the Cretan Zeus, unlike his Olympian counterpart, was believed to have died and been buried. It is possible to drive to the summit of Mt. Juktas, and you will find the turn for the ascent on your right just over 1km south of town on the road to Vathypetro. The mount's peak sanctuary is thoroughly fenced-off, but the panoramic vistas at the top are stunning and you're likely to see local birds of prey hovering overhead.

PRINCIPAL SITES

The Minoan Villa of Vathypetro

The situation of this gracious Minoan villa, with commanding views of the Mesara Plain, is exquisite, which is perhaps the primary reason for at least pausing and gazing, whether or not you decide to enter and explore the site.

Constructed in the Late Minoan or New Palace Period, this country estate illustrates clearly the tasteful comfort enjoyed by the prosperous Minoan gentry. Its self-sufficiency is suggested by the olive and grape presses, the ample store-room, the pottery kiln, the weaving equipment, and the household shrine that are among the finds unearthed on the site. This was a home that had and did it all, in a setting that was perhaps its greatest treasure.

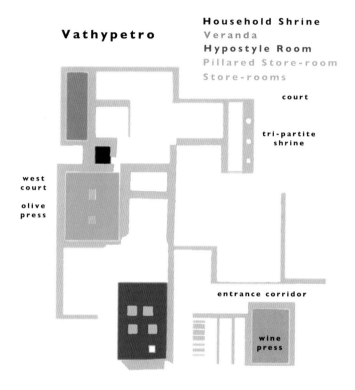

Vathypetro

Household Shrine
Veranda
Hypostyle Room
Pillared Store-room
Store-rooms

court

tri-partite
shrine

west
court

olive
press

entrance corridor

wine
press

As you will not be provided with a site map, the basic diagram offered above will give you some initial bearings in finding your way through the villa's remains. The footpath from the main road enters from the upper right of the diagram, i.e. from the north-east. One caution as you explore the ruins or decide to enter: there may be some quite spirited bees swarming about, which are most likely to leave you be, but if you are allergic this may be one site you will want to forego.

Located just over 6km south of Archanes Tues–Sun 08:30–14:30. € Signposted from Archanes, you will see it on the right as you drive south in the direction of Peza and Pirgos. It is on your way to Phaestos.

The Minoan Palace of Phaestos

Phaestos is a magnificent site, cresting a steep rocky outcrop high above the Plain of Mesara. In myth and literature, Phaestos is said to have been the palace of Rhadamanthys, the younger brother of Minos. This was unquestionably one of the great centers of Minoan wealth and power from the time of the first palaces. In fact, it is conjectured that Phaestos once controlled the south-central region of Crete, with the Mesara Plain as its heartland and Kommos to the south as its port. Whether Phaistos was ever wholly independent of Knossos, however, is unclear, though there seems to be little doubt that the island became increasingly centralized across the Minoan centuries, with the state and palace of Knossos as its capital.

Phaestos is the second largest of the great Minoan palaces, occupying 8,400 square meters or roughly two acres atop a settlement site that can be traced to the Neolithic Period. It enjoys spectacular views of the Mesara valley to the south and east and Mt. Ida to the north. The magnificent main entry to the palace with its monumental stone staircase and grand double-porch Propylon are unique among the Minoan palaces and they are only the beginning of the wonders here. Its central court, mostly paved with slabs of porous stone, is comparable in scale to that of Knossos. The stepped structure in its northeast corner is thought to have been a sacrificial altar. The west court and the theatral area are also noteworthy for their scale and fine design. The royal residential suite is found at the palace's north end, where it looks out upon Mt. Ida. An independent complex in the northeast corner of the site, where the famous clay Phaestos Disk was uncovered, seems to have been, at least in part, a sacral area and in the Archaic Period is thought to have included a temple of Rhea. The site plan included with your entrance ticket will help you find your way among the labyrinthine complexity of the palace, but remember to allow yourself to get lost as well; for that is often the beginning of discovery. There are countless details (plumbing, giant pithoi, inscribed stones, etc.) here to notice, admire, and wonder about. Unlike Knossos, this massive and magnificent palace is wide open for exploration and resides in a breathtaking location, often observed from above by soaring birds of prey.

It is interesting to reflect briefly on the very different choices made by the archaeologists who first dug at Knossos and Phaestos. Both excavations were begun in 1900: by Arthur Evans at Knossos, and by F. Halbherr and L. Pernier at Phaestos. While Evans chose to re-envision and partly restore Minoan Knossos, the archaeologists of the Italian Archaeological School and their successors were more modest in their interventions. Admittedly, there are many differences between Phaistos and Knossos, but surely one of them is the size of the footprint left by those who unearthed them. It is telling, we believe, that it is so rare to visit or discuss Knossos without the name and work of Evans coming to the fore, while the names and lives of his peers and counterparts at Phaistos are, like the Minoans who lived here millennia ago, all but forgotten amidst its mute stones. Consequently, the meticulous excavation and unobtrusive reconstruction of Phaestos release and inspire the imagination of the informed visitor to resurrect and inhabit the original palace in the mind's eye and then leave it be for others to do the same.

Located 2km south of the main southern highway, between Mires and Tymbaki (30-28920-42315). Open daily 08:00–19:30. € (Joint tickets available for Phaestos and Aghia Triada. €€)

The Minoan Palace-villa of Aghia Triada

First excavated in 1902 as an extension of the work at Knossos, Aghia Triada remains a mildly puzzling yet attractive site. A second palace so near Phaistos as to be a neighbor raises the issue of redundancy and at the least a question of nomenclature. While Aghia Triada in many respects meets palatial standards, it does so in miniature, hence the curious title of "palace-villa" preferred by some scholars. The extraordinary finds unearthed at Aghia Triada (like Zakros, never plundered), including fine figured frescos and the famed sarcophagus, bear testimony to its importance and wealth, whatever we call it. It's relationship across time with Phaistos remains a matter of speculation. A further puzzle surrounding this site is the fact that after the destruction of the Minoan palaces, Aghia Tridha recovered and thrived in the Post-palatial Period, as did the port town of Kommos to the south. It is thought that during this period, Aghia Triada replaced Phaestos as the administrative center for the region.

The structures on or adjacent to the site of Aghia Triada are quite complex, spanning as they do several millennia. There are pre-palatial tholos tombs, as well as palatial components from the First, Second, and Post-palatial Periods. Mycenaean influence was strongest in the last stage, of course, as represented by a megaron or great hall, the first Cretan instance of this characteristically Mycenaean element.

Aghia Triada, apart from its Minoan ruins, offers a quiet retreat after the massive, sun-baked, and often crowded site of Phaestos. Here you will find a view of the sea, ample shade, and numerous benches, frequently used for naps by weary tourists. To reach the cemetery, walk left after leaving the main gate of the site and make your way a short distance around the side of the hill. There you will find two pre-palatial tholos tombs and one rectangular chamber tomb. At the time of writing, though, it is well fenced-in and thus a rather fruitless venture.

Located little more than a stone's throw, or more precisely just shy of 3km, from Phaestos (30-28920-91360). Open daily 08:30–15:00. € (Joint tickets available for Phaestos and Aghia Triada. €€) Exit the the far end of the Phaestos car park and bear right at the fork, following the slope of the hill.

The Minoan Port of Kommos

Minoan Kommos was the sole regional port serving Phaestos and Aghia Triada. It seems to have been spared the island-wide catastrophe of the mid-15th century and actually flourished in the Post-palatial Period, when it may have been under the jurisdiction of Aghia Triada. In Minoan times, Kommos is assumed to have been linked to both Phaestos and Aghia Triada by a road, a portion of which still survives on-site here.

Today, Kommos lies behind a fence while under on-going, periodic excavation. Quite a bit of the site can be

Mesara Bay from the Minoan port of Kommos

surveyed quite easily, however, through the fence, particularly from the beach side. Until those excavations are complete and the site is published and opened, there is perhaps no point in saying more here than that Kommos was once an important and prosperous port town. In the meantime, for explorers of ancient sites, Kommos also serves as a convenient pretext, if one is needed, for an end-of-day swim in a marvelous setting.

Located roughly 8km southwest of Phaestos on Mesara Bay. Fenced site. After leaving Phaestos and coming to the main north-south road turn left (from Aghia Triada turn right). After 3.5 km, you will reach the village of Pitsidia. It is best to drive clear through Pitsidia (ignoring all in-town signs to Kommos or Kommos Beach). Then, at the top of a hill 1.5km beyond the village, you will see on your right a road and sign for the archaeological site. Take this and you will be at the Kommos site and its beach in a matter of minutes.

BED AND BOARD

In the Phaestos area there are a number of villages and towns in which you might happily spend the night. One that you might have heard all about is Matala, which we strongly recommend your avoiding. It was once quite stark and beautiful, but it has been ruined beyond recognition. Somehow in the conversion from hippie to hip it lost its way and became rather horrid.

VORI is a village only 4km north of Phaestos. Driving west on the road from Mires to Tymbaki, turn right (north) at the sign for the Museum of Creten Ethnology and continue on to Vori. Although Vori is not a tourist town, Margit Venetikos offers a friendly welcome at her homey and spotless Pension Margit (30-289-209-1129, fax 30-289-209-1539). € While some of the rooms are small, they all share a communal kitchen and a patio for guests. Follow signs to the museum, go past the museum sign at the church, bear left at the fork by Rex Bookshop, take a left after the Grill House, and you will see Margit's sign on the right past Ariadne's market. Snacks can be had in the village square and there is a relaxed family taverna down from the square toward Tymbaki where grandma cooks while the kids do their homework.

ZAROS is a mountain village within reasonable driving range of Phaestos. You'll find it on the map north of Mires and will notice that there are several routes you might take. Just beyond the village is the Idi Hotel (30-289-403-1301) www.votomos.com € with an indoor pool and a taverna that serves their own fresh trout. Check a number of the clean, simple rooms to find one you like in their varied complex and ask about hot water off-season. Further up the road is a spring-fed lake, the source of Zaros bottled water, a delightful taverna, and a network of hiking trails.

AGIA GALINI lies another 27km along the well-traveled and by now familiar east-west road from Phaestos. Once a very sleepy and utterly idyllic fishing village it is now an extremely popular seaside resort, offering a host of places to stay. If this is your chosen destination, we recommend your reserving a room well in advance at the Glaros Hotel (30-283-209-1151) www.glaros-agiagalini.com, € halfway down the hill to the harbor, with fresh, unpretentious balconied rooms, studios, and swimming pool. Next door to the Glaros is the Fevro Hotel (30-283-209-1275, fax 30-283-2091475) € offering simple, clean rooms behind a glorious cascade of bougainvillea. For your evening meal, with its array of inviting tavernas, you are spoiled for choice here in Aghia Galini; so it's best to follow your own nose and pick the one that pleases.

DAY NINE

Today begins the home stretch of your Minoan explorations. If your Day One coincided with ours, on a Sunday, then today is Monday and thus a day mostly for driving and exploring modern Crete, as nearly all archaeological sites and most museums are closed. In case this is not Monday, we list below one recommended site which you will pass on your way back to the north of the island.

Today is also is a day of decision. You may head with us, as it were, to Khania, which we recommend, or spend the night instead in Rethymnon, which involves less driving and has a fine archaeological museum open tomorrow morning, or lastly

Khania Harbor

you could decide to head straight for Iraklio, either for your return to Athens and home or to travel to Santorini, which is a highly recommended side trip (see below). All of these options, however, take you first on the same road north to the national highway, where you will either turn left for Khania, turn right for Iraklio, or go straight into Rethymnon center. Beginning from just outside Aghia Galini, your journey north to the national highway intersection is 50km. From there it is 72km west to Khania and 78km east to Iraklio.

PRINCIPAL SITES

The Late Minoan Cemetery of Armeni

To date, more than 220 tombs have been revealed in this remarkably extensive, well-planned late Minoan cemetery. The shaded oak-grove setting is quite lovely, a welcome respite from driving. Many of the tombs are open, and it is possible to descend deep into some of the impressive Mycenaean-style chamber tombs, for which you will want to bring a flashlight. The number, scale, and craftsmanship of these rock-cut tombs are truly impressive. The cemetery (outside the fence to the right of the entrance) also contains

one tholos tomb. The mix of Mycenaean and Minoan tomb types and burial customs here gives clear evidence of the mingling of these two cultures in the Late and Post-palatial Periods.

When we were here in 2005 the site was being significantly upgraded, as it well deserves, to attract and accommodate more visitors.

Located just over 5km south of Rethymnon. Traveling north from Aghia Galini it will be on your left. Open Tues–Sun 08:30–15:00. No fee.

The Minoan Palace and Town of Kydonia

This is a level or facet of Khania which, apart from a few relatively modest archaeological digs in progress on Kastelli Hill, you will not be able to visit or explore in the contemporary city. Western Crete, in general, has not been the traditional focus of sustained, extensive investigation by Bronze Age archaeologists, at least by comparison with the energy and resources lavished on the eastern half of the island. With the discovery of such dazzling archaeological sites and treasures at Knossos, Phaestos, Malia, and other major Minoan foci in the east, the west's Minoan past and legacy have been largely overlooked and unexplored. Additionally, time is usually not kind to ancient sites. In heavily settled areas, time marches on and over them. Here in Khania, the areas of great interest now lie beneath the second largest city of Crete, which means that discovering the past would entail demolishing the present. Even before the modern city took shape in the 19th and 20th centuries, however, Greeks, Romans, Byzantines, Venetians, and Turks all added their own layers above what seems to have been, in the Bronze age, a major Minoan center known in antiquity as Kydonia, as evidenced in Linear B tablets unearthed at Knossos, as well as in later ancient texts.

Kydon, the Minoan founder of Kydonia, was said to be the grandson of Minos, and many or even most Minoan scholars today are convinced that his palace lies under Kastelli Hill just in from today's harbor, perhaps at or near the Plateia Aghias Aikaterinis, where excavations have produced a range of evidence to support this conviction. It is argued that with the decline and eventual demise of Knossos, Kydonia, after either surviving or rapidly recovering from the crisis of the mid-15th century, only rose in importance, perhaps signaling a shift of power from the east to the west of the island. Then, as now, it seems to have been the administrative and commercial center of western Crete.

If Kydonia must remain mostly buried by modern Khania, it could hardly be eclipsed by a more charming city, at least in the old town. This is a most inviting and delightful place to spend a night, or a week for that matter. The harbor, especially at night, is pure enchantment. As most of old town is prohibited to cars, it is best to park your car at the free harbor lot and take in old Khania on foot.

Khania Archaeological Museum

The first thing you will notice and admire about this museum is its remarkable building, originally part of the Venetian monastery of St. Francis and later sequentially converted into a mosque, a cinema, and a storehouse, before assuming its present form and function in 1963. Its holdings span the Neolithic, Minoan, and Archaic Greek to Roman Periods, representing the long and rich habitation of Khania and its surrounds. While the holdings of this museum are very modest by comparison with those in the museum at Iraklio, they are helpful in understanding and appreciating the Minoan legacy in western Crete.

Located in from the harbor on Khalidon Street (30-28210-53033). Open daily 08:30–15:00. €

BED AND BOARD

In the atmospheric old town you can find a wide selection of spic-and-span, artistically decorated rooms, some with antiques and romantic wrought-iron beds, in the five properties operated by Ifigenia Rooms and Studios (30-282-109-4357) www.ifigeniastudios.gr. € Ask for a quiet room, especially if in the harbor-side property, with a balcony and a view so as to enjoy the ever-changing scene in the neighborhood's colorful pedestrian streets. The welcoming Hotel El Greco 47–49 Theotokopoulou St. (30-282-109-4030) www.elgreco.gr € is spotless and, though the bathrooms are a bit small, the rooms are ample and bright.

You will enjoy an excellent meal, enthusiastic service, and a sunset view overlooking the Venetian port at the harborside Taverna Patari € next to the old Mosque. If you can pull yourself away from the harbor, however, you will find exceptional authentic cuisine at To Karnagio, 8 Plateia Katekhaki, a favorite with locals.

CRETAN SCRIPTS

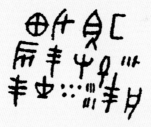

Found mostly on seal stones, sealings, and pottery, Cretan hieroglyphics, bearing little resemblance to Egyptian hieroglyphs, have been unearthed at a number of palaces, such as Knossos, Phaistos, Malia, and Petras. The above glyphs are from the Phaistos disc, which may be dated to approximately 1600 B.C.E.

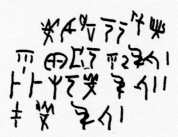

Linear A script, the script of the new or second palaces, first appeared in the early or mid-17th century and was in use perhaps until the end of the Neopalatial Period. Derived from the earlier hieroglyphic script, it was a syllabic system that also relied on ideograms.

The Linear B Script was introduced during the Late Palatial Period from the Greek mainland and has been found almost exclusively among the ruins at Knossos. It was deciphered by Michael Ventris with John Chadwick in 1953 and found to be a form of early Greek, mostly used for keeping accounts.

[If you've opted, instead, to stay in Rethymnon, then we can make the following recommendations: Centrally placed in the old town, a stone's throw from the port, the spruce Hotel Fortezza 16 Melisinou St. (30-283-105-5551) www.fortezza.gr € has a pool and plain but tasteful rooms with balconies. For those who would like a refined atmosphere, the Palazzo Rimondi 21 Xanthoudidou St. (30-283-105-289) www.palazzo rimondi.com €€ in the old town has suites and a small pool. There are basic, tidy rooms with small bathrooms and a warm welcome to be had at Atelier Rooms to Rent 27 Chimaras St. (30-283-102-4440) above the pottery studio and shop of Frosso Bora and her gifted icon-painter husband. Ask for a room with a balcony. The Atelier is located off the pedestrian walkway at the top of the Fortezza in the old town, around the corner from the Archaeological museum. The harbor is lined with tavernas serving fresh seafood with a picturesque view or you can consider the line-up of summer restaurants along the beach.]

DAY TEN

Nothing remains now in the Minoan itinerary but to find your way back to Iraklio and from there to Athens. That is, unless you decide to take the recommended side trip sketched below.

SIDE TRIP

The Island of Santorini and the Ancient Town of Akrotiri

No argument should be required for a visit to Santorini if time and resources permit. Santorini is unique and simply unforgettable. It also represents your one chance to walk down actual Bronze Age streets and peer into nearly intact Minoan houses in the extraordinary ancient site of Akrotiri. Often described as the Greek Pompei, Akrotiri was buried and preserved in volcanic ash for nearly 3,500 years due to the catastrophic eruption that devastated the island of Thera (Santorini) around 1500 B.C.E. Santorini, or "Thera" as it was

known until the Italians renamed it, was then a thriving Minoan colony, satellite, or trading partner in the southern Aegean. Its precise political relationship with Crete is debated, but there is no disagreement over the profound stamp of Minoan civilization on every aspect of life in Akrotiri. Consequently, it survives — though at this writing, it is closed for restoration work—and serves as an accidental time-capsule for Bronze Age Crete at the peak of its influence and power.

To research and consider this side trip more thoroughly, refer to Days Three and Four of Itinerary Four (page 305). What you will not find there, however, is how to reach Santorini directly from Crete. As it turns out this is an easily accomplished goal. Olympic Airways (www.olympic-airways.gr) offers several direct flights each week from Iraklio to Santorini; but it is also quite pleasant and convenient to cross by sea unless bad weather and rough seas intervene. In summer there are multiple daily sailings, including ferries operated by Minoan Lines (www.minoan.gr) and catamarans operated by Hellenic Seaways (www.hellenic seaways.gr) and Sea Jets (www.seajets.gr). Catamarans make the journey in roughly 2 hours, and high-speed ferries in twice that time.

ITINERARY TWO

MYCENAEAN CIVILIZATION:
THE PELOPONNESE 1500–1100 B.C.E.

PRINCIPAL SITES

"Essential Athens"....*Temple of Olympian Zeus, Acropolis Museum, Theater of Dionysos, Odeion of Herodes Atticus, Acropolis, Agora, National Archaeological Museum, Goulandris Museum of Cycladic Art*

Nafplio....*archaeological museum*

Tiryns....*Mycenaean acropolis*

Mycenae....*focal acropolis of Mycenaean civilization*

Mycenae....*archaeological museum*

Treasury of Atreus....*Mycenaean tholos tomb*

Argos....*theater, agora, and archaeological museum*

Korinthos....*ancient city and archaeological museum*

Akrokorinthos....*ancient mountain fortress*

Nemea....*sanctuary of Zeus and stadium*

Epidavros....*sanctuary of Asklepios, theater, stadium*

Asini.... *Mycenaean coastal acropolis*

Lerna....*early Helladic settlement and fortress, "House of the Tiles"*

Menelaion....*sanctuary of Menelaos and Helen*

Sparta.... *archaeological museum, acropolis, theater*

Pylos.... *Mycenaean acropolis and tomb of Nestor*

Hora....*archaeological museum*

Olympia....*sanctuary of Zeus and stadium*

Olympia....*archaeological museums*

SIDE SIGHTS

Peloponnese....*Wine Roads of the Peloponnese*

Pellana....*Mycenaean acropolis (of Menelaos?)*

Sparta....*Museum of the Olive and Greek Olive Oil*

Mistras.... *medieval city*

ARRIVAL IN ATHENS

This itinerary, like the three others in this guide, begins in Athens, with arrival in Athens' new Eleftherios Venezelos International Airport. Unlike its predecessor, "Venezilos" or "Spata" (as it is commonly known) is well designed, easily negotiated, and linked directly to the city center by both Metro and rail lines, as well as by taxi and bus. Before leaving the airport, you will do well to stop by the EOT (Greek National Tourist Organization) office in the arrivals hall and pick up free copies of their Athens map, cultural events guide, and other free hand-outs, such as up-to-date lists (for Athens and Greece) of current openings and closings at every state archaeological site and museum. Also ask for a free "Athens Public Transport Pocket Map"; and, if they don't have one for you, try the ticket counter at the Syntagma Metro station. If you miss or take a pass on the airport tourist organization office, there is another very helpful EOT office, several minutes' walk from Syntagma, at 26a Amalias (30-210-331-0392), open Mon–Fri 09:00–19:00, Sat–Sun 10:00–16:00.

Since all of the Athenian hotels recommended here are located in or near the traditional, in fact ancient, district known as the Plaka, we will assume that you will be seeking a bus or Metro to Syntagma or Constitution Square, which adjoins the Plaka. The airport bus to Syntagma runs roughly every twenty minutes, takes about an hour, and costs just over €3 per person, while the Metro leaves every thirty minutes, takes a half hour, and costs €10 for two persons. In general we avoid Athenian taxis whenever possible and we are not alone in this. They have a dire and mostly well-deserved reputation for unarmed theft. I have heard the view expressed more than once that Athenian taxi drivers ought to be required to wear masks to alert the unsuspecting visitor to the true nature of their profession.

As an alternative to the plan above, you may decide to fetch your rental car at the airport upon arrival and drive at once to Nafplio, beginning this itinerary there (see Day Three) and therefore postponing Days One and Two until the end of your trip. There are advantages to each of these options. Our logic is that, jet-lagged and unfamiliar with Greece, you may not be inclined to get behind the wheel on a Greek highway as soon as you touch ground in Greece. Another consideration is that, assuming you arrive on a Saturday and spend Sunday and Monday in Athens before driving to Nafplio on either Monday evening or Tuesday morning (we recommend Monday evening), you will be able to take advantage of the fact that the principal Athenian sites and museums are open both of these days, while you would likely be facing some Monday closures in the Peloponnese if you went there directly. In summer, it is also the case that Nafplio is often overrun by Athenians on weekends, as it is a favorite getaway from the city; and, as a result, Nafplio loses an appreciable share of its accessibility and charm. It is a good deal easier on weekdays to find a bed, a table, a parking space, an ample patch of sand on the beach, as well as peace and quiet when it's time to sleep (something that will take on unusual importance if your body clock is not yet set for Greek time).

Days One and Two

Days One and Two in this itinerary correspond directly to the first two days in "Itinerary Three: Classical Civilization" found on pages 223 through 258. In case you are already familiar with Athens and its treasures or for some other reason prefer to skip or reduce your time in Athens, simply make your way to Nafplio and proceed to Day Three. Depending on which form of transport you choose for your journey to Nafplio, you may need to cut short your second day in Athens and visit the sites you missed when you return from Nafplio.

Bed and Board

Our recommendations for lodging and eateries in Athens may be found in on pages 212 through 215. At this point you will be spending between one and three nights here, as determined by the particulars of your arrival in Athens and departure for the Peloponnese.

Travel to the Peloponnese

Decisions, decisions. Now you have another one to make regarding the time and method of transport to Nafplio. Our recommendation is that on Monday evening you return to the airport by bus or preferably by Metro (both leave from Syntagma), pick up your pre-booked rental car and drive to Nafplio, a 170km journey that will take anywhere between two and three hours, depending how far down you press the accelerator. Regardless, if you leave the airport by 7pm, you'll have plenty of time to check into your hotel, refresh yourself, and find a restaurant (remember that Greeks customarily begin their evening meal when many northern Europeans and Americans are going to bed). Your other options involve taking a bus or hydrofoil to Nafplio, neither of which is direct and both of which will take about 4 hours. During the day and evening there are numerous buses departing central Athens for Nafplio from the Peloponnese Bus Station (Stathmos Leoforia Peloponnisou 30-210-512-9233 www.ktel.org). Weather permitting, i.e., in the absence of rough seas, hydrofoils bound for Nafplio leave Zea Marina, Piraeus, in the late afternoon on most days. For schedules and fares call: 30-210-453-6107 or go to: www.dolphins.gr.

We will assume that you have taken our recommendation, avoided the nightmares of driving in Athens or tacking your way to Nafplio in a bus or hydrofoil, picked up your car at the airport, and are now at the wheel. The drive to Nafplio should be straightforward and painless, even enjoyable. Be sure to have some loose euros ready at hand to pay tolls along the way. Follow signs for "Athina" (Athens) out of the airport, take Route 62 until you come to the new E94 toll road, which has made a breeze of bypassing Athens for the Peloponnese. On the E94 follow signs at first to Athina until you have the opportunity to follow signs to Elifsina and Korinthos. After 122km, as you near Korinthos (just after you cross the Isthmus into the Peloponnese), turn left onto E65. After 25km on E65, outside of Archaia Nemea, turn left again on the road signposted for Nafplio, where you will arrive in another 32km. Follow signs to the center, and the harbor or port in particular, where you will find ample free public parking. Here, along the waterfront, even in summer, there's always a convenient spot available on week nights.

Depending on whether you arrive in Nafplio on the evening of Day Two or the morning of Day Three, this will be your base for either three or two nights, and you will be glad for that. Nafplio is just about everyone's—insider and outsider alike—hands-down favorite spot in the Peloponnese. Spilling down a steep, rocky hillside to the water's edge, the old town has more charm and surprises than you could possibly consume in several days or several weeks.

Following the War of Independence, this was modern Greece's first capital for six years (1828–1834), until the seat of government was transferred to Athens. Even today, this concentrated city of 10,000 presents itself to visitors with much of the pride, vitality, elegance, and would-be majesty that one might expect of a nascent nation's first city. At the same time, Nafplio, like Greece, is as ancient as it gets in southeastern Europe, with remains reaching back to the Paleolithic. Its legendary namesake founder, Nafplios, was no less than a son of Poseidon, and one of the two fortresses perched above the modern city is called Palamidi, after the son of Nafplios.

In myth, Hera, queen of the gods, in her capacity as a fertility goddess, came to Nafplio every year to bathe in the waters of a local spring, which annually restored her virginity. Regrettably, these waters have not been known to convey the same boon on mortals. In the Mycenaean age, Nafplion is conjectured to have been the fortified port for nearby Argos, and indeed a Mycenaean cemetery has been unearthed on Palamidi's slopes. It is also claimed to be the port to which Helen and Menelaos returned together from Troy a decade after the most fateful elopement or abduction (which it was remains unresolved) of Greek antiquity. According to Euripides, this was where and when they learned of the murder of Clytaemnestra and Aegisthus by their nephew Orestes.

Today, however, the heart of the city is in its central plateia, Plateia Syntagma, just in from the harbor, where every evening the children of the city scramble wildly in countless unscripted, simultaneous games involving balls and

Nafplio rooftops from the Byron

balloons and wheels of every sort, while everyone else from teens to the wizened only watch—the games, each other, the full spectacle. If you wonder why we chose Nafplio as your base, spend a few after-dark moments in the Plateia Syntagma and you will know.

BED AND BOARD

We recommend staying in the captivating Venetian old town with its bustling central plateia, narrow, cobbled lanes, colorful walkways, and admittedly endless flights of steps. While there is free public parking along the harbor, some of the lodgings in steeper locations offer drop-off areas for luggage or even private, more convenient parking. You might inquire into parking when you book your room in advance.

The King Othon Hotels (I & II), 4 Farmakopoulou St. (30-275-202-7585) & 5 Spiliadou St. (30-275-209-7790) www.kingothon.gr € enjoy a prime location on the Plateia Syntagma, just in from the harbor. Tasteful rooms, a bountiful breakfast, and helpful owners assure a most pleasant stay in the historic dwellings. The Pension Acronafplia, 34 Papanikolaou (30-27520-24481) www.pensionacronafplia.gr €/€€ provides a wide variety of rooms and apartments in three different locations; so check out their offerings and decide what appeals to you. The lavishly decorated Hotel Ilion, 4 Efthimiopoulou & 6 Kapodistriou St. (30-275-202-5114) www.ilionhotel.gr €€ with its romantic rooms invites visitors to "Live its calmness to enslave every sensation" with cupid-adorned Jacuzzi rooms and attentive service. The Byron, (30-276-202-2351) 2 Platonos St. www.byronhotel.gr €€ offers tasteful, simple, reliably spotless rooms in a quiet corner of the old town. For optimal space, ask for a room with a view or one with a balcony. When dropping off your luggage, drive most of the way by ascending Sigrou St. from the harbor and then turn onto Papanikolaou to the Plateia Agia Spyridonos where you can park long enough to deliver your bags to the hotel. Otherwise, bring along a llama. At the top of the town the sparkling Pension Marianna, 9 Potamianou St. (30-275-202-4256) www.pensionmarianna.gr € has a stellar view of the city's enticing quilt of rooftops and the bay below; but not every room comes with this view. Best to put in your request early for a sea-view. Regardless, the lovely tent-topped patio, where a generous breakfast buffet is laid out every morning, will allow you to feast your eyes as well as fill your stomach. To reach the Marianna by car from the harbor, turn off Bouboulinas onto Polizoidou St. in the direction of the Akronafplia Fortress and park in the lot adjacent to what is now a vacant, defunct hotel. Proceeding on foot a short distance to the walled entrance to the old town you will see a sign pointing the way to the Pension Marianna.

Among the many options for old town dining our favorite is the unassuming Taverna Old Mansion, Palio Arhontiko € for the delectable "real thing" and for daily live music in the summer. It is tucked away at the corner of Ypsilantou and

Sidaou. The Taverna Vasilis €, wedged into a line of its competitors on Staikopoulou St., has substantial, satisfying food and affordable fixed menus for two. Savouras €€ and Arapukos €/€€ are both favored by locals and visitors alike for the freshest fish on the waterfront. Hellas Restaurant €/€€ in the lively Plateia Syntagma pairs classic Greek fare with a front-row view of all the action on the monumental square: kids romping, neighbors gossiping, teens courting, seniors reminiscing. Whatever its temperature on arrival, your food is likely to get cold and forgotten here as you put down your fork and gaze. There's also the risk of a soccer ball landing in your soup.

DAY THREE

Why save the best for last? Why not first? Today, after a relatively brief stop at the acropolis of Tiryns, we suggest that you make your way to the magnificent hilltop citadel of Mycenae, the timeless epicenter of Mycenaean civilization and the legendary palace of Agamemnon. In following this order and route, you will follow ancient practice and protocol; for, at the height of Mycenaean power, visitors traveling by sea and bound for Mycenae would arrive first at Tiryns, Mycenae's port authority, as it were, and then proceed overland along the Mycenaean road linking the two. To picture this clearly, you will have to place the sea much closer to the acropolis of Tiryns than where you find it today.

Depending on how much time and will remains for exploring after your visit to Mycenae, you may wish to go on to the Sanctuary of Zeus at Nemea, site of the Nemean Games, and one of the nearby wineries (see Day Four). Nemea, after all, is known not only for its ancient games but also for its outstanding wines. Whatever you choose to do after Mycenae, your return will take you through Argos, which has claimed to be the oldest city in Europe and left its powerful imprint many times across the scroll of Greek antiquity. Lastly, if the sun has not yet set, this may be the day for you to discover Nafplio's long, sandy, and splendidly situated Blue Flag beach (Karathona) to which you can either drive in a matter of ten or fifteen minutes or walk within an hour. The road loops around the back of Akronafplia and Palamidi, while the walking route (4km) leads south along the harbor and then follows the water all the way. There is also a public bus to take you there.

One final note: for today's explorations, be sure to bring with you a reasonably powerful flashlight/torch, for reasons that will become clear.

PRINCIPAL SITES

The Mycenaean Acropolis of Tiryns

This impressive World Heritage Site suffers on several levels from its proximity to Mycenae, which so outshines it that Tiryns is by comparison overlooked, under-funded, and left to gather dust. Its ancient pride and enduring wonder are its massive cyclopean fortification walls, whose footprint measures roughly 750m. Regrettably, they are no longer safe nor accessible to admire up close. Nevertheless, even at the distance to which we are kept, they are startling in their craftsmanship and scale, once flatteringly compared by Pausanias to the pyramids of Egypt. In fact, these walls, completed by the end of the 14th century B.C.E., were all that were said to have survived of the citadel over 800 years later when Argos assaulted and took Tiryns apart in 468 B.C.E. Today they stand partially reconstructed at about half of their original height, estimated to have been 20m; in thickness, they range mostly from 8m to 11m.

The silent walls of Tiryns might hold their visitors captive for days if only they could speak and tell the stories of what they have seen since their erection. To mention only one, Herakles, a crazed hero given to fits of madness, hurled to his death the young prince Iphitos, who had alone defended Herakles' claim to a bride he had rightfully won and wrongfully been denied. Other stories involve such towering figures as Bellerophon, Dionysos, Melampos, Perseus, and, of course, the Cyclops, the walls' own architects and builders.

In ancient times it was possible to ride into the citadel in a chariot, mounting a spacious ramp 5m in width; but today you must leave your car outside the site and walk to a break in the enclosing fence where there is an entrance kiosk. Site maps are not provided and the site is poorly signed; so we have provided below a basic diagram of the site and its highpoints for the sake of orientation and discovery. Entry is from the east side of the site. Once inside the circuit walls, the point of attention is the upper citadel, comprising the palatial residence of the king of Tiryns. We will mention here just a few of the architectural details which are of particular interest and which you might otherwise overlook.

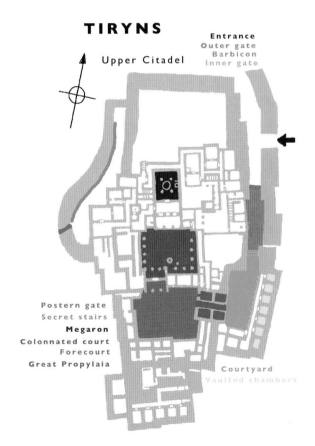

TIRYNS

Upper Citadel

Entrance
Outer gate
Barbicon
Inner gate

Postern gate
Secret stairs
Megaron
Colonnated court
Forecourt
Great Propylaia

Courtyard
Vaulted chambers

The principal entrance takes you through two defensive gates, separated by a barbican, and into a spacious courtyard. If, instead of turning right through the Great Propylaia, you proceed directly ahead at this point and then down a set of stairs you will discover a cyclopaean tunnel with corbelled roof and side chambers. This is one of the site's marvels and is either indicated poorly or not at all. From here you can retrace your steps to the propylaia (double-porched entryway) and make your way through the forecourt and colonnaded court (take note of the round sacrificial altar) into the megaron (great hall), whose roof was once supported by wooden pillars (their stone bases are preserved and visible). The central clay hearth and some of its once painted surface are evident, as is the base of the royal throne. It was here that the king of Tiryns once received his guests and emissaries.

As you examine the stones of Tiryns be sure to look up now and again to take in the view from the citadel's elevated prospect. It is a commanding view in more sense than one and suggests, along with the citadel's steep massive walls, that the man on the throne was a man of considerable clout, admittedly in the shadow of the great king of Mycenae but luminous all the same.

Located at the northern edge of Nafplio on the road to Argos (30-27520-22657). Signposted on right. Open daily 08:30–15:00. €

There are also two additional and affiliated Mycenaean sites nearby: a tholos tomb and a massive dam that is one more testimony to the Mycenaeans' remarkable engineering skills and accomplishments. Neither of these sites, however, in their present state will adequately reward your efforts to find and examine them. Far better to proceed at once to Mycenae, which lies less than 9km ahead. Returning to the road and direction that you took just now from Nafplio, keep going straight instead of bearing left to Argos. You will see signs first for the modern village of Mikines and then, after 2km, for the archaeological site of Mycenae.

The Acropolis of Mycenae

The modest elevation of the Mycenaean acropolis, at only 278m above sea level and no more than 50m above the limestone plateau below is misleading, for it didn't get any higher than this in the Mycenaean world. This was the powerful epicenter of a civilization and empire that once controlled the Aegean and Ionian seas, established colonies throughout the Mediterranean, and whose direct and indirect trade connections took them or their products as far east and south as Mesopotamia and Nubia and as far west and north as Central and Eastern Europe, Britain, and Scandinavia. The Mycenaeans reached Sicily and the Lipari Islands as early as the 16th century, and Ischia soon afterwards; then, once they and no longer the Minoans presided over the Aegean, the Mycenaeans established for themselves what may have been colonies or perhaps only trading posts in the Near East, most notably in Syria, Palestine, and Cyprus. Mycenaeans are thought to have fought with the Egyptians in the early 16th century against the Hyksos, and, in the late 13th century, to have returned among the "Sea Peoples" to invade Egypt and the Levant, completing the collapse of what had been a remarkably prosperous and relatively stable period for the entire region.

While the Argolid was the focus, the fist as it were, of Mycenaean clout, the Greek mainland was strewn with Mycenaean fortresses, each with its own king, representing a widely dispersed yet functional confederation, often reinforced by blood and linked by an extensive system of Bronze Age roads. As a chain of command, these roads appear to have begun and ended here, at Mycenae. Among the mainland citadels and palaces of Mycenaean Greece, in addition to Mycenae and Tiryns, were Asini, Argos, Midea, Sparta, Pylos, Athens, Thebes, Orchomenos, and the largest of all, Gla. The Mycenaean islands, too, had their kings and citadels—Melos,

The epithet "Mycenaean" is currently used to designate the world of ancient Greece in the Late Bronze Age (c. 1600–1200 B.C.E.), and "The Mycenaeans" is a parallel term for the human agents active in that particular development of Hellenic civilization. The usage is essentially modern, stemming from the unparalleled trove of gold artifacts and other precious objects found at Mycenae in 1876 by Heinrich Schliemann, and now on display in the National Archaeological Museum in Athens.

Schliemann recovered the artifacts when he excavated a circle of six "shaft graves" situated within the massive walls of the Bronze Age citadel. His discovery confirmed that Homer had been right to call Mycenae "rich in gold," but his belief that one of the gold death masks recovered from a grave showed the "face of Agamemnon" has to be rejected on chronological grounds. As commander of the Greeks at Troy, Agamemnon's *floruit* must be placed c. 1200 B.C.E., while the treasures of the shaft graves cemetery date from before 1500 B.C.E.

Mycenae was clearly an important place in the 16th century B.C.E., but the sources of its wealth are problematic, and we do not know the names of its early rulers. After the transition from Bronze Age to Iron Age, c. 1100 B.C.E., Mycenae sank into insignificance though it did continue to exist as a minor village.

It is a surprising fact that the only occurrence of the term "Mycenaean" in Homer comes in the *Iliad* (XV.638,643), where it characterizes Periphetes, a minor Greek hero slain by Hector. The ethnic terms normally used by Homer are: Argives, Danaans, and Achaeans. "Argives" underlines the importance of the Argolid, where, in addition to Mycenae, other major centers existed at Argos and Tiryns. "Danaans" had the specific meaning of "subjects of Danaos," a king of Argos, but was also applied more generally to the Greek host. 'Achaeans' comes nearest to being a general term for "Greeks," and one may note that when the Romans turned Greece into a province of their empire they called it "Achaia." It is also interesting to observe that Odysseus, when interrogated about his identity by Polyphemos, describes himself and his crew as "Achaeans" attempting to make their way home from Troy (*Odyssey*. IX,259ff.).

In marked contrast with the peaceable Minoans, the Mycenaeans displayed a strongly militaristic ethos. It has been well said of them that "their pedigrees were short, but their spears were long." Their traditions included memories of an internecine struggle between the Argolid and Thebes known as the Seven against Thebes. Their citadels were surrounded by defensive walls that can still amaze by their strength and sophistication. Their art featured lion hunts, hand-to-hand combat, and cities under siege.

The political geography of this Mycenaean world is detailed in a remarkable "poem within a poem"—the Catalogue, or Muster List of ships and commanders who went to Troy (*Iliad*.II.484–759). The date and authenticity of the List have been endlessly debated, and will not be re-argued here. The present writer believes that it originated as an oral compilation considerably older than the *Iliad*, that it was memorized and handed on by a succession of bards, and that its historical value is high. It lists some 180 locations from which the troops came, includes the names of 46 commanders (nearly half of them with patronymics and other biographical details) and records 16 tribal groupings (Boeotians, Phocians, Locrians, etc.). The number of ships conveying each contingent is also given, amounting in all to 1186, and so underpinning Marlowe's famous apostrophe to Helen: "Was this the face that launched a thousand ships…?" Study the Catalogue with the aid of a good atlas of the ancient world, and you will find that, in effect, it provides a gazetteer of the combined might of the Mycenaean world at war.

—*J.V. Luce, Trinity College Dublin and the Royal Irish Academy*

Crete, and Ithaka, to mention only a few. Never was this vast consortium more visible or destructive or memorable than in the Trojan War, once thought to be a free flight of poetic fancy but, thanks to the archaeologist's spade, ever more widely acknowledged to have been a momentous clash of great Bronze Age rivals. This war, sizeable on the ground and limitless in the imagination, was launched from here, by Mycenae's Agamemnon, *wanax* (high king), ranked as a peer among the super-powers of the day—the Hittites, the Assyrians, and the Egyptians.

The mythographers, poets, and playwrights of the ancient world and the last three millennia have all conspired, it seems, to bestow upon the walls and treasures of Mycenae more splendor and significance than they or we can bear. They have also splashed the stones of Mycenae with blood and cast over the house before you a thick shroud woven of violence and betrayal. The compulsory tales on this theme focus on several generations of what may just be the most dysfunctional family ever in print. We hear of the slaughter of innocents, cannibalism, ambition, adultery, regicide, matricide, angry demanding ghosts, and swarms of unspeakable, avenging Furies circling this house and family, hounding its offspring, crying out for still more slaughter, as if only fresh blood can remove an old stain. If we need any convincing that power corrupts and that absolute power corrupts absolutely, the family history of the Atreids will do the job.

Back to the bleached stones. The hill before you, while inhabited in modest, hardworking fashion since the Neolithic, reached its peak between 1300 and 1200 B.C.E. in the Late Bronze Age. The cyclopaean walls girding the Bronze Age fortress were constructed in three phases dated approximately 1350, 1250, and 1225 B.C.E. The Atreids, those who raised this modest mound into a pinnacle of power, were not enthroned here from the beginning, however. The traditional founder of Mycenae was Perseus, a son of Zeus, who enlisted the Cyclops to build the great walls here to gird what was to be his capital. The last of the line of Perseus was the infamous Eurystheus, who died violently without issue and without wide regret. Atreus, his brother-in-law became his successor and through him the scepter passed to Agamemnon.

The walled site of Mycenae was a fortress, a royal residence, an administrative center, and a cult center, as well as housing storerooms, workshops, a military garrison, and a royal grave complex. It was surrounded by a town and a number of important burial sites, including both shaft graves and chamber tombs. The site map below locates the most important and visible of these, except for the Treasury of Atreus, which lies beyond this map, a very brief walk down the road towards town. It is listed separately below.

No site plan is provided with your entrance, but the entire site is exceptionally well presented and explained in a series of panels that direct and inform you as you make your way into and through the citadel along a well-designed network of concrete paths, ramps, and steps. After passing through the site's modern entry point, we recommend that you proceed directly, along the original Mycenaean road, to the Lion Gate, after noting, on your right, Grave Circle B. When excavated in 1952, this site yielded 15 royal shaft graves (most containing multiple remains and all but one previously undisturbed) pre-dating or roughly contemporary with those in Grave Circle A, inside the walls. After exploring the citadel, we suggest that you visit the exceptionally fine museum on site, take a

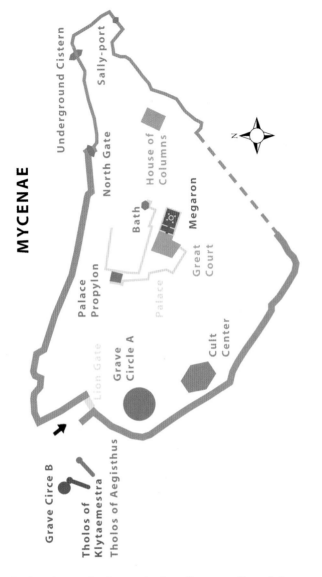

MYCENAE

Underground Cistern
Sally-port
North Gate
House of Columns
Bath
Megaron
Palace Propylon
Great Court
Palace
Lion Gate
Grave Circle A
Cult Center
Grave Circe B
Tholos of Klytaemestra
Tholos of Aegisthus

break for lunch or refreshment in the adjacent café, and then walk to the magnificent Treasury of Atreus. Finally, before returning to your car, if time, energy, and interest persist, explore the tholos tombs named after Mycenae's most infamous couple, Clytaemnestra and Aegisthus.

The walls of Mycenae, though actually less impressive than those at Tiryns, will seem more so, because you can stand directly against and beneath them and so experience their unimaginable magnitude. Approach, they say, is almost everything; and this approach must have instilled a sense of insignificance into the common visitor. Overhead is the famed Lion Gate with two rampant lionesses mounting a column that likely represents an ancient tree or pillar goddess. As at

Tiryns, this gateway was designed for chariots. Today, however, everyone—kings and tourists alike—enters on foot.

As you pass under the Lion Gate, notice the pivot holes dug into lintel and threshold to support and hold two massive doors; note too the holes into which the bar sealing the doors would have been slid into place. Next, to your right is Grave Circle A, one of the focal sights here, whose stunning contents are displayed in the National Archaeological museum. Most of the dazzling treasures of Mycenae—"rich in gold" Homer called it—were unearthed here. It is also interesting to note that the burial gifts found in Grave Circle A included objects originating from places as diverse and far afield as Mesopotamia, Syria, Egypt, Nubia, Anatolia, Northern Europe, and Afghanistan. This fact, as much as the pricelessness of the finds, testifies to the stature and reach of the kings buried here.

> They were born just like us from a womb.
> And like us they became bride and groom.
> But the king and his queenie
> In ancient Mycenae
> Wound up in a beehive-style tomb.
>
> —*Sheila B. Blume*

At this point we will leave you to explore the citadel and palace unaccompanied, as it were, except for the signs and panels provided on the site. As you ascend the ramp, however, into the upper citadel and the royal palace, conjure the scene drawn by Aeschylus in his *Agamemnon*, when the great and murderous king returning triumphant from Troy trod underfoot raw red silk into his own familiar halls, where his own wife and queen hacked him down with an axe like a rotten stump. Then, as you peer over the cyclopean walls, realize that Mycenae's greatest king was likely never buried in royal fashion in any of the citadel's grave circles or vaulted tholos tombs, but instead hurled, with his Trojan lover Cassandra, over the walls to be picked at by vultures and worried by local dogs.

> I stand now where I struck him down. The thing is done.
> Thus have I wrought, and I will not deny it now.
> That he might not escape nor beat aside his death,
> as fishermen cast their huge circling nets, I spread
> deadly abundance of rich robes, and caught him fast.
> I struck him twice. In two great cries of agony
> he buckled at the knees and fell. When he was down
> I struck him the third blow, in thanks and reverence
> to Zeus the lord of dead men underneath the ground.
> Thus he went down, and the life struggled out of him;
> and as he died he spattered me with the dark red
> and violent driven rain of bitter savored blood
> to make me glad, as gardens stand among the showers
> of God in glory at the birthtime of the buds.
> —*Aeschylus,* Agamemnon, *1379–1392,*
> *tr. Richmond Lattimore*

One final tip. Don't miss the corbelled underground cistern at the far northeast corner of the citadel, which although it descends to great depths is one of the high points of Mycenaean engineering genius. The tunnel cuts into solid rock down through the citadel, out through the fortification wall, finally connecting to a natural spring by way of clay conduits. This aqueduct guaranteed a fresh water supply to the fortress, even under siege. You will need a flashlight for your cautious descent. The well-worn steps can be quite slippery, so proceed slowly with care and see how far you can get. We have never explored the full extent of the shaft.

....
Located just north (2km) of the modern village of Mikines (30-27510-76510). Open Tues–Sun 08:00–19:30 and Mon 12:00–19:30. The entrance fee and ticket for the citadel provides access also to the on-site archaeo-logical museum, as well as the nearby Treasury of Atreus.
....

Mycenae Archaeological Museum

When you enter this beautifully designed museum, the first thing you will notice after exploring the citadel in the heat of the day is probably the air-conditioning; but after that you will discover a scale model of the site, which will help you put together into a coherent whole the various sights you have seen so far. This museum, while it does not contain the most spectacular finds from Mycenae and the nearby area, which you have already seen in the National Archaeological Museum, nevertheless displays roughly 2,500 objects discovered in the citadel and its surrounds. The instructional panels are particularly well-written and illuminating, providing finely distilled commentary on the Mycenaean world, its history, and its material remains.

Located on site at Mycenae. Open Tues–Sun 08:00–19:30 and Mon 12:00–19:30. Entry free with ticket to archaeological site.

The Treasury of Atreus

One of the great masterworks of Mycenaean architectural design and engineering, this is a perfectly stunning exemplar of the tholos tomb, with its characteristic *dromos* (uncovered passageway) and its *tholos* (beehive burial chamber). This, like the other tholos tombs at Mycenae,

yielded no significant grave goods, as they had long since been plundered. But in this case the structure itself is a treasure, the largest and most exquisite of the roughly 100 known tholos tombs in Greece. It has been attributed to Atreus, though it precise dates and first inhabitants are a matter of speculation and debate. Some date it to roughly 1350 B.C.E. while others place it a century or more later.

The dromos here is 36m in length and the inner lintel stone weighs in at roughly 120 metric tons. The tholos measures 14.5m in diameter and at its center soars to a height of 13m. The corbelled roof of this chamber is a wonder, whose technique can be described but whose impression cannot. North from the center of the tholos there is a small secondary rock-cut chamber. Whether this or the larger tholos originally held the remains of the dead is unknown, since the tomb was found empty and entirely despoiled.

We and others have seen an owl standing sentinel over the entrance to the tomb; so be sure to look for this most appropriate guardian when you visit.

Located a short walk from the citadel. Open Tues–Sun 08:00–19:30 and Mon 12:00–19:30. Free entry with a combined ticket to the archaeological site of Mycenae and its museum.

For your return to Nafplio, we recommend that you take a different road, one that passes through Argos. After leaving the archaeological site of Mycenae and passing through the village of Mikines, ignore the road that you took earlier from Nafplio and take instead the next road to your left (south) for Argos (10km). Apart from items displayed in the Argos Archaeological Museum, there are no significant, readily accessible Mycenaean remains in Argos. Regardless, for readers of Homer and Thucydides, Argos retains its ancient aura as a site of great legendary and historical import. On its approach the sight of the Larissa is impressive; and its theater, one of the grandest in all of ancient Greece, is worth an admiring drive-by gaze if nothing else.

The Theater, Agora, and Archaeological Museum of Argos

Continuously inhabited since prehistory, Argos was one of the most powerful and illustrious Greek states from the Mycenaean through the classical age, a proud legacy that endures in the fact that the entire region or *nome*—the Argolid—bears its name. Today, however, apart from this, few traces of its former stature survive.

Two Argive citadels—the Aspis (100m) and the Larissa (276m)—once occupied the summits above the ancient town, but they have long since been eclipsed by subsequent structures. On the Larissa, once the site of Argos's principal citadel, there stands a more recent *Kastro* (fortress), erected by the Byzantines and Franks and enlarged by the Venetians and Turks. The main reason for ascending the Larissa, though, is for the unparalleled view it offers over the entire Argolid and the Gulf of Nafplio. Near the foot of the Aspis, on the ridge called the Deiras, it is possible to find a number of ancient remains, most notably those of the Temple of Apollo Deiratiotes (Athena of the Ridge) and the Temple of Athena Oxyderkes. If you wish to find these sites or ascend the Larissa, take Tsokri St. north from the center of the town. The Deiras and its sites will be signposted on the right at the edge of town; and, just beyond the town, the road to the Larissa is on the left. In both cases it may require a bit of searching to find your way, as the crucial signage here as elsewhere is often minimal, defaced, turned, or otherwise rendered unhelpful. These are all open sites with no designated hours and no fees.

En route from Mycenae back to Nafplio you will pass the ancient agora and theater on the northwest edge of Argos. The agora ruins are, in their current state, all but unintelligible to the less than fully informed eye, but there are a handful of convenient parking spaces directly in front of them, where you can pause to take in the most impressive ancient theater of Argos, which once held as many as 20,000 spectators.

Dating from the late 4th century B.C.E. it was enlarged and enhanced by the Romans. While it falls outside the time-focus of this book and itinerary, it is nonetheless impressive in its scale and worth a pullover.

Open Tues–Sun 08:30–15:00 (30-27510-68819). € This ticket provides entry to the agora, theater, and also the archaeological museum in the town of Argos.

The Argos Archaeological Museum, if time permits, deserves a brief visit, as it contains some important finds from Argos, its environs, and the wider region. The nearly complete set (helmet and cuirass) of late 8th-century bronze armor, a 7th-century pottery fragment depicting the blinding of the Polyphemos, and material from the Early Helladic site of Lerna are among its most important holdings. Also, be sure to note the museum's figurative door panels, the fine work of a local artist. The downside here is that nearly all of the text in the museum, from exploratory panels to exhibit labels, are in Greek or Greek and French. The Lerna material, however, is accompanied with English text.

The museum is located across from the central square of Argos, Plateia Ahiou Petrou (30-27510-68819). Open Tues–Sun 08:30–15:00. €

Just a reminder that Nafplio's Blue Flag Karathona beach awaits you, offering revival and refreshment at the end of a long "ruinous" day.

DAY FOUR

The sites we have in mind for this day do not include any significant Mycenaean remains; so, depending on your timetable and priorities, you may decide to pass on Day Four and advance instead straight to Day Five. As explained earlier, the riches of the Peloponnese are not confined to the Mycenaean period; for, after its stint as the center of Mycenaean civilization, it continued to play a vitally important role in Greek antiquity, from the archaic through the Roman period. Consequently, our focus in this itinerary, like all of the others in this book, is intentionally split, here with one eye on Peloponnesian antiquity and the other eye on Mycenaean antiquity. We like to imagine that the result is three-dimensional clarity, rather than blurred confusion; but we will let you be the judge of that.

The first two sites suggested for exploration today are, not surprisingly, archaeological, while the third is, oddly enough, agricultural. All are in their own way ancient. First, there is Corinth, or Korinthos, one of the great centers of power and influence throughout the Greek world from the archaic through the Roman period. Next we turn to the Sanctuary of Zeus at Nemea, which gave its name to the bi-annual Panhellenic games founded there in the 6th century B.C.E., as well as to the wines of the region, famed in the ancient world and touted to this day. We suggest that you consider completing your day with a tasting tour of local vineyards and wineries, where you will learn a bit about viniculture and winemaking, ancient and contemporary. Lastly, since this day will include an optional steep climb to the ancient mountaintop citadel of Akroko-rinthos, where keeping your feet under you can be a challenge, be sure to bring along your walking stick, if you have one. As recommended earlier, the telescoping type with a solid, sharp point provides the best support.

Setting out, then, from Nafplio, you will take the same road that you took yesterday toward Mikines and ancient Mycenae, but remaining on it this time an additional 12km until you reach the major toll-way, which you will take in the direction of Korinthos and Athina. Note that you are entering the toll-way at what will later be your exit for ancient Nemea. (If you wish to avoid the toll, you can take the side road via Hiliomodi, which comes up 2km before this major motor-way.) Once on the motorway, proceed 19km to the exit for Ancient Corinth (Archea Korinthos), which lies about 2km to the west. Archea Korinthos, you will discover, refers both to the archaeological site and to the modern village that surrounds the site. In fact, less than 5 percent of the ancient city has been excavated, while the remaining portion still lies beneath the modern village and its environs.

PRINCIPAL SITES

The Ancient City and Archaeological Museum of Korinthos

While this site seems to have been occupied from as early as 4500 B.C.E., it does not clearly emerge as a major political and commercial center until the 8th century B.C.E., when it first took full advantage of its strategic location at a critical land-sea crossroads. Controlling land traffic between the north and south of the Greek mainland, as well as the east-west sea trade, Corinth rose to be, along with Athens and Sparta, one of the three great centers of power in early 5th century Greece, a position which it soon lost when it became a rival and enemy of Athens. Across its turbulent history, Corinth reached the top and touched bottom a number of times, in part because it had an uncanny knack for choosing the wrong allies and the wrong enemies in a range of lethal rivalries and conflicts. In 146 B.C.E. it was reduced to near rubble by the Roman general Mummius and lay there for another century until Julius Caesar resurrected the city in 44 B.C.E., thus setting Corinth once again on the path to prominence and prosperity. As the new capital of the Roman province of Achaea, comprising most of Greece, it became known for the good life, as Romans (and not Christians) understood the term. Among its most famous ancient visitors was the Apostle Paul, whose scolding and inspiring words to the undisciplined Christian community of Corinth have been preserved as sacred scripture. For eighteen months, from the end of 50 C.E. to the middle of 52 C.E., he lived in Corinth in the house of

a fellow tentmaker, preaching the gospel of Jesus mostly to poor Jews and Greeks in a city where they were surrounded daily by luxury and license. The one preserved Corinthian monument of sorts to Paul is the *bema* (public rostrum) in the agora or forum, quite possibly the platform from which the Roman proconsul of Achaea in the mid-5th century, named Gallio, dismissed as frivolous the charges brought against Paul by the worthies of the local synagogue (Acts of the Apostles xviii.12–16).

From the above sketch of Corinth's ups and downs, it is clear why most of the remains in evidence today date from the Roman period. The most notable exception is the archaic temple of Apollo, of which seven adjacent standing columns (out of an original thirty-eight) survive. The original temple here was constructed in the mid-7th century and is said to have been one of the first Greek temples to support a tile, not a thatched, roof. The visible remains today are from the second, Doric temple, constructed a century later in the mid-6th century.

Long before the ministry of Paul, the beneficence of Caesar, or the Macedonian occupation, Thebes received a number of notorious outsiders. It was to Corinth that the abandoned infant Oedipus was brought to be fostered in the king's palace as the adopted heir to the throne. This was the adoptive home of Medea after she had fled her own homeland with her reckless and unreliable husband Jason. When the same Jason later abandoned her for a younger, more suitable wife, Medea, we are told, incinerated her husband's princess bride, slaughtered her own children as a way of cutting out Jason's heart and leaving him to live with the pain, and made her exit in a sky chariot drawn by dragons. Ancient Corinth was indeed not without its moments of color and chaos. Today, however, more in the tradition of Sisyphus, another of Corinth's sons, general hardworking tedium seems to hold sway in what is admittedly a lusterless backwater.

The site map provided with your entrance ticket to the site of ancient Corinth will help you find the other landmark remains in the agora and vicinity, such as the odeon, the theater, the Peirene Fountain, and the Fountain of Glauke, whose reservoir once held 64,000 liters of water. The Asklepion lies off the top of the map, 500m to the north of the theater. The modest archaeological museum, located near the entrance to the excavations, provides both shade and some very interesting finds.

Located 7km southwest of the city of Korinthos in the modern village of Ancient Korinthos (Archaea Korinthos), signposted from the motorway (30-27410-31207). Open daily 08:00–19:30. €€

A visit to the modern, appealing village of Ancient Corinth is both inevitable and recommended. It offers a number of small shops catering to tourists and also some inviting, shaded tavernas, where you can escape the sun, recover from the morning's efforts, and nourish yourself for the afternoon's excursions. If you decide to settle in here for lunch, we highly recommend that you sample the enticing Cypriot specialties and traditional home cooking at Taverna Dionysos. You can't miss it on your right if you walk several minutes along the main road away from the archaeological site.

The Ancient Mountain Fortress of Akrokorinthos

Like so many of Greece's high spots (in this case 575m), the principal reason for making this climb is the view from the top rather than the view of the top. And the view from here is truly astounding, on a clear day one of the finest in Greece. Be sure to bring a map and a compass so that you can locate what you are seeing.

The only approach to this massive fortress (it stretches across 60 acres) from below was secured by a trivallate system of circuit walls, each with its own gate. An outer moat and guardhouse, as well as inner towers provided additional security on this rocky peak which by itself was already eminently defensible. The summit of the fortress is today still held by a restored Turkish tower house, or keep. On the highest of the mount's two peaks, you may be able to locate as well the scant remains of an ancient temple of Aphrodite, later the site of a Byzantine church, and lastly a mosque. When Aphrodite held sway on the peak, hers was a notorious shrine; for her worship took the form of sacred sex performed by as many as a thousand dedicated prostitutes. Today the only delights available on the summit may be found in the café situated just below the immediate ascent to the fortress area, the last point to which you can take your car.

Located just south of ancient Korinthos. While a trekking path leads up from the archaeological site, its is a steep climb with little or no shade. I once collapsed with heat stroke on this climb; so it is difficult for me to recommend it. It is only a short ascent, on the other hand, by car. Turn left out of the archaeological site and then right when you come to the signposted road winding up to the summit. Open daily 08:00–17:00. No fee.

The Sanctuary of Zeus and Stadium of Nemea

This peaceful and appealing site, situated on a plateau in the Nemean river valley, was from the early 6th century B.C.E. a precinct sacred to Zeus, a place of pilgrimage for all Greeks. Here, every two years in the late summer, the Nemean Games took place—one of the four great Panhellenic festivals celebrated in the Odes of Pindar. The other three precincts and festivals were at Olympia and Isthmia in the Peloponnese, and Delphi in central Greece.

Nemea was occupied from the early Neolithic, and may have been tied to Mycenae in the late Bronze Age. Following the demise of Mycenaean civilization, Nemea did not reemerge as a significant permanent settlement until the Roman Period. This was in large part due to the annual flooding to which the site was subject. Only in the late summer was it sufficiently dry and suitable to host the festival and games that still bear its name. As a seasonal site, ancient Nemea and its festival were controlled by the town of Kleonai. The Games were eventually moved to Argos, and the sacred precinct lay in ruins by the end of the 5th century B.C.E., as the site had been the scene of a  pitched battle, perhaps between forces from Sparta and Argos.

Nemea and its Games are tightly woven into a tapestry of ancient myths. The "Seven Against Thebes"—en route to retrieve the kingdom of Oedipus for his son Polyneikes—were said to have stopped here and to have inadvertently occasioned the death of the infant Opheltes, struck by a serpent as he lay on a bed of celery leaves. The child's death cast Nemea at once into profound mourning. In honor of the infant, the Seven conducted funeral games; in doing so, they founded the Nemean Games, whose funereal origins were preserved in the Games' later traditions that included judges robed in black and victory crowns made of wild celery sprigs. Many centuries later, in the Roman period, the founding of the Games was attributed to Herakles and linked to the tradition of his first labor, the slaying of the Nemean lion, a feat which the Greeks of antiquity had not associated with the Games.

Quite recently, a contemporary revival and reenactment of the Nemean Games was undertaken by the site's chief archaeologist for 30 years (1974–2004), Stephen Miller, of the University of California at Berkeley, who in multiple summers assembled 700 runners from 45 nations to raise the dust in the ancient stadium here, running not naked but clad in white tunics, for the honor of being crowned, as in the past, with wreaths of wild celery.

Ancient stadium of the Nemean Games

In the sacred precinct, or sanctuary, the focal monument in antiquity and today is the Doric Temple of Nemean Zeus, surrounded by whatever remains of a sacred cypress grove, a long monumental altar (east of the temple, where athletes and trainers made their offerings and swore their oaths before competing), nine *oikoi* (treasuries) double the size of those at Olympia, a guest house, kilns for the manufacture of roof tiles, a bath house, a 6th century C.E. basilica, and the hero shrine containing the so-called "Tomb of Opheltes" west of the bath house. There are also the foundational remains of dwellings

thought to have belonged to the priests of the shrine. If you visit the on-site museum first, you will find a detailed and very helpful scale model of the site, which will assist you in visualizing the site and orienting yourself within it.

The excellent museum here is situated on your right as you enter the archaeological site. The museum's scale model of the site mentioned above is an appropriate place for you to begin your explorations. The exhibits and explan-atory panels in the museum provide a rich introduction to the site, its history, and its surrounds. And, if you've always wondered how ancient runners managed to leave their marks at the same moment without the blast of a starting gun, there is a video illustrating the ingenious starting gate (*hysplex*) used in the Nemean Games to send the competitors on their way.

The stadium area is located within a short walk from the precinct site. Turn left off the access road to Ancient Nemea and the stadium entrance will be on your right. You may also drive to the stadium site, where there is a small but usually adequate parking area.

This stadium at Nemea was constructed in the Early Hellenistic period after the games were restored here from Argos. Remains in the stadium area include: the *dromos* (running track); the *theatron* (spectator seating and judges platform); the *krypte esodos* (vaulted tunnel), complete with ancient graffiti, through which athletes entered the stadium; and the *apodyterion* (locker room), where competing athletes (runners, wrestlers, boxers, jumpers, discus and javelin throwers...) prepared and waited for their entry into the stadium. It is clear from finds, especially coins, unearthed in the stadium, that fans from rival cities sat in separate sections of the stadium seating. Near the stadium, the location of the ancient hippodrome has been found, yielding evidence that it once hosted chariot races. Even the reservoir which once held enough water for an estimated 150 competing horses to drink their fill has been uncovered.

The stadium site is designed now as a small archaeological park with a series of sixteen viewing points from which the various elements of the stadium can be appreciated, especially with the help of a book on sale in the museum entitled *The Ancient Stadium at Nemea*, by Stephen G. Miller.

Located 2km north of the modern motorway exit and 6km east of the modern village of Nemea or Nea Nemea (30-27460-22739). Site and museum open Tues–Sun 08:00–15:00. Summer hours may include an afternoon opening on Mondays and an extension to 19:00 Tues–Sun. €

SIDE SIGHT:

Wine Roads of the Peloponnese

The "Wine Roads of the Peloponnese" comprises an association of 40 wineries from nine different regions designated as: Gerania, Corinth, Argolis, Arcadia, Achaia, Kefalonia, Ilia, Messinia, and Laconia. The region with the greatest number of participating vintners is Corinth, in which the Nemean wineries are included.

Nemea, producing both red and white grape varieties but known best for its reds, represents the largest and oldest viticultural zone in the Peloponnese, and in all of Greece for that matter. Some say that wine production here reaches back as many as 7,000 years and once supplied the palace citadel of Mycenae. Its signature grape is the Agiorgitico, which grows only in this region. A local white grape, Roditis, is responsible for Nemea's fine, though less touted, white wines.

Several of the finest Nemean wineries, both open to the public for tours and tastings, are very near the Sanctuary of Nemean Zeus: the first of these is the Palivou Estate (30-327460-24190 www.palivos.gr) less than a kilometer from the archaeological site; another fine winery, also located in Ancient

Nemea, is the Papaioannou Estate (30-27460-223138); lastly, the Lafkiotis Winery (327460-31000 www.lafkiotis.gr) is located 3km east of Ancient Nemea in Ancient Kleonai and is open daily 09:00–16:00. We especially recommend the Palivou Estate. The wines of Georgos Palivos have won so many medals in European competitions that they have to rotate their display of award plaques for lack of wall space. Additionally, they are quite gracious to visitors; and, even for their finest wines, their direct sale prices by the bottle are quite reasonable. Their tasting room is open daily 10:00–18:00.

When you visit your first Peloponnesian winery, ask for a free copy of the brochure entitled "Wine Roads of the Peloponnese" produced by ENOAP, the Wine Growers' Association of the Peloponnese, so that you might locate and learn about the other participating wineries scattered throughout the Peloponnese.

Day Five

The principal destination today is the archaeological park at Epidauros (written "Epidavros" as it is pronounced in modern Greek), where you can fruitfully spend several hours exploring and perhaps picnicking. After that, we suggest that you investigate the ancient coastal citadel at Asini and then, if you like, wile away the remainder of the afternoon on the nearby beach. You will find the road east to Epidavros at the north end of Nafplio. En route to the Asklipion Epidavrou (as it is indicated on your map), you will see (after 14km) signposted on your left a cyclopean arched bridge, dating from the Late Bronze Age. It is worth pulling over and taking a look at this fine surviving example of Mycenaean engineering. To avoid confusion, be forewarned that in addition to the "Asklipon Epidavrou" (your destination) there are also "Archea Epidavros," "Apo Epidavros," and "Nea Epidavros" all in close proximity to each other.

PRINCIPAL SITES

The Sanctuary of Asklepios, Ancient Theater and Stadium at Epidauros

Ancient stadium, Epidauros

The Sanctuary of Asklepios at Epidauros, one more of Greece's many World Heritage Sites, is idyllically situated in a well-watered, densely vegetated plain girded by mountains—Arachnaio and Velanidia (ancient Titthion) to the north and Charani (ancient Kynortion) and Koryphaia to the south. Known in antiquity as the Sacred Grove, the site still has the character of a shaded grove, providing the pleasant tranquility one would associate with a place of healing. Quite apart from its extensive and dramatic ruins, today's archaeological park has a special appeal of its own, a fine spot for a quiet stroll or an extended picnic. In fact, you would do well to plan ahead and bring your own lunch provisions, as there is currently nothing but a concessions stand here, whose offerings are hardly in keeping with a site associated for thousands of years with health and recovery.

While the surrounding area is replete with Mycenaean remains, this site first appears on the archaeological record near the beginning of the 5th century B.C.E. The earliest inscribed offerings left by patients, as well as the first record of the Great Asklepieia (the Epidaurian Festival celebrated every four years) may be dated to this period. Prior to this, as early as 1600 B.C.E. in the Early Mycenaean Period, there appears to have been a cult on nearby Mt. Kynortion devoted to the healing god called Maleatas, whose name and powers Apollo later (in the Geometric period) absorbed into his own, becoming known locally as Apollo Maleatas. Only in the classical and Hellenistic periods did Asklepios—a newcomer from the north—occupy center-stage, becoming the focal god of healing at Epidauros. He had started out as a mere mortal, a king of Thessaly skilled in medicine, a skill he handed on to his two sons, Machaon and Podaleiros, who appear in the *Iliad* leading a Thessalian contingent from Trikka and Oichalia to Troy. In fact, when Menelaos is wounded in battle, it was this same Machaon who was summoned to attend to the commanding general's wounds. In subsequent centuries the status of Asklepios was enhanced, as he became first a demigod—tutored, as was Achilles, by the centaur Chiron—and finally a god. At one point his powers of healing were so great that he was able to resurrect the dead and did—a practice which threatened to overthrow the scheme of things, blurring the line between gods and mortals—so Zeus is said to have stepped in and struck Asklepios dead.

Regardless, the Sanctuary of Asklepios remained a place of benign miracles, of recovery if not of resurrection. In the Asklepion's first centuries, the healing that it offered was understood to be the gift of the god and not the result of advanced medical practice. The officials here were priests, not physicians. Healing was believed to come from the hand of the god in ritual sleep. Those suppliant patients who brought their diseases or wounds here were first expected to undergo certain preparatory rites and ordeals and then to sleep in the Abaton—the sacred intensive care unit, as it were—where the god would visit patients during the night in dream and either bring instant healing or convey instructions for the treatment that would surely bring healing. The healed and recovered were then expected to make appropriate offerings to the god according to their means and to bear testimony to their miraculous healing. Many of these testimonies were inscribed in stone at the Asklepion, and roughly seventy of these have survived to the present.

Later, especially in the Roman Period, the emphasis shifted from divine miracle to human medicine—transforming, or at least expanding, the Asklepion from a cult place into a hospital and spa. The Asklepion had, in truth, been for centuries a

complex site offering a range of diversions and delights to its
visitors in addition to healing for its patients. Every four years
it hosted the Great Asklepeia, the Festival of Epidauros,
founded in 480 B.C.E., which included the Epidaurian Games,
some of whose victors were celebrated by the poet Pindar. At
least one aspect of the Epidauros Festival—the dramatic—was
revived in 1954 and survives to this day. Every July, a series of
plays, mostly from the canon of ancient Greek drama, are
performed here by the National Theatre of Greece as well as by
a number of visiting international theater companies and guest

Pine glade, Epidauros

artists. For advance details regarding the Epidauros Festival, go to: www.hellenicfestival.gr or contact the Hellenic Festival Box Office in Athens at 39 Panepistimiou (30-210-322-1459).

An onslaught of Goths in 395 C.E. began the full destruction of the sanctuary. Christian dismantling and conversion of the site, aided by two severe earthquakes in the 6th century C.E., left Epidauros in ruins until its excavation

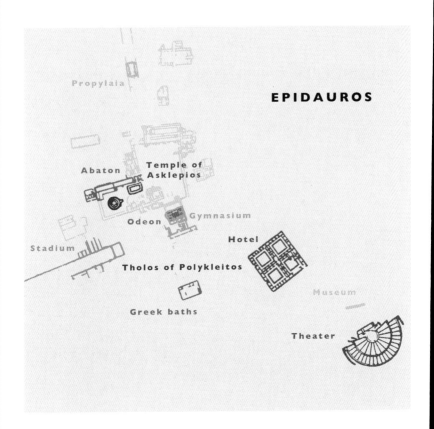

EPIDAUROS

Propylaia

Abaton

Temple of Asklepios

Odeon

Gymnasium

Stadium

Hotel

Tholos of Polykleitos

Museum

Greek baths

Theater

and reconstruction began in 1879, a slow process of recovery that continues to this day. In fact, as we write, a number of the most important structures are being partly and judiciously restored, in an ambitious project to resurrect the Asklepion to at least a small share of its former splendor.

In its present form, Epidauros constitutes an extensive archaeological park comprising several principal sites: the Asklepion, the theatre, the stadium, and the archaeological museum. The most impressive of these today is the Hellenistic theater, not the largest but surely the most perfect and intact ancient theater in Greece, preserving the full, circular orchestra, and possessing legendary acoustics. No doubt someone will be putting this legend to personal test when you visit. If not, stand in the center of the orchestra and merely whisper to someone else, standing in the fArthest, top-most seat in the house. You will find that your voice will carry, as will the sound of a single coin dropped at your feet. If not, it is the hearing of your listener rather than the acoustics of the theater that need to be examined further. Next in importance and scope is the Sacred Grove, the

Asklepion where for many centuries old and young, women and men, brought their diseased, broken, wounded, or wasting bodies and spirits in the hope of respite and renewal. This site is well provided with informative panels to help you make sense of the complex and easily confusing ruins; and, even better, there is an ambitious endeavor underway to partially restore many of the central monuments here, such as the Tholos of Polykleitos, the Stoa of the Abaton, the Temple of Asklepios, and the Hestiatorion complex. There is no plan, however, to invite sacred snakes back into the site, where they were once thought to have played a crucial cultic role in the healing process. The well-preserved stadium, resembling that at Olympia, retains some of its stone and rock-cut seating. The small archaeological museum offers a number of architectural reproductions and sculptural casts, as well as some interesting finds from the site, including inscribed testimonies to cures and ancient surgical instruments.

Located 25km east of Nafplio, signposted from main Nafplio-Archaia Epidavros road (27530-23009). Site and museum are open daily 08:00–19:30. €€

The Mycenaean Coastal Acropolis of Asini

The ancient acropolis of Asini, also known as Kastraki, is perched on a promontory measuring nearly 50,000 square meters and reaching a height of 52m above sea level. The earliest settlement on Asini may be dated to the Neolithic period. Excavations have uncovered a flourishing late Bronze Age acropolis, a lower town that extended to nearby Barbouna Hill, a late Mycenaean cemetery. Rich finds from these sites have provided convincing evidence of Asini's early trade contacts with the wider Aegean and Mediterranean. In the 1990s a Mycenaean wreck, with cargo from Crete and Cyprus, was discovered in these waters only 14km southeast of Asini. Another indication of her importance in the Late Bronze Age is the fact that Asini, together with a cluster of other Mycenaean centers of power in the Argolid, including Argos and Tiryns, was credited by Homer with having launched eighty ships to Troy under the command of King Diomedes, son of Tydeus

Bay of Tolo, from Asini

and one of the greatest of the Greek warriors. After the demise of the Mycenaean civilization at the end of the Bronze Age, Asini recovered some of its early prosperity in the 8th century B.C.E., only to be laid low again, this time by Argos in the First Messenian War. Asini, however, survived to rise again in the Hellenistic period, when the fortification walls visible today were constructed. Most of the important finds unearthed in excavations on the Asini acropolis and in nearby sites are on exhibit in the Nafplio Archaeological Museum.

Located on the Bay of Tolo between two beaches on the Kastraki headland 3km south of the modern village of Asini, signposted "Ancient Asini" from the Nafplio-Tolo Road (30-27520-2750). Daily 08:30–15:00. No fee.

From Epidauros, retrace your earlier drive from Nafplio, but turn left after 22km onto the Tolo road. After another 5km, before you reach Tolo, you will see a sign for Ancient Asini. Immediately adjacent to the site there is small, sheltered beach and a quite luring local fish taverna named after its location: "Kastraki." After exploring the site, you'll want to linger here, whether on the beach or at a table overlooking the sea, or

Out of Salamis Aias brought twelve ships and placed them
next to where the Athenian battalions were drawn up.
    They who held Argos and Tiryns of the huge walls,
Hermione and Asine lying down the deep gulf,
Troizen and Eïonai, and Epidauros of the vineyards,
they who held Aigina and Mases, Sons of the Achaians,
of these the leader was Diomedes of the great war cry
with Sthenelos, own son to the high-renowned Kapaneus,
and with them as a third went Euryalos, a man godlike,
son of Mekisteus the king, and scion of Talaos;
but the leader of all was Diomedes of the great war cry.
Following along with these were eighty black ships.
              —*Homer,* Iliad, *II.550–568,*
                     tr. Richmond Lattimore

both. Your return route will take you back to the Epidauros
road, where you will turn left and, in less than 10km, find
yourself back in Nafplio.

Day Six

After breakfast and an early morning visit to the city's
Archaeological Museum, it will be time to check out of your
hotel and leave Nafplio far behind for an excursion south to
Sparta, one of the most resonant names in Greek history. In late
Mycenaean times, Sparta (not to be confused with the modern
city) was, of course, the reputed home of Helen and Menelaos,
who together surfed the most turbulent and resilient marriage
in Greek history. On the way there, should you choose the
wildly scenic route that we recommend, you will visit the
fascinating yet often overlooked site of Lerna as well as the
captivatingly pristine mountain village of Kosmas. The
alternative route, if time and ease are your principal concerns—
would take you from Nafplio to Argos to the major motorway
south as far as Tripoli, where you would exit onto the road
heading directly south to Sparta, for a total of 120km.

    Assuming that the weather is suitable for mountain driving
and that you welcome a bit of adventure, you will follow the
costal road 12km from Nafplio, first to Myli (stopping at Lerna)

and then another 66km to Leonidio, where you will turn right and inland to ascend the Parnonas Mountains on a journey whose vistas are likely to make your eyes pop and whose hairpin turns and sheer drop-offs may once or twice turn your knuckles white. Not to worry. After 29km your intrepid spirit will receive its due reward in the form of the peaceful mountain peak village of Kosmas (elevation 1200m), where you can enjoy a shaded lunch under one of the seven majestic plane trees gracing the central plateia. There are a few tavernas serving authentic mountain fare, or you can sit facing the mountains and enjoy a picnic, if you thought to bring one along (with this in mind, Myli, adjacent to Lerna, is the perfect place to gather such provisions in advance). After a pause at Kosmas, you will then make your way another 65km down the west slopes of Parnonas into the Laconian plain and the fertile Eurotas River Valley to Sparta. Just before reaching Sparta, however, you will turn left to follow the east bank of the Eurotas River southeast several kilometers, where you will see the Menelaion signposted on your left. This route, in sum, will have added 50km, several hours, and considerable adventure to what would otherwise have been an uneventful, if efficient, drive through central Arcadia into Laconian Sparta.

PRINCIPAL SITES

Archaeological Museum of Nafplio

The first thing to strike any visitor to this museum's collection is the magnificent building that houses it. Occupying the west end of Nafplio's stately marble-paved central plateia, this early 18th century structure began its long career as the arsenal for the Venetian fleet. What will strike the visitor's eye upon entering the museum in the future is yet to be revealed, as the entire building is currently closed indefinitely for major restoration and refurbishment. In all likelihood, however, it will reopen by the time this book is released.

The museum's most respectable collection included finds from Nafplio, Mycenae, Tiryns, Asini, Midea, Dendra, and

Nafplio rooftops

other sites in the region, ranging from the Paleolithic to the Roman periods. As is the case with most local and regional museums, it is unable to display the most important discoveries from these sites, as these have long since been sent off to the National Archaeological Museum in Athens. That said, the nearly complete set of bronze 15th-century Mycenaean armor from Dendra, the necropolis belonging to the acropolis of Midea, is all but unique, and includes an intact wild boars-tooth helmet, as described by Homer. Other important and intriguing items include: a 12th-century Mycenaean figurine from Asini, idols and frescos from the cult center of Mycenae, a terracotta mask from Tiryns, and stone menhirs from the cenotaph of Midea.

Located on the west side of Plateia Syntagma (30-27520-27502). Opening date and times to be determined. €

Early Helladic Settlement and Fortress of Lerna and the "House of the Tiles"

The earliest Neolithic settlement of this site dates from the early 6th millennium B.C.E., and there is evidence of activity as late as the classical and early Hellenistic periods, comprising some 5,000 years of occupation. The unique importance of Lerna, however, lies in what it tells us, and the questions it raises, about life in Early Helladic Greece. Most surprising are its one-of-a-kind encompassing fortifications, predating the earliest Mycenaean citadels by over a thousand years.

Beginning as a small village, Lerna grew to a community of perhaps as many 150 houses, with an approximate population of 800. It is a complex site with many layers, as one would expect from a site occupied for many millennia. In the simplified site diagram below, shades of red indicate remains dating from Lerna III (3rd millennium), shades of blue remains from Lerna IV (end of 3rd millennium), and shades of green remains from Lerna V and VI (20th–16th centuries). The site is well signed to help you find your way and understand what you see.

The center and jewel of this small complex is the structure known as the "House of the Tiles" (named for its terracotta roof tiles) that by prehistoric standards is palatial in scale and may have served as the administrative center for the surrounding area in the Early Helladic Period. In design and apparent function it appears to anticipate later Minoan and Mycenaean palaces.

Finds unearthed on the site include items from Troy, Crete, and the Cyclades, evidence of its wide trading contacts, as well as seals suggesting a system of taxation. Two royal Mycenaean stone-lined shaft graves inserted later into the site bear testimony to the continued significance of Lerna in the late Bronze Age. The earliest burials unearthed within the site date from the Early Neolithic period. Many objects from Lerna are exhibited in the Lerna Collection in the Argos Archaeological Museum.

Lerna surfaces more than once in Greek myth. When Poseidon set aside his anger over an earlier affront and resolved to make the Argolid fertile again, it was here at Lerna that he struck the parched earth with his trident and brought forth three springs for the daughters of Danaos. Here too, in a nearby cave, Herakles found the dreaded Hydra and, for his second labor, proceeded to slaughter it one head at a time. When, at last, it lay at his feet, he dipped his arrows in its blood, allowing him to bring instant death to mortals and to inflict on immortal gods wounds that would never close but would fester instead, forever. Later, this site belonged to the cult of Demeter and the Lernaean mysteries, which may be traced back to belief that it was here that Hades descended into the underworld with his captive Kore, leaving her mother to weep and pound the earth in grief.

Located just beyond (less than 1km) the center of the village of Myli on your left as you drive south (30-27510-47597). Open Tues–Sun 08:30–15:00. Note that the sign for the site is quite small and easily missed, and the left turn into the entrance is rather sharp and abrupt.

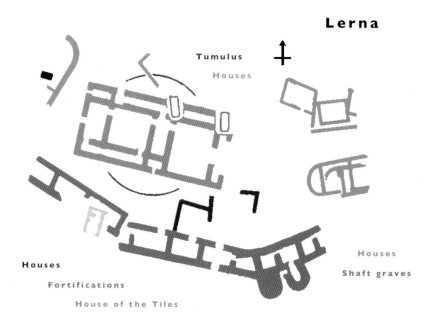

Lerna

Tumulus

Houses

Houses

Shaft graves

Houses

Fortifications

House of the Tiles

HYDRA
The murderous serpentine bitch of Lerna
With too many heads to count,
Made a great bonfire,
And provided the tips of his arrows with venom,
    Making an easy triple kill of the monstrous
        herdsman of Erytheias,
The one with two extra bodies.

—*Euripides*, Herakles, *419–424, tr. R.E. Meagher*

The Menelaion

The ancient name for this area is Therapne, and it is rich in Mycenaean remains. Here on an elevated ridge of Mt. Parnon, rising above the River Eurotas, there are signs of an extensive Mycenaean settlement. Some have claimed this to be the actual site of the palace of Menelaos—that is to say, Homeric Sparta. Just below and northeast of the summit occupied by the hero shrine of Helen and Menelaos, you will come upon the ruins of a Mycenaean mansion or palace of modest scale. This structure went through several building phases beginning, it seems, in the 15th century and was finally destroyed by fire at the close of the 13th century B.C.E.

There is clear evidence that the Menelaion, the hero shrine of Helen and Menelaos, occupies the site of a cult of the tumultuous royal couple dating from the late Bronze Age. No part of the visible present structure, however, pre-dates the Geometric period, and most everything you see is from the classical period or 5th century B.C.E. Some of the ancient offerings unearthed here may be seen in the Sparta archaeological museum, in Room 4.

As with so many ancient sites the most spectacular surviving feature here is the location offering, stunning views in this case, of Mt. Taygetos to the west. This much has not changed since shining Helen, vilified in life and deified in death, and her star-crossed spouse were perhaps laid to rest but surely worshipped here. A place of pilgrimage for many

The Menelaion, Therapne

centuries—from the Mycenaean to the Roman period—this ridge may be as close as we can come to setting foot in Mycenaean Sparta, where Paris first set eyes on Helen and Menelaos vowed to take her back.

Located roughly 5km southeast of Sparta. Open Tues–Sun 08:30–15:00. No fee. Approaching Sparta from the east, turn left on the Geraki road just before crossing the river and entering the town. After roughly 4km look for a signposted road on your left for the Menelaion and the church of Aghios Ilias. On this narrow winding road you will climb to the church, where you will leave your car, as you must make the rest of the way up by foot (approximately 15 minutes). As you climb you will see the site ahead on your right, prominently situated on a height overlooking the Eurotas Valley below.

The Ancient Acropolis and Theater of Sparta

Dorian Sparta, one of the great powers of ancient Greece, is all but lost to view today. Like Thebes—its only true equal on the field of 5th century phalanx warfare—ancient

Spartan warrior, possibly Leonidas, 5c B.C.E.

Sparta lies buried beneath a lackluster town that whispers nothing of its former fame. Anyone steeped or even briefly dipped in ancient Greek myth and history inevitably comes to Sparta expecting to experience a goose bump or two upon arrival. And it may happen, if you allow your imagination to wrestle reality to the ground. Sparta, remember, was never known for architecture or the arts. It had relatively few monuments. Unlike Athens, Sparta was not a first-rank tourist destination in the ancient world, any more than it is today.

Classical Sparta saw no need for walls. Its distance from the sea, together with the natural fortress formed by Taygetos to the west and Parnonas to the east made sudden attack unlikely; and for centuries its was madness for any rival to meet the red-cloaked Spartiate warriors in battle. They were the invincibles and their city could not have been more impregnable if it encased itself in stone.

There is, however, a modest archaeological park on the site of Sparta's ancient acropolis, which makes for a pleasant early evening stroll. The setting, amidst olive groves, is quite lovely, and at least two remains—that of a 6th-century B.C.E. Temple of Athena Chalkioikos, Athena of the Bronze House) and a 1st-century theater—merit some exploring. Whatever you see and do, though, be sure to spend time with the trees.

Ancient theater, acropolis of Sparta

Olive trees grow to startling old age and, like Greek ruins, defy time and age in the most beautiful ways. Many of these trees are centuries old and deserve, if not a hug, at least your wonder and attention.

The Spartan acropolis is reached easily on foot from the center of Sparta. Walk north on Paleologou, the town's central nort–south thoroughfare, until you reach the modern football stadium fronted by a row of shields and a monumental statue of the hero Leonidas. Follow the track to the left, passing through the stone gate of the late-Roman fortification walls once encircling the acropolis into the olive groves beyond. If you continue to bear left (northwest) you will come to the Roman theater, whose distinctive feature was its once movable stage; and just north of the theater you will find what little remains of the Temple of Athena. The ruins to the east belong to a 5–7th-century C.E. Christian basilica.

Located at the top (north end) of Paleologou Street to the left (west) of the stadium (30-27310-28275). Open Tues–Sun 8:30–15:00. No fee. These are the officially announced hours; but, in our experience, the fact seems to be that until darkness sets the people of Sparta and visitors are free to stroll through the olive groves and ruins.

Regrettably, the nearby ruins of the Sanctuary of Artemis Orthia, the notorious site of one of ancient Sparta's more sadistic ancient pedagogical rituals, has slid into such current disarray and neglect that it does not reward a visit at this point. The tomb of Leonidas, as well, is a disappointment, as it is defaced with graffiti and its small enclosure often badly littered. The Shrine of Apollo and Hyakinthos at modern Amykles offers negligible ruins, though it enjoys a lovely site. It's location, however, does match that of the Menelaion, and with time at a premium, we don't recommend seeking it out.

SIDE SIGHT: *Pellana—The Possible Mycenaean Acropolis of Menelaos*

If your love of the road is insatiable, and you fancy an early evening adventure into the Laconian countryside, Pellana is your destination. It is the latest, and many say most likely contender for the site of Homeric Sparta, the palace-citadel of Helen and Menelaos. In ancient epic as well as later classical drama, Menelaos was the decidedly second-fiddle brother of Agamemnon, a reputation supported by the enduring obscurity of his royal site. It is his wife Helen, the infinitely

For I suppose that if Sparta were to become desolate, and only the temples and the foundations of the public buildings were left, that as time went on therewould be a strong disposition with posterity to refuse to accept her fame as a true exponent of her power. And yet they occupy two-fifths of the Peloponnesus and lead the whole, not to speak of their numerous allies outside. Still, as the city is neither built in a compact form nor adorned with magnificent temples and public edifices, but composed of villages after the old fashion of Hellas, there would be an impression of inadequacy. Whereas, if Athens were to suffer the same misfortune, I suppose that any inference from the appearance presented to the eye would make her power to have been twice as great as it is.

—*Thucydides*, Peloponnesian War, *I.10.2*,
tr. Richard Crawley

more desirable, if not less dangerous sister of Clytaemnestra, who perhaps keeps the search alive. Other candidate sites have been the area adjacent to the Menelaion and Vapheio.

There is a not yet a great deal to see at Pellana, still under excavation, and it requires a good deal of uphill bushwhacking to see what is there. But if it's a matter of an inner and irresistible Homeric need to step foot on the same soil as Helen (and we do not make light of this, having made the pilgrimage ourselves), then by all means set out. The drive is remarkably beautiful and will convince you that the rural Laconian landscape is among the loveliest in Greece. What you will find when you get there is an obvious acropolis bearing the footprint of a palatial structure at its summit, girded by fortification walls. Five rock-cut chamber tombs are located nearby, and below the citadel lie the ruins of a prehistoric town. A portion of Room 7 in Sparta's archaeological museum is dedicated to the site and discoveries at Pellana.

To reach modern Pellana without misstep it's best for you to follow closely your own *Road Editions* map. That said, it's mostly the last 300m that are the challenge and this level of detail is beyond any map and requires once again keen eyes and a good nose for ruins. For the simplest route take the Tripoli road north out of Sparta for roughly 12km, turning left on the road signed for Selasia. Stay on this road for 16.5 km through Selasia and Pardalia to Pellana. A more scenic route takes you off the main road at the north limit of Sparta town in the direction of Kastorio (22km from Sparta) and from Kastorio another 5km through Koniditsa and Perivolia to Pellana. Once in the modern village of Pellana, from the center of the village turn right at the lower church on a road posted in Greek for the "Μ ΚΗΝΑΙΚΟΙ ΤΑΦΟΙ ΚΑΣΤΡΟ" (Mycenaean Tombs and Citadel). As you walk on this road you will soon see on your left the lower Mycenaean town and looming above it the acropolis. The tombs are up on the left of the excavations between the town and the citadel. There is no prescribed or direct path to any of these ruins; so it's a matter of finding the way with which you are most comfortable or least uncomfortable. You may have to avoid various farm animals—either loose, fenced, or staked. We encountered nothing dangerous, only muddy. It may be that years from now, if and when this site is more extensively excavated and confirmed to be the palace of Helen, you will be able to say that you were there when it was an all but secret glint in archaeologists' eyes; and from that perspective the mud will hardly matter.

Located 28km northwest of Sparta. Open site. No fee.

Bed and Board

Most of the public lodging in Sparta is, well, Spartan, and best avoided unless your purse requires pinching. Our recommendations are a modest cut above the rest, for which we hope you will thank us. Central Sparta's prime lodgings include: the Menelaion, 91 Paleologou (30-273-102-2161) www.menelaion.com €€ with its gracious neoclassical facade, cooling pool, and bright, spacious rooms; and the contemporary Maniatis Hotel, 72–76 Paleologou (30-273-102-2665) www.maniatishotel.gr €€ with smaller, more stylish rooms and with its own highly touted Zeus Restaurant €/€€. Since both of these hotels face Sparta's "main street," you would do well to ask for a quiet room, though in the Maniatis the quieter rooms are also smaller. If you're smarting from the cost of your lodging, you may recoup some of your losses at dinner by paying less for more at the street-side Restaurant Elysseus €, a brief walk north of your hotel at 113 Paleologou. This is our pick, both for its friendly welcome and its exceptional home cooking, which includes researched and revived ancient dishes such as classic Spartan eggplant and pork. You also won't be disappointed with your meal or your bill at Diethnes €, nearly next-door at 105 Paleologou, serving delicious traditional dishes prepared with care and appreciated by locals.

Day Seven

After relatively brief visits to Sparta's two museums of special note, both of which are easily reached on foot from your hotel, it will be time to check out of your hotel and Sparta for a long and most memorable day's drive. The principal route to your next destination (the west coast port of Pylos) will take you up and over one of the most dramatic mountain ranges in Greece, the legendary Taygetos, which has been towering over you since your arrival in Sparta. En route, you may wish to stop and explore Mistras, one of Greece's most famed attractions but well beyond the chronological scope or interest of this book. You will want to take your time crossing Taygetos, both because of its tortuous high-rise turns and because of its stunning vistas. You will also want to stop for a picnic and to buy from a roadside stand possibly the most amazing honey you will ever encounter. The more ramshackle the stand and the more aged the vendor the better. The old ways are what you want when it comes to Taygetos honey, so thick you nearly need to cut it. Take our word, it will never crystallize, though unless you've had your sweet tooth pulled your jar has no chance of surviving long enough to prove us wrong. Remember to pack suitable provisions in Sparta if you see a picnic in your future as you set out to the mountains. The route to Pylos is followed quite easily on the map. The first leg is due west from Sparta to Kalamata (58km), and the second leg cuts southwest across Messenia from Kalamata to Pylos (51km) via Messini and Handrinos.

Alternatively, we also suggest below a most enticing detour, if you have the time to spare, that will take you south through Messenia, in antiquity the land of Sparta's *helots* (rebellious serfs) subdued by the invading Dorians and forced to work the land to feed the Spartan war machine. This route—remote and fascinating—skirts the Taygetos and explores, instead, the Mani Peninsula, before finding its way up the western coast to Pylos. The choice is yours. If you have an extra day or two and want to experience a more remote, pristine, and starkly stunning corner of Greece that you won't forget, then this side trip is for you.

PRINCIPAL SITES

Archaeological Museum of Sparta

Sparta's small and quite interesting neo-classical archaeo-logical museum is attractively situated in a rose garden and sculptural park just east of Odos Paleologou. Here you will encounter an engaging assortment of finds from all of the local Mycenaean and Spartan sites you've visited as well as those you've skipped. The votive reliefs Helen and Menelaos, and the Dioskouroi, Helen's celestial twin brothers; the bust of a Laconian warrior; said to be Leonidas; the painted clay head of a woman from the Spartan acropolis; and bronze idols from the Menelaion are among the items of special interest. Perhaps most remarkable, however, is the extensive collection, displayed in Room 4, of terracotta masks from the Sanctuary of Artemis Orthia, thought to be clay copies of the originals worn by young boys for their initiation rituals.

Located at 71 Aghiou Nikonos, in a square just east of Sparta's central plateia, across Odos Paleologou and before your reach Odos Aghios Nikolaos (30-27310-28575). Open Tues–Sun 08:30–17:00. €

SIDE SIGHT: *Museum of the Olive and Greek Olive Oil*
This is Sparta's newest museum and, though already open to the public, it is still under development. Only a short walk from your hotel as well as from the archaeological museum, this little gem—the only museum of its kind in Greece—is well worth a visit. Its unique focus is on the olive, its history, and its place in

Greek life. Surely you have noticed how the olive tree follows you nearly everywhere in Greece. That all but omnipresent glint of silver outside your car window as you drive through the Greek countryside, or on either side of your path as you explore ancient sites on foot is, of course, from its leaves catching the sun and shimmering in the breeze. It might be argued that the only thing ancient Greece had more of than olive trees was rocks. Between the olive and the grape, one could almost say there was barely room to walk in the more prosperous regions of ancient Greece, and this fact has only lost some of its force since then. It is estimated that the city-state of Athens alone, at its peak in the mid-5th century, possessed between 5 and 10 million olive trees. Sparta too, was and is a major olive producer. In fact, Greece remains today, as it was in antiquity, one of the most important olive and olive oil producers in the world. It was with the olive (and the grape) that Greece first entered world trade, and it might be said, with some forgivable exaggeration, that the story of Greece and the story of the olive are inseparable. It is that story—from the earliest fossil olive leaves from Santorini dated to 50–60,000 years ago to the most advanced olive presses and pharmaceuticals of the 20th century—that this museum seeks to tell. In little over an hour you will learn everything you never guessed you needed to know about the olive and, in doing so, you'll understand that much better the land and history you've been exploring for the past six days.

Located off Odos Paleologou at 129 Othonas-Amalias (30-27310-89315) www.piop.gr. Open Tues–Sun 10:00–18:00. €

SIDE SIGHT: *Medieval City of Mistras*

The road to Mistras (6km northwest of Sparta) represents only a brief detour off the Sparta-Kalamata road over Taygetos and, for anyone particularly interested in medieval Byzantine Greece, this may be a must. Mistras was one of the last great centers and strongholds of the Byzantine Empire. In fact, the coronation of the last of its emperors, Constantine XI, occurred here in 1449. The extensive fortified city that emerged here and spread down the mountainside across centuries began on the summit with the kastro, or castle, constructed by Franks in 1249 and controlled by Greeks from 1262 until it was overrun by the Turks in 1460. Under Byzantine control it grew to be a flourishing, fortified city, whose palace, basilicas, villas, and chapels have provided a great sprawl of impressive ruins to be explored today. Among the most important monuments here are the kastro and its walls; the restored Palace of the Despots; the Basilica of St. Demetrios, the churches of Sts. Theodore, Our Lady of Hodegetria, Aghia Sophia, Our Lady Evangeslistria; the Monasteries of Our Lady Peribleptos and of Our Lady Pantanass; as well as a number of impressive urban estates. There is also an on-site museum.

If you decide to explore Mistras, prepare yourself for a good bit of rigorous climbing, as the site spills down a steep mountainside. You will also want to prepare for the heat in summer, with sunscreen, hat, and an ample supply of water. Here, as elsewhere, check the opening hours in effect at the time of your visit.

Located 6km northwest of Sparta, signposted from town (30-273-108-3377). Open daily 08:00–19:30. €

BED AND BOARD

First, a few brief words about Pylos. This small modern port is selected here merely to provide a picturesque place to recover from the day's journey and to spend a pleasant night before exploring Homeric Pylos in the morning. That said, it may in its own right qualify as a destination; for it has considerable present charm and historical interest. Besides its attractive central plateia and popular town beach, it boasts a small archaeological museum and two castles. In the Peloponnesian War of the 5th century B.C.E., this was the site of an Athenian base on hostile Spartan soil, from which the Athenians tried to foment rebellion among Sparta's helots, or slaves. At the southern extremity of the bay, on the sea-girded strip of land known as Sfakteria, the supposedly invincible Spartans suffered their most humiliating defeat of the war in a battle that nearly brought an end to the conflict that ripped apart Greece for 27 years. Over two millennia later, Pylos was the site of another historic and devastating engagement—the

Battle of Navarino—when the combined fleets of Britain, France, and Russia destroyed a coalition of naval forces led by Ibrahim Pasha, sinking 53 ships and killing an estimated 6,000 of his men.

A short stroll from the central tree-covered square of Pylos, on the main road into town from Kalamata, you'll see on your left the well-tended Hotel Karalis, 26 Kalamatas St. (30-272-302-2960, fax 30-272-302-2970) with bright, fashionably designed rooms, balconies, and expansive views of the harbor. An attractive seasonal alternative (closed Nov–Mar), operated by the same owners, is the more secluded Karalis Beach Hotel (same phone and fax). It is located by itself at the south end of town, between the sea and the stone fortress. What this hotel has that others in Pylos do not is its edge-of-the-sea location. The contemporary, balconied rooms here literally hang over the sea as it crashes against the rocks below. The sea vistas from your room and from the hotel's spacious terrace lounge are unmatched anywhere in Pylos; but, of course, if you require silence to sleep, the sea just outside your slider is unlikely to oblige.

For excellent fish and traditional Greek dishes The 4 Ephones €/€€, across from the swimming pier, is the place to enjoy waterside dining and the fresh catch. Away from the water, just one street in from the harbor near the Hotel Karalis, the Restaurant Gregoris € offers home-cooked flavor some meals in a charming taverna setting.

Detour: The Mani

This is one of the most remote and alluring regions of Greece and we can propose a modest excursion which will enable you to explore and enjoy some of what it has to offer, from the bleak beauty of its rocky, barren landscape dotted with unique stone tower houses, to steep seaside cliffs, quaint seaside villages, and isolated, pristine beaches. In brief, we propose that you drive south along the eastern edge of Taygetos to Gythio (42km), cutting southwest from there across Messenian Mani to Areopoli (25km), and from there drive north (44km) along the southwestern coast of the Peloponnese to Kardamyli. This lovely oasis—wedged between mountains and the sea—

offers everything you could reasonably want for a memorable stay of a night or a week. If you love hiking, swimming, and being spoiled with spacious, sea-view accommodations and great food, you won't find it easy to leave after only a day.

The gracious and helpful Fotis and Anna Paliatseas operate two idyllic seaside hotels in the village of Kardamyli: The Liakoto and the Anniska Sea Front Hotel Apartments (30-272-107-3600) www.anniska-liakoto.com at the foot of the rugged Taygetos. Both appealing hotels enjoy marvelous views of the sea to their front and the Taygetos mountains to their back. The range of accommodations on offer includes tasteful studios and one- or two-bedroom apartments. All of these are spacious, with well-stocked kitchenettes, and verandas or balconies. Each unit is invitingly furnished with traditional Greek textiles and art, and is, at some risk of overstatement, divinely comfortable. (Can you tell we love this place?) The Liakoto has, in addition, two suites and an outdoor pool. Continental breakfast is available if you can't face shopping the night before for local treats and making your own coffee in the morning. There are many delightful tavernas in town. The Taverna Kiti, facing the sea and overlooking the village pier, is our personal favorite. This is an exciting area for trekking, so be sure to ask your hosts upon arrival for a free guide to local trails which begin practically outside your door. If you're staying only one night, be sure to arrive in time to climb to Aghia Sofia via the Old Kardamyli museum. Be forewarned that this spot is in high demand in summer from "repeat offenders" i.e., those who came once on a whim and now come every summer for a week or two; so you will want to secure a room in advance, if you choose to make the Mani a part of your Peloponnesian explorations.

However long you stay in Kardamyli, you will eventually rejoin the Mycenaean itinerary in Kalamata, roughly 28km north of here on the coastal road, enroute to Pylos (see Day Seven above). Since Homeric Pylos, your next destination site, is closed Mondays, you will need to time your visit there, and thus your stay in Kardamyli, accordingly.

Day Eight

There are only two major sites on today's roster—the Palace and Tomb of Nestor and the associated archaeological museum in nearby Hora—followed by a not so very long drive north to Olympia, your next and final base for two nights. Before leaving the town of Pylos, you may wish to visit the Turkish fortress, the Neo Kastro, or the local miniature archaeological museum; but unless you are inexplicably drawn to these, we would recommend your setting out straightway for Mycenaean Pylos, signposted off of the main coastal road north of Pylos. Departing Pylos from the central Plateia, you will come upon this road on your left, 2.5km outside the town. You will then come to Nestor's Palace in roughly another 17km. After leaving this site, which includes the so-called tomb of Nestor, you will proceed another several kilometers north to the town of Hora. The archaeological museum displaying many finds from the Pylos site and its surrounds is on the north edge of town, a couple of minutes beyond the central plateia. More specifically, as you enter the town of Hora coming from Nestor's site keep the plateia on your left and continue north perhaps a kilometer; and just when it seems you have left the town behind you will see the rather unimposing archaeological museum on your left.

After completing your museum visit, you will return to the town center, turning right at, or rather just beyond, the central plateia, keeping it on your right. This is the main road north, eventually to Patra via Gargaliani, Filiatra, Kyparissia, Zacharo, and Pyrgos. You will see, as you approach Pyrgos, that there are several routes that you might take diagonally to Archaea Olympia. We recommend the turnoff (signposted Ancient Olympia on right) approximately 16km south of Pyrgos at Krestina, scenically following the River Alphios. The entire day's trip, from the town of Pylos to the town of Archaea Olympia, without any unanticipated excursions to which you might be tempted, will come to approximately 125km.

As you will no doubt confront hunger at some point in your journey from Pylos to Olympia, we would suggest either that you have a bite in Hora or provide yourself with the makings of an en route picnic. Hora's shops offer all you will need, or you will find, soon after leaving Hora, on your right a LIDL store and beside it another large market, in which you will be overwhelmed with edible options. Along the coastal Pyrgos road as you continue north you will have numerous opportunities to turn left (east) to seek out a beach for your picnic. As you will see on your map, the roughly 40km coastal span from Kyparissia to Pyrgos is one long beach, with over a dozen well-marked access roads.

Helios, leaving behind the lovely standing waters,
rose up into the brazen sky to shine upon the immortals
and also on mortal men across the grain-giving farmland.
They came to Pylos, Neleus' strong-founded citadel,
where the people on the shore of the sea were making sacrifice
of bulls who were all black to the dark-haired Earthshaker.
There were nine settlements of them, and in each five hundred
holdings, and from each of these nine bulls were provided....

Now the Gerenian horseman Nestor led the way for his sons
and his sons-in-law back to his splendid dwelling.
   But after they had reached the glorious dwelling of the king,
they took their places in order on chairs and along the benches,
and as they came in the old man mixed the wine bowl for them
with wine sweet to drink which the housekeeper had opened
in its eleventh year and loosed the sealing upon it.
   The old man mixed the wine in the bowl and prayed much,
pouring a libation out to Athene daughter of Zeus of the aegis.
   When they had poured and drunk, each man as much as he
wanted, they went away each one to sleep in his own dwelling,
but Nestor the Gerenian horseman gave Telemachos
the dear son of godlike Odysseus a place to sleep in
upon a corded bedstead in the echoing portico.

—*Homer,* Odyssey, *tr. Richmond Lattimore, III.1–8; 386–399*

PRINCIPAL SITES

The Mycenaean Acropolis and Tomb of Nestor

Perched atop the hill of Epano Epano Englianos, the Mycenaean palace of Nestor is, in fact, the best preserved of all the Mycenaean citadels. Although its visible remains appear to be far less impressive than those at Mycenae, Nestor's palace was and is roughly comparable in size to that of the Great King (*Wanax*) Agamemnon. Comparable too were the fleets that these two high kings took with them to Troy, as the Achaean armada assembled for its assault on the fortified love nest of Helen and Paris. Homer places 100 ships under Agamemnon's command and ninety under the grey and garrulous Nestor, that most revered and memorable Mycenaean motor-mouth, who tirelessly reminded the current generation of just how far short they fell of their fathers and forefathers, present company included.

An immediately striking difference between the palace of Nestor and that of Agamemnon is the absence of any appreciable fortification walls. Like the earlier Minoan palaces, it may be that this site was felt to have little need of defensive walls; but there is some initial evidence that the lower city, as yet largely unexcavated, was protected by circuit walls. Regardless, the palace of Nestor eventually met its end in a great fire, which brought both destruction and preservation, as over 600 Linear B clay tablets in the palace archives were hardened against time in the flames that consumed all else. These tablets, mainly administrative in content, give weight to the claim that Pylos was in the late Mycenaean period the capital of a prosperous, extensive, and unified Messenian state.

On site today, the covered area comprises the central palace building, originally two storics, containing the megaron, or throne-room, approached through a double propylon, an inner court, and a vestibule. A site map provided with your entrance ticket will assist you in finding your way through the remains and visualizing the character of each space and its contents, from the king's throne to the king's bathtub. The fresco fragments

preserved in the Hora museum suggest the vivid splendor of the palace, perhaps enough to occasionally gladden the heart of an old king who had seen too much of war and of the rivalry and corruption that came with it.

Of special note is the raised circular hearth (4m in diameter) in the center of the megaron, as well as the painted floor that surrounded it. On the northeast side of the megaron is where the king's throne once sat; and, beside it, on the king's right, you will see a depression in the floor, marking out a narrow channel, roughly 6 feet in length. It is speculated that this was used for royal libations, which would flow from beside the throne and collect in a shallow pool carved in the floor.

The tholos tomb on the site, to the right of the entrance booth, is the largest such royal tomb in the area and seems to have been in use from the mid or late 16th century to the 13th century B.C.E., serving as a family tomb. As many as 17 burials have been associated with the site; and, despite rather thorough looting in the ancient period, some grave goods have survived to be displayed in the museum at Hora. Except for it scale and proximity to the palace, there is no evidence to support or dismiss claims that this is the tomb of Homeric Nestor.

Located 17km north of modern Pylos on the road to Pyrgos (30-27630-31437). Open Tues–Sun 08:30–15:00). €

The Hora Archaeological Museum

This unimposing museum, despite is modest size, contains some important finds from the site of Nestor's palace at Englianos and its adjacent tholos tombs (only one of which is accessible), as well as from the surrounding Messenian countryside. As always, the finest finds from this area are to be found not here but in the National Archaeological Museum in Athens.

Room I contains finds from a number of Mycenaean tombs in surrounding Messenia, including swords, daggers, bronze vessels, gold cups, and jewelry. In Room II you will find an assortment of remains from the site of Nestor's palace and tomb. There is an illuminating scale model of the palace, as well as fresco fragments from the palace, together with reconstructions, including a Mycenaean battle scene, and casts of some of the Linear B tablets from the royal archives. There is also the requisite profusion of pottery, especially drinking cups, which flows into Room III. Room III also offers some very interesting bronze finds from the Vagenas tholos tomb, south of the palace complex.

It will not take very long to examine this museum's offerings, but it will serve to complete your experience and heighten your appreciation of the palace site at Englianos.

Located 4km north of the Palace of Nestor on the edge of Hora town (30-27632-31358). Open Tues–Sun 08:30–15:00. €

BED AND BOARD

In a town bursting with hotels, the Hotel Pelops, 2 Varela (30-262-402-2543) www.hotelpelops.gr € stands out. The obliging Spiliopoulos family recently renovated their central, spotless lodging, and its rooms are as tasteful as they are spacious. The family occasionally offers set menu dinners and always a buffet breakfast worth waking up for. We especially recommend a bright corner room with balcony overlooking the local church. If the Hotel Pelops is full, the Neda Hotel, 1 Karamanli St. (30-262-402-2563) www.hotelneda.gr € has simple, attractive rooms and a rooftop restaurant overlooking the town. The Olympia Palace, 2 Praxitelous Condili St. (30-262-402-3101, fax 30-262-402-2525) € € on the main street has bright, inviting rooms, but for a silent night be sure to ask for a room off the street. If it's blazing hot and you must have a pool then the Best Western Europa Hotel, 1 Drouva (30-262-402-2650) www.hoteleuropa.gr € € is the place to stay, though it is a significantly out of town, requiring that you drive to everything else.

Olympia is no culinary mecca, but there is also no need to starve or otherwise punish yourself here. We enjoyed some very satisfying meals at two tavernas recommended to us by opinionated, well-fed locals. On Odos G. Doumas, at the taxi stand off the main street, we can personally vouch for the Aegean Cafeteria Restaurant's € more unusual, well-prepared Greek dishes, and for the Taverna Melathron's € truly superior souvlaki and local wine. Their simple menus may be the closest you'll come to down-home, authentic Greek fare in Olympia's tourist-town tavernas.

An after-dark suggestion: Every summer, throughout the months of July and August, the town of Ancient Olympia hosts the Olympia International Festival, featuring an exciting array of Greek and European musicians, dancers, and theater companies in performance at the Floka Theater, an outdoor, ancient-style amphitheater situated just above the town center. The summer's offerings typically include a couple of ancient Greek plays performed by the Greek National Theater or one of Greece's fine regional theaters. Since most theatrical performances here are in modern Greek, you will want to familiarize yourself with the play in advance. In the case of ancient plays, if you come with the plot and central characters fixed in your mind, you should be able to enjoy fully this rare opportunity to experience classical drama coming to new life before an appreciative Greek audience as the intervening millennia vanish into insignificance before your eyes. The Floka Theater can be reached on foot in 20–30 minutes from the center of town, depending on your pace. Much of the trek is uphill and you will be returning long after dark; so be sure to wear light colors and bring a flashlight with you, as a portion of the walk is along a road. To find out what's on and when, ask your hotelier for a copy of the festival calendar or search in advance at: www.cultureguide.gr

DAY NINE

Be sure to set out today with sunscreen, a hat, lots of water, and comfortable shoes, as you will likely be on your feet and in the sun until sunset. Fortunately, the sites and museums of Olympia are all within a brief walk of town and your hotel, so you can easily retreat at any point in the day for a meal, a cool drink, or a siesta. The archaeological park of Olympia is one of Greece's finest. It is vast and pleasant, offering splendid sights and ample shade. The central must-see attractions are, of course, the sanctuary of Zeus, the Olympic stadium, and the new archaeological museum. These are all well-provided with explanatory panels, maps, and plaques, so you can easily find your way and make sense of the archaeological sites and museum exhibits. Olympia, another of Greece's World Heritage Sites, is supremely visitor-friendly and self-revealing; nevertheless, some introductory notes and a general locator map here will no doubt be helpful and illuminating.

We recommend that you spend the morning hours on the site, before the heat and crowds of the day reach their peak. Then after a midday break for lunch and/or siesta, you can explore the museums of Olympia as long and thoroughly as time, energy, and concentration permit.

For look, that laureled head
compels me to this God-appointed debt,
to blend the many voices of the lyre,
the crying of flutes and disposition of words,
fitly: for Ainesidamos'
    son. And Olympia too
                calls for my song.

—*Pindar*, Olympian 3, *tr. D.S. Carne-Ross*

PRINCIPAL SITES

The Sanctuary of Olympian Zeus and the Olympic Stadium

Olympia is the oldest and arguably the most revered pan-Hellenic sanctuary in Greece. After all, Zeus was the high god, the unrivaled sovereign over all of the Olympian deities, who comprised his household, an extended family as quarrelsome and dysfunctional as they were sublime and powerful. The sacred precinct of Olympia lies at the foot of the Hill of Kronos (named for Zeus' infanticidal father) wedged between the River Alphios and its tributary, the River Kladeos. This site was settled and inhabited without interruption from the early third millennium B.C.E., and was already a cult center in the late Mycenaean period, when the shrine's first focus, it is thought, fell on King Pelops and his wife Hippodaemia, from whom the Peloponnese—the "Island of Pelops"—received its name. Even from this earliest period, the rituals of the sacred precinct were accompanied by athletic contests of at least regional significance. Some say that Pelops founded the games, while others attribute them to the hero Herakles. Regardless, the enduring irony and wonder of the games was that men came here not only to worship the shining heroes and luminous gods but to reveal their own splendor as well. The victorious few arrived at Olympia as mere mortals and departed as near gods, immortalized by their awesome achievements in the stadium and hippodrome.

During the early centuries of the sanctuary, the cultic focus of the sacred precinct was expanded, in part under Cretan influence, to include a broader spectrum of gods and heroes, including Gaia, Kronos, Rhea, Eileithyia, Themis, and Herakles. Eventually, perhaps by 1000 B.C.E., Zeus occupied the highest chair, as it were, at Olympia, as he did on Olympus. It is said that the earliest contest in his honor was a foot race for which the feet of his cult image served as the finish line. The first recorded Olympiad was held in 776 B.C.E. and from then on every four years for twelve centuries. A recently unearthed plaque containing the names of victors from late antiquity has led scholars to date the last ancient Olympiad near the end of the 5th century C.E. The ancient Olympic festivals occurred in late summer and lasted five days, though the contestants were required to arrive a month earlier and to train for thirty days under the close supervision of the *hellanodikai* (judges). A strictly enforced Olympic truce protected athletes and visitors alike from any violence or harm both in their travels and in their celebration of the festival. Participation in the games was limited to Greek-speaking males, while any free men regardless of race or tongue were free to watch. Slaves and married women were prohibited from entering the sanctuary and stadium. Unmarried girls, however, were admitted to the games as spectators and, on a day of rest for the male athletes, competed in running races in honor of Hera. Unlike the male athletes, these young girls did not compete naked but wore, instead, short, revealing tunics. Both for young men and for young women, then, the games were an opportunity to gaze and wonder at the most fit and beautiful bodies in motion and struggle that the Greek-speaking world produced.

Only the names of victors were recorded and preserved. There were no silver or bronze medals, as it were, only gold medals or, more precisely, laurel crowns. If you were not first, you were last. Record times and distances were not kept; so we have no way of knowing how fast these Olympians ran or how far they jumped or threw javelin or discus. If we can judge anything from their long-jump pits, however, they far surpassed modern jumpers in at least that one event. One

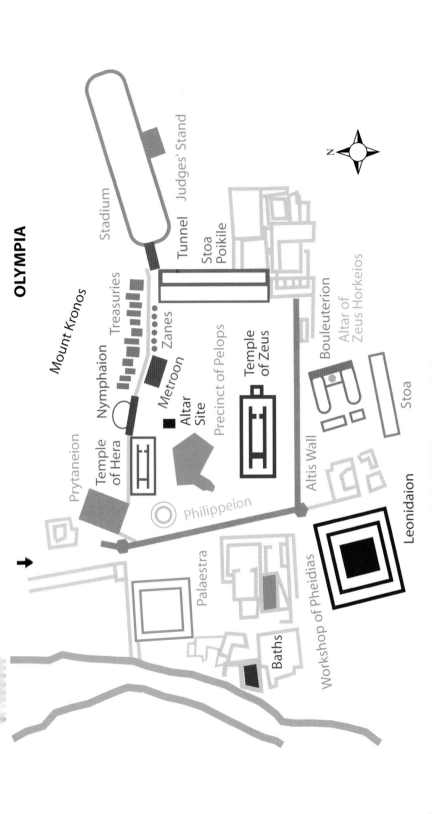

OLYMPIA

Mount Kronos

Stadium

Judges' Stand

Tunnel

Stoa Poikile

Treasuries

Nymphaion

Zanes

Metroon

Altar Site

Precinct of Pelops

Temple of Zeus

Bouleuterion

Altar of Zeus Horkeios

Stoa

Prytaneion

Temple of Hera

Philippeion

Altis Wall

Leonidaion

Palaestra

Workshop of Pheidias

Baths

N

legendary Greek jumper is recorded as having overleapt with ease a 50-foot jumping pit, which would mean that he surpassed the current world record by more than 20 feet. The fact that ancient jumpers ran into their jumps carrying hand weights which they jettisoned in such a way as to propel them further may account for the phenomenal distances that they were able to achieve. The ancient games included foot races of various lengths, boxing, wrestling, a brutal no-holds-barred, fist-and-foot fight called the *pankration*, horse races, chariot races, and the pentathlon (running, jumping, wrestling, and the throwing of discus and javelin).

While the games brought fame to some, they meant infamy for others, especially for those who were found to have violated their Olympic oaths (taken at the altar of Zeus Horkeios) and cheated in the games. Those who lost in the games suffered oblivion and were soon forgotten; but the cheaters, like the winners, were sure to be remembered, for their deeds were inscribed where they would be seen for centuries. Be sure to note on your left, before you enter the entrance tunnel to the stadium, a row of stone platforms or bases known and labeled as the *Zanes*. These once supported statues of Zeus paid for with the fines exacted from those caught cheating in the games. They also bore the names and offenses of these disgraced miscreants, written in stone. This avenue of infamy served to remind anyone entering the stadium, whether athlete or observer, that not only the judges but Zeus too was watching.

Across many centuries, the sanctuary, or "the Grove" (*Altis*) as it was called, from its modest beginnings grew in scale and importance to become a shrine of pan-Hellenic significance, drawing the pious, the curious, and the competitive from every corner of mainland Greece, the islands, the colonies, as far west as Italy and France, and as far east as Egypt and the Black Sea. One of the earliest monumental structures within the sacred enclosure was the 7th-century Doric Temple of Hera, the Heraion, one of the first known examples of monumental temple architecture in

Top: Temple of Zeus, Olympia
Bottom: The Krypte, the entrance tunnel to the stadium, Olympia

Greece, containing in its cella (central part) colossal sculptures of Hera and her husband Zeus. The Grove and its surrounds were indeed from the Archaic period through the Hellenistic and Roman centuries an ever-expanding building site where monuments of every sort, sacred and secular—from temples, altars, shrines, and votives to treasuries, gymnasia, baths, and elite lodgings—rose up to honor the gods and to highlight their benefactors. The full span of the precinct's history was preserved in these monuments and in the art that adorned them. The Pelopeion (Precinct of Pelops), for example, preserved the memory of Pelops, the earliest legendary king of the region, who is said to have won his wife in a chariot race; and the canon of Herakles' labors was fixed in stone here on the greatest of Olympia's monumental structures, the temple of Olympian Zeus. A number of states and famed individuals too left their mark and their stories here. Gela, Byzantium, Megara, Syracuse, Samos, Sikyon, and other Greek states, mostly outside Greece proper, built treasuries or miniature temples and stashed them with an assortment of gear, trophies, and offerings. Later, Philip of Macedon and his son Alexander celebrated in stone their victory at Chaironeia with the circular Philippeion; and still later, in the hippodrome, the Roman Emperor Nero reveled in another sort of victory when he wiped out in the chariot race and claimed, all the same, the victor's crown, a distinction of which he was posthumously stripped. Olympia is clearly steeped in stories millennia deep, most of which are lost. Here, only fragments, whether of story or stone, remain.

The undisputed gem of Olympia was, to be sure, the Temple of Zeus, constructed largely from the spoils of nearby Pisa between 472 and 457 B.C.E. The work of a local architect, Libon of Elis, this was one of the largest temples ever built in Greece, with 13 Doric columns along its sides and six at either end. The two pediment groupings were carved of Parian marble. The roof tiles, instead of terra cotta, were also made of marble from the island of Paros. The metopes, front and rear, depicted labors of Herakles; and it was this selection that henceforth formed the canonical twelve. However magnificent the shell, however, it was the pearl within that stunned the ancient world; for there within the cella sat the

Lord of the Gods enthroned. This sculptural masterpiece—Olympian Zeus carved and fashioned of marble, gold, and ivory—was the work of Pheidias, whose on-site workshop lies just outside the sacred precinct or Altis to the west. Pheidias, whose sculptures adorn the Parthenon, surpassed himself here at Olympia creating this colossal cult image numbered among the seven wonders of the ancient world. Nearly forty feet in height, the head of the seated figure nearly scraped the ceiling; if the god had ever decided to stretch his legs and stand, he would have gone through the roof. Tragically, nothing of this masterwork, apart from its memory, survives. The same is true of perhaps the most sacred of ancient monuments within the Altis, the sacrificial altar of Zeus, on which 100 bulls were slain and offered as part of the Olympic festival. Only a small ritual portion of each victim, however, was offered to Zeus, while the rest was roasted and divided among the festival participants. It is said that the accumulated ashes from these sacrifices and from the sacred hearth of the Prytaneion (the dwelling of the sanctuary's officials) formed over the centuries a great mound on which further sacrifices were offered.

Apart from the monuments mentioned above, there is much to explore, discover, and learn at this extraordinarily rich and diverse site; so be sure to leave time to get lost, find your own way, and stumble upon the unexpected. You may want to save one last burst of energy as well to test and show your stuff on the field of glory in the ancient Olympic stadium. Or you may just prefer to watch. There are always willing contestants who find the challenge of the field and the roar of imaginary ghosts irresistible; so pull up a patch of grass as the ancient spectators did (only the judges had seats) and think ancient thoughts.

One final note: to save you looking for it, the hippodrome (horse track), which once accommodated 44 chariots and thus 176 horses was washed away in antiquity by the River Alphios and is likely never to be excavated and restored.

Located on the southeast edge of the modern town of Ancient Olympia (30-26240-22517). €€ Combined ticket for site and museums. Open daily 08:00–19:30 with shorter hours off-season.

The Archaeological Museums of Olympia

There are three museums of note in Ancient Olympia focused on the ancient precinct and games: the new Archaeological Museum; the Museum of the History of the Olympic Games in Antiquity; and the Museum of the History of Excavations at Olympia. The last of these is so professionally specialized as to be of little interest to the general reader or visitor, even those all but addicted to ancient ruins. We recommend that you conserve your museum energies and focus them first on what is usually referred to as the "new" (1970s) museum, which is undeniably one of the finest archaeological museums in Greece. Recently renovated, relit, and redesigned for the 2004 Olympics, this museum is now better than ever. After exploring its exceptional collection, if time and interest remains before you call it a day, spend some limited time in the Museum of the History of the Olympic Games in Antiquity, whose collection and presentation are quite engaging and informative.

Some of the finest finds from the precinct of Zeus cannot be seen either here in the Olympia museum or in the National Archeological Museum in Athens, for they have long since been removed to the Louvre in Paris, where they remain. They were claimed, or more accurately looted, by the site's French excavators in the first half of the 19th century. After the French excavations at Olympia were halted by the Greek government, the French were eventually replaced by German archaeologists, whose successors continue to dig at Olympia to this day. To be sure, the despoiling of Greece's ancient treasures hardly began or ended with this episode. It is a story of plunder that began in antiquity and whose final chapters are yet to be written.

That said, the archaeological museum of Olympia offers a treasure-laden walk through the history of Olympia, from the prehistoric period through the Roman and post-Roman era. Your way is well marked here and enhanced with excellent presentation panels. Visual overload is all but a forgone conclusion, as nearly every exhibit and item is worthy of close attention and deep appreciation; so you may want to

pace your visit and save yourself for the most dramatic pieces
and for those of greatest personal interest to you.

The sculptural ornaments from the Olympic Temple of
Zeus are sure to rank high on anyone's list of priorities, as is
the Hermes of Praxiteles and the Nike of Paionios, all but two
carved of Parian marble. The collection of bronze figures and
weaponry—Geometric and Archaic—is exceptional. In the
classical gallery there is an item of great historical
significance: the helmet of Miltiades, worn by him as he led
Athens to victory over the Persians at Marathon and then
dedicated by him to Zeus as an offering of thanks. Next to it
is the only known piece of booty to have survived from that

momentous battle, a bronze Assyrian-style helmet worn and left by a Persian warrior who either fell or fled in defeat.

Located a short walk north of the archaeological site (30-26240-22529). €€ Combined ticket for site and museums. Open Tues–Sun 08:00–19:30 and Monday 12:30–19:30, with shorter hours off-season.

You may wish to complete your day with a brief visit to the Museum of the History of the Olympic Games in Antiquity which opened its doors for the first time in 2004 and whose exhibits tell the full story of the Olympic Games. The items selected—everything from musical instruments to chariot wheels—and the accompanying explanatory panels are excellent, providing a clear and vivid chronicle of the origins, history, and character of the ancient pan-Hellenic festivals and games, held not only here at Olympia but also at Delphi, Nemea, and Isthmia. Unless you are already running on empty, we encourage you to pay at least a brief visit here, where you are bound to learn and be fascinated by more than you ever thought there was to know about the great athletic *agones* or contests of ancient Greece.

Housed in a striking Neoclassical building a short walk northeast from the archaeological site. No extra fee as yet. Open Tues–Sun 08:00–19:30 and Monday 12:30–19:30, with shorter hours off-season.

DAY TEN

Today's only official task is to find your way back to Athens and the Eleftherios Venezelos International Airport, where you will return your rental car. For this you will need a detailed, preferably *Road Editions*, map of the Peloponnese. Without allowing for side-trips or stops, planned or un-planned, the drive will take at least six hours. We recommend a route north to the coast and then east along the Patra-Korinthos motorway. The first leg of this route is remarkably beautiful and will reveal to you stunning, fertile landscapes that you would likely never expect to encounter in the Peloponnese.

From Olympia town take the scenic (green) road north and east past the archaeological site (on your right) in the direction of Miraka and Lalas. Roughly 20km north of Lalas and just north of Marmara, you will turn west to Panopoulos and then north to Stavrothromi and still further north in the direction of Patra. A few kilometers south of Patra you will come upon and join the major tollway to Korinthos. Do not exit at Patra but remain instead on this coastal motorway straight through to Korinthos and Athina. As you cross the isthmus and approach Athina you will stay on this motorway past the city, exiting only to follow signs to the airport.

ITINERARY THREE

CLASSICAL CIVILIZATION:
ATHENS AND ATTIKA 480–336 B.C.E.

PRINCIPAL SITES

Temple of Olympian Zeus

New Acropolis Museum

Sanctuary and Theater of Dionysos

Odeion of Herodes Atticus

Acropolis....*Propylaia, temple of Athena Nike,
Parthenon, Erechtheion, archaeological site museum*

Areopagos....*site of ancient council*

Ancient Agora....*temple of Hephaistos, stoa of Attalos*

National Archaeological Museum

Goulandris Museum of Cycladic Art

Delphi....*sanctuaries of Apollo and Athena Pronaia, and
archaeological museum*

Piraeus....*archaeological museum*

Aegina....*temple of Aphaia and archaeological museum*

Brauron....*sanctuary of Artemis and archaeological museum*

Marathon...*Athenian tumulus and archaeological museum*

Rhamnous....*temple of Themis, temple of Nemesis,
ancient fortress town*

Pnyx....*site of ancient democratic assembly*

Hill of the Muses....*prison cell of Socrates*

Kerameikos....*ancient cemetery and archaeological museum*

Sounion....*sanctuary of Poseidon*

ARRIVAL IN ATHENS

This itinerary, like the three others in this guide, begins with arrival in Athens' new Eleftherios Venezelos International Airport. Unlike its predecessor, "Venezilos" or "Spata" (as it is commonly known) is well designed, easily negotiated, and linked directly to the city center by both Metro and rail lines, as well as by taxi and bus. Before leaving the airport, you will do well to stop by the EOT (Greek National Tourist Organization) office in the arrivals hall and pick up free copies of their Athens map, cultural events guide, and other free hand-outs, such as up-to-date lists (for Athens and Greece) of current openings and closings at every state archaeological site and museum. Also ask for a free "Athens Public Transport Pocket Map"; and, if they don't have one for you, try the ticket counter at the Syntagma Metro station. If you miss or take a pass on the airport tourist organization office, there is another very helpful EOT office, several minutes' walk from Syntagma, at 26a Amalias (30-210-331-0392), open Mon–Fri 09:00–19:00, Sat–Sun 10:00–16:00.

Since all of the Athenian hotels recommended here are located in or near the traditional, in fact ancient, district known as the Plaka, we will assume that you will be seeking a bus or Metro to Syntagma or Constitution Square, which adjoins the Plaka. The airport bus to Syntagma runs roughly every twenty minutes, takes about an hour, and costs just over €3 per person, while the Metro leaves every thirty minutes, takes a half hour, and costs €10 for two persons. In general we avoid Athenian taxis whenever possible and we are not alone in this. They have a dire and mostly well-deserved reputation for unarmed theft. I have heard the view expressed more than once that Athenian taxi drivers ought to be required to wear masks to alert the unsuspecting visitor to the true nature of their profession.

From Syntagma you will be able either to walk or to take the Metro to your hotel so as to check in and leave your bags. Already, no doubt from multiple sources, you have heard that it is best not to succumb at once to jet lag but rather to resist gravity and remain awake until more or less your normal bedtime. Fortunately, Athens is a city that both inspires and rewards tireless exploration, so it should not be altogether impossible to stay vertical until dark.

Bed and Board

It's nearly safe to say that there are no inhabitable bargains in Athens, at least not if location matters. Athens boasts lowly to lavish accommodation, and all of it is costly. That said, room rates fluctuate wildly depending on the season; so don't hesitate to dicker until the sun goes down if bargaining is in your blood or personal repertoire. A tip to the timid: hotels offering reservation via the Web often list reduced rates. Regrettably, however, many of the more modestly priced, and thus affordable, hotels communicate only by fax and/or phone. The good news is that in Athens nearly all of these will be able to do basic business in English. Keep in mind that in high season—July and August—the most desirable hotels may be fully booked well in advance, so it is best to arrange for your lodgings in Athens well ahead of your arrival.

We suggest staying in or close to the attractive, old (really old!) precinct of the inner city known as Plaka. From here you can walk to the city's major archaeological sites and enjoy a plethora of cafes, shops, and pedestrian walkways. Plaka occupies much of what was the walled city of Athens in the 5th century and today comprises the core of the tourist zone. This fact should not deter you, however, as whatever charm Athens possesses is mostly concentrated here. Until you reach the remote mountainous or coastal suburbs, the rest of Athens is a matter of uncontrolled sprawl with little appeal for most visitors. One nearby exception is the neighborhood known as Kolonaki, an upscale, chic enclave with more than its share of designer labels and people who at the very least find themselves dazzling.

But you need a place to stay, and here are our recommendations. If money is no option, then the lavish Electra Palace Hotel (30-210-337-0000) www.electrahotels.gr €€ on the edge of Plaka and Syntagma Square at 18–20 Nikodimou Street is the place to stay to feel spoiled and lack nothing. If there are more than two of you or if you want to spread out in your

space, then the AVA Hotel (30-210-325-9000) www.avahotel.gr
€€ with immaculate apartments and suites, some with views
from balconies, and a most helpful staff is a perfect choice.
AVA plans to add a roof garden and a small gym in the
upcoming year. The AVA Hotel is located in the Plaka, just up
from Hadrian's Arch at 9–11 Lysikratous Street. Another fine
option at the edge of Plaka—and the foot of Dionissiou
Areopagitou (the pedestrian walkway that winds around the
side of the Acropolis and the Plaka), is the Parthenon Hotel
(30-210-640-0720) www.airotel.gr. €€ It is just off Amalias
Street and around the bend from the Acropolis Metro station
at 6 Makri Street. While there are no spectacular views, it is
convenient and very clean, with quieter back rooms and small
balconies.

The superior Herodian Hotel (30-210-923-6832)
www.herodion.gr €€ and its more modest sister the Philippos
Hotel (30-210-923-6114) www.philipposhotel are both stylish
and deeply comfortable. While they are set well away from
the action in a quiet residential area behind the Acropolis
Metro Station, they are very near Dionissiou Areopagitou
(the pedestrian walkway mentioned above). The Herodian
Hotel is at 4 Rovertou Galli Street, just off of Mitseon Street,
which in turn is off of Dionissiou Areopagitou; and the
Philippos Hotel is at 3 Mitseon Street.

On a more modest scale, the Hotel Acropolis House (30-
210-322-2344) www.acropolishouse.gr € offers breakfast and
simple lodging in an historic mansion on the edge of Plaka. Its
address is 6–8 Kodrous, a short walk from Syntagma down
Mitropoleos Street, then left on Voulis Street, which turns into
Kodrous. Acropolis House is on the corner to your right.
Another basic Plaka accommodation is the Phaedra Hotel
(30-210-323-8461; fax 30-210-322-7795)€ overlooking the
small square of the 11th-century church of Ayia Ekaterini at
Adrianou and Cherefondos Street. It has a roof garden with
an Acropolis view, and while its rooms are small they have
balconies. Breakfast is extra. The Phaedra is an easy walk
from the Acropolis Metro Station. Turn left out of the station
and then right to the Dionissiou Areopagitou pedestrian
walkway, which you cross to Vyronos, then right on

Lyssikratous to Cherefondos Street. It can also be reached on foot from Syntagma down Amalias Avenue and right on Lyssikratous.

Athens is teeming with eateries of all sorts. The Plaka is awash with tavernas vying to satisfy your appetite and tap your funds. Often waiters will go to great dramatic lengths to lure you to their menu and their tables. Needless to say, it pays to be strong and to resist until you find what you want. If you walk on by, their disappointment will pass in seconds; not so yours if you succumb to pressure and make an unfortunate choice. Best to play the field before making a commitment. Meanwhile, beware of low fixed prices accompanied by an often hidden and exorbitant cover charge, levied for the view or the live music. Just because you can't eat the scenery or the atmosphere doesn't mean you won't be expected to pay for them. We advise that you take your time, wander at will, work up an appetite, inform your instincts, and then follow the inner voice that eventually shouts "this is it." Either that, or you can let us point you to a few of our favorite finds:

In Plaka, Platanos € at 4 Diogenous Street offers generous portions of authentic and well-prepared Greek dishes. Also in Plaka, the excellent Palia Taverna tou Psara, the Old Tavern of Psara's €€ at 16 Erehtheos Street is a very popular local restaurant with delicious seafood, a wide range of appetizers, and a lovely terrace. Then, on the very edge of Plaka, just off Syntagma at 44a Voulis, there's an easily overlooked hole-in-the-wall taverna, the Paradosiako €, serving among other things the finest grilled octopus we've ever had. This place has no need to announce itself and doesn't bother; avid locals can find it blindfolded. If you go to the above address, you'll know it when you see it—a handful of small tables on the sidewalk, rarely an empty seat, and no one trying to get you to look at the menu. If all the tables are taken, it's worth the wait.

Outside of Plaka, off the Dionissiou Areopagitou, across from the walkway entrance to the Parthenon, the Dionysis-Zonar's €€ restaurant is a popular refuge for the weary, the thirsty, and the famished. In the heat of the day its grape vines and pine trees offer welcome shade from the scorching sun, and at night the vista of the illumined Parthenon is quite spectacular from this vantage.

Further along, past the entrance to the Parthenon, the Dionissiou Areopagitou walkway changes names to become Apostolou Pavlou. Here, on a corner location at #23, just before you come to the busy cafe scene of Thissio, you'll find the charming Filistron € serving memorable light fare and a wide selection of Greek wines from 6:00pm Tues–Sun, with grand views of the Acropolis from their rooftop terrace.

Outside the tourist zone, to explore some of the finest dining Athens has to offer, one need look no further than the famed Spondi (30-210-752-0658) €€ 5 Pironos for exceptional fare and impeccable service in luxurious surroundings. Spondi is located in the Pangrati area behind the Panathenaic Stadium. Varoulko (30-210-522-8400) €€ 80 Pireos, in Gazi, offers exceptional seafood and meat dishes from their Michelin Star-studded chef. It is beyond the ancient cemetery, Keramikos, on the busy thoroughfare to Piraeus harbor. Needless to say, if you decide for either of these upscale options, you would do well to dress to match the cuisine and make a reservation.

Lastly, whether for picnic fare or the sheer spectacle, you may want to pay a visit to the city's covered central market, focused on Athinas Street and spilling into the surrounding side streets, between Monastiraki and Omonia Square. This mecca for all things edible has it all: bins of bright, aromatic spices, baskets and trays of luminous fruits and vegetables, tubs of glossy olives, great rounds of Greek cheese, and stalls groaning under the day's catch of fish and seafood. How you will long for a kitchen of your own after a stroll here! Don't save this for the last stop of your day, as many of the vendors are gone by mid-afternoon.

SOME PRELIMINARY THOUGHTS ON ATHENS

This itinerary, while concentrating on Classical Greece, confines itself (apart from an excursion to Delphi) to the much narrower focus of Attika, the ancient city-state of Athens. This is for several reasons. The first is practical.

Many first-time travelers to Greece are disinclined to take the wheel of a rental car and navigate Greek roads on their own, tracing their days and their routes on a map. One person's holiday can be another person's Hades. Many are those who prefer a fixed base, where they unpack once, venturing out each morning and returning each night to a familiar bed. Timidity, however, is not the only reason for spending a week in the Greek capitol. Athens, on her own merits, deserves a long stay, especially since its Olympic makeover. The return of the Games to their motherland in 2004 provoked a frenzy of preparations, from housecleaning to major new construction; and Athens was the principal focus of this dramatic refurbishment. Greeks, known both for their national pride and their hospitality, won't invite the world to visit without first making an Olympian fuss at home. And it shows. Athens has never looked better or been more inviting, at least not within my memory.

But there is a still more compelling reason to concentrate our exploration of Classical Greece on Athens. Athens was undeniably the epicenter of the Classical Greek world. Although ancient Greece was never truly united—not even when fighting their arch-enemies the Persians—Athens made herself the focus of attention then, as she does now. Whether revered or reviled, whether hailed as the savior of Greece or denounced as its oppressor, ancient Athens held the 5th-century headlines, as it were. At her Periklean peak, Athens was the most powerful of the Greek city-states, the most ambitious, the most feared and, by many, the most admired. Her four-drachma piece—the "silver owl"—was the standard currency of Hellas, the "dollar" of the Greek world. Her radical democracy—offering every citizen not only the vote but also voice in government, access to office, and equality before the law—was a provocation to the rest of the Greek world and beyond, a glove thrown down in challenge. You were either with Athens, or you were against her. For a time during and after the "great" and "good" wars against the Persian empire, Athens held the high ground in more ways than one. She was the fist of the Greek free world and its most prosperous economic engine. She was also a laboratory of

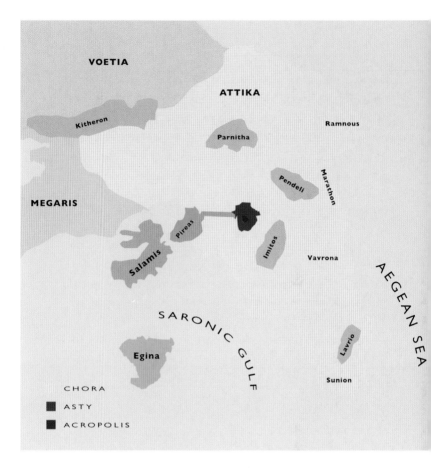

aggressive, muscular democracy, as keen to preach as to practice her beliefs. Though roughly the size of Luxembourg or Rhode Island, Athens in the 5th century was on its way to becoming a world power. The great flowering that represented the golden age of Classical Greece occurred more than anywhere else on her soil, so it is little wonder that both archaeologists and tourists should want to plant their shovels and unpack their bags here.

Already we are ahead of ourselves. Some very fundamental questions confront us. What do we mean by the ancient polis, or city-state, of Athens? The typical Greek polis was comprised of several geographically concentric parts: the acropolis, the asty, and the chora. We begin at the center, with the acropolis. This was, as its name suggests, an elevated site, walled and monumental in scale. Many of the most eminent city-states began as Mycenaean domains with an acropolis or hilltop citadel at their administrative, military, economic, and cultic center. This was true, for instance, of Athens, Thebes, and Sparta, to mention three of the greatest powers of the Greek 5th century. In the Mycenaean Period, it was the *wanax* or king who resided on the acropolis and presided over his realm from his megaron or great hall. Few of these citadels and kings survived the general disaster that marked the end of the Bronze Age in the East Mediterranean; but here Athens was already an exception. She survived and made her way through the ensuing centuries intact and inviolate. Her legendary founder-king Theseus left to her the comparatively vast chora or countryside of Attika, diverse yet unified, a cohesive state centered in the asty or city of Athens. Eventually, the kings were deposed and replaced by gods and goddesses, whose temple residences were modeled on and often stood over the megara of their mortal predecessors.

Classical Athens, then, had long since disposed of her kings. The ultimate welfare and direction of the state was now in the hands of her patron deity, Athena, who ruled and watched over the city from the Acropolis, which was now in its walled entirety a sacred precinct. Below the Acropolis and encircling it was the asty, the city of men, the urban core of the polis. Until the Persians first invaded the Greek mainland in 490 B.C.E. it was not customary for an asty or city center to be walled; but the enduring Persian threat as well as increasingly hostile rivalries between city-states inspired the fortification of Athens and many other Greek cities. Within its walls every city required certain public spaces in which to conduct its essential civic life and business: the temple, the agora, and the theater. Without these a city was not a city. The temple or temples on the Acropolis were where the gods lived and where they were ritually attended to by those whose well-being they held in their hands. The agora was the "commons" where the people of the city conducted their affairs—political, legal, and commercial. The agora, then, contained places of deliberative and legislative assembly, law courts, markets, shops, as well as stone "billboards" and public monuments. Later, when Athens moved from a narrowly representative government to a radical democracy it needed a dedicated place of assembly (the *Pnyx*) that might accommodate as many citizens as would likely show up to be heard, to listen, and to vote regarding everything from taxes to declarations of war. Finally, there was the theater—at once a sacred precinct and a place where both the brightest and the darkest layers of the human were revealed and confronted. This was a place of culture and of healing where music, dance, and poetry found a unique fusion in Classical tragedy and comedy.

Following the ill-fated Persian invasions of 490 and 480 B.C.E., however, as the 5th century progressed, Athens soon grew beyond itself, indeed beyond the size and shape of any traditional polis or city-state, into an imperial power. Redefining and asserting herself as a sea power, or rather as *the* sea power in the region, and seizing a unique post-war opportunity for moral, military, and economic leadership in the Aegean, Athens followed in the footsteps, or more accurately the wake, of Knossos and Mycenae in establishing a maritime imperium, or thalassocracy. For a traditionally agricultural people, this was a bold, if not blind, leap in which one foot led while the other trailed. It was one thing, after all, to grow olives and grapes and quite another to grow an empire. For whatever reason—some combination, no doubt, of personal brilliance and irresistible message—the people of Athens followed where Perikles led them: to empire, to war, and (posthumously) to ruin. In the half-century between the second Persian invasion and the outbreak of the Peloponnesian War (480–431 B.C.E.), Athens assembled an empire of roughly 300 "member" or subject states from whom she exacted annual tribute in addition to the expectation of military service. At the height of her power in 430 B.C.E., Athens had more military might (heavy and light infantry, triremes or battleships, and cavalry), more wealth (liquid assets and reserve funds), and way more attitude than any of those who resented and resisted her. In fact, Athens had more strategic resources than nearly all of her rivals combined. Perikles was for a time indeed the "first citizen" of Athens, and Athens was the "first city" of Greece.

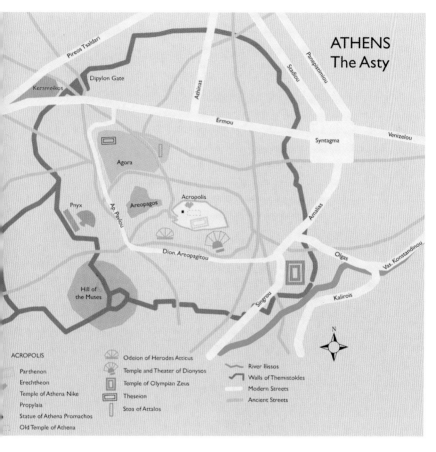

ATHENS
The Asty

ACROPOLIS

Parthenon
Erechtheon
Temple of Athena Nike
Propylaia
Statue of Athena Promachos
Old Temple of Athena

Odeion of Herodes Atticus
Temple and Theater of Dionysos
Temple of Olympian Zeus
Theseion
Stoa of Attalos

River Ilissos
Walls of Themistokles
Modern Streets
Ancient Streets

The point of this brief excursus is this: like (Egyptian) Thebes, Persepolis, Rome, and London, Athens was once an imperial city. This is why, even in ruins, she dazzles the eye and ignites the imagination, as Sparta, Corinth, Thebes, and other Greek powers of her day do not. Today, as then, they offer nothing resembling the spectacle of Athens. Her visual splendor was, it seems, an integral component of Perikles' imperial design for his city; so, in the mid 5th century, Perikles made the case that Athens should look the imperial power that she was. While her impregnable walls already instilled fear, he wanted her towering beauty to inspire the love of her citizens and the admiration of everyone else who would ever set eyes on her. His imperial building program, focused on the Acropolis and agora, began with the Parthenon, one of a few candidates on anyone's list for the most perfect flower of human architectural genius and skill.

PERIKLES TO THE PEOPLE OF ATHENS, 431 B.C.E.

"Our constitution is called a democracy because power is in the hands not of a minority but of the whole people. When it is a question of settling private disputes, everyone is equal before the law; when it is a question of putting one person before another in positions of public responsibility, what counts is not membership of a particular class, but the actual ability which the man possesses. No one, so long as he has it in him to be of service to the state, is kept in political obscurity because of poverty...

When our work is over, we are in a position to enjoy all kinds of recreation for our spirits. There are various kinds of contests and sacrifices regularly throughout the year; in our own homes we find a beauty and a good taste which delight us every day and which drive away our cares. Then the greatness of our city brings it about that all the good things from all over the world flow in to us, so that to us it seems just as natural to enjoy foreign goods as our own local products....

Our city is open to the world, and we have no periodical deportations in order to prevent people observing or finding out secrets which might be of military advantage to the enemy. This is because we rely, not on secret weapons, but on our own real courage and loyalty....

Our love of what is beautiful does not lead to extravagance; our love of the things of the mind does not make us soft. We regard wealth as something to be properly used, rather than as something to boast about. As for poverty, no one need be ashamed to admit it: the real shame is in not taking practical measures to escape from it. Here each individual is interested not only in his own affairs but in the affairs of the state as well: even those who are mostly occupied with their own business are extremely well-informed on general politics—this is a peculiarity of ours: we do not say that a man who takes no interest in politics is a man who minds his own business; we say that he has no business here at all....

Taking everything together then, I declare that our city is an education to Greece... Mighty indeed are the marks and monuments of our empire which we have left. Future ages will wonder at us, as the present age wonders at us now. We do not need the praises of a Homer, or of anyone else whose words may delight us for the moment, but whose estimation of facts will fall short of what is really true. For our adventurous spirit has forced an entry into every sea and into every land; and everywhere we have left behind us everlasting memorials of good done to our friends or suffering inflicted on our enemies.... fix your eyes every day on the greatness of Athens as she really is, and... fall in love with her..."

—*Thucydides*, Peloponnesian War, *II.37–43, tr. Rex Warner*

A few concluding words now about the ordinary people of Athens, whose everyday, lusterless lives were lived out hundreds of feet below the sublime splendor of the Acropolis. The total population of Athens, in the first third of the 5th century, may have reached 350,000, of which fewer than 15% were citizens. Until late in the Peloponnesian War when citizenship was awarded more liberally, blood and gender alone determined a citizen's claim to a vote in the assembly and all that went with it. Only males whose father and maternal grandfather were Athenian citizens would have their names inscribed in the civic rolls. The remaining 85% of the population—women, slaves, immigrants, and resident aliens—were welcome and in many cases integral to the state. They were participants, not bystanders, in the life of Athens—but they were not citizens, which meant, for example, that they could not vote or hold public office and that their legal rights were severely abridged. Athenian democracy, in short, gave unprecedented power (*kratos*) to the people (*demos*), true enough, but defined "people" to include only a sliver of the population. In doing so, however, Athens was more liberal than any state of its day. Only in the 20th century did its civil rights begin to compare unfavorably with the majority of modern nation states. Most urban Athenians, citizens or not, lived modest lives in architecturally humble households. The typical Athenian city-house faced inward on a central court, where you would be likely to find an altar to Zeus Herkeios, Zeus guardian of the household. Marble was reserved for temples and public monuments. Private homes, on the other hand, were commonly constructed of sun-dried mud brick and wood beams, with mostly dirt floors, and a terra-cotta tile roof on wooden rafters. There were no private palaces, not even starter-mansions equivalent to those that litter today's American suburbs. The Athenians, it seems, had not yet learned to equate ego or self-worth with domestic cubic feet. Even in their most stunning public monuments, crafted in gleaming, translucent marble, they paid greater attention to proportion and harmony of form than to sheer magnitude. Size matters to empires, to be sure, when it comes to money, armies, and territory; but it matters little to the mind or the soul. And, from all that we can see at our remove, imperial Athens honored the mind and recognized the soul's needs, which may be why both still find an elusive haven in her ruins.

DAY ONE

Why save the best for last? Even if we were to recommend that you wait several days before exploring the Acropolis, you would surely ignore our advice. Once in Athens, the lure of the Acropolis is irresistible. Look up and it is there, silent as a Siren. Without having yourself bound, as Odysseus did, to something immoveable, you will inevitably begin to move towards the Acropolis, which in this case is surely the right thing to do. Before setting out, however, we have a word of caution. The steps, ramps, and rocky surfaces of the Acropolis are indescribably slick, worn smooth by millions of pedestrians as well as by the elements, so wear shoes that make sense. Traction (grip) and ankle support are crucial. Sneakers or boots make sense; smooth-soled sandals or heels do not. Also keep in mind that nearly all of today's sites are virtual frying pans; so, in summer, hat, sunscreen, and water will separate survivors from suicides. With a touch of foresight and perhaps a slight sacrifice of fashion to practicality, you will be ready to launch into what is almost bound to be one of the most memorable days of your life. To make it even more memorable, you may wish to bring along a copy of your favorite Greek drama, in order to read a bit of it to yourself as you sit or stand in the place where it was first performed.

Since we recommend that you begin your day with a brief visit to the Olympeion, the Temple of Olympian Zeus, we will direct you from Syntagma, an orientation point already familiar to you from your first arrival in central Athens. With your back to the green plateia, or square (west), and facing (east) the Tomb of the Unknown Soldier, turn right (south) and walk along Amalias. If you have not yet stopped in to the EOT (Greek National Tourism) office, you will soon find it on your right at 26a Amalias (30-210-331-0392, open Mon–Fri 09:00–19:00, Sat–Sun 10:00–16:00)—the one-stop source for free maps, booklets, and answers to your touristic questions.

Otherwise, keep walking another few minutes until you see, on your left, the enclosure containing the Olympeion, or the Temple of Olympian Zeus and, as an added Roman bonus, Hadrian's Gate, also known as the Arch of Hadrian.

PRINCIPAL SITES

The Temple of Olympian Zeus

Even in its mostly tumble-down condition, the Olympeion—the largest temple in mainland Greece—can almost take your breath away. Its sheer scale, nearly a kilometer in circumference, is startling. No wonder it took 700 years to complete. There was, admittedly, a large span—mostly defined by inactivity—between the first stage of its construction during the tyranny of Peisistratos the Younger in the late 6th century B.C.E. and its final completion by Hadrian in 124/125 C.E. Inspired by the gigantic temples of Ephesos and Samos that easily dwarfed their architectural cousins on the mainland, Peisistratos resolved to double the size of an earlier temple that stood on this site. His original plan in the Doric order was later abandoned in the late 2nd century B.C.E., when a Roman architect, Decimus Cossutius, reconceived and retrofitted the 104 Olympeion with Corinthian columns in Pentelic marble. The Doric order, after all, had reached its perfection of form and embodiment in the Parthenon, and achieved perfection often discourages repetition. The Ionic order—developed in Asia Minor and on the islands of the Aegean, where temples often dwarfed in size those of the mainland—was better suited to the mammoth scale of the Olympeion; and the Corinthian order is identical to the Ionic apart from the introduction of the ornate acanthus capital. In this order, the Olympeion is without rival and stands, or rather lies fallen, as its most extravagant expression. When completed, it housed a massive gold and ivory cult image of Zeus, noteworthy more for its size than its form, if we are to take the 2nd century C.E. itinerant Pausanias at his word.

The precinct of the Olympeion—one of the most ancient in Athens—contains a number of other monuments and remains. Most of those still visible date from the Roman Period. Near the entrance to the site, however, you may notice a surviving section of the 5th-century fortification walls raised at the urging of Themistokles, walls brought down by Spartan occupiers to the sound of joyous piping at the end of the Peloponnesian War near the end of the 5th century B.C.E.

The most obvious Roman monument here is, of course, the Gate or Arch of Hadrian, who treasured Athens and her culture as one of his most prized imperial possessions. With an acknowledging bow or nod to the past he had carved on the west side of his gate the words: "This is Athens, ancient city of Theseus" while on the east side he updated the record with the words: "This is the city of Hadrian, not Theseus." The exact meaning of his words remains a matter of debate. He may have been dividing the city into east and west, one half for him and one half for Theseus. Or he may have suggested that Theseus was bygone, like the setting sun, while his reign, like the rising sun in the east, brings a new day to Athens. The latter reading seems the more persuasive. Emperors, after all, prefer not to go fifty-fifty with others, even if they're dead.

The Olympeion is included in a package ticket for the Archaeological Sites of Athens. Assuming this is your first visit to one of these sites, purchase your inclusive ticket here and use it for the Theater of Dionysos, the Acropolis and its site museum, the Ancient Agora, Kerameikos, and the Roman Agora.

....

Entrance from Leoforos (Avenue) Olgas, off of Leoforos Amalias (30-210-922-6330). Open daily 08:00–19:30. €€

....

When you leave the Olympeion precinct, cross over Amalias to the west side and turn left. Almost immediately you will see the pedestrian walkway Dionysiou Areopagitou veering off on your right. Follow this walkway a few minutes until you see off to your left the New Acropolis Museum and on your right the entrance to the Theater of Dionysos.

The New Acropolis Museum

This latest addition to the cultural largesse of Athens has yet to open its doors. It was conceived and designed first and primarily as a fitting receptacle for the notorious Elgin Marbles—"notorious" because they represent a stunning instance of national grand larceny—in anticipation of their *nostos* (return) to Greece from their current installation in the British Museum. The Elgin Marbles—more appropriately referred to as the

Parthenon Marbles—comprise a sizeable collection of stunning relief sculptures stripped from the pediments, metope, and frieze of the Parthenon in 1806 by Thomas Bruce, 7th Earl of Elgin, who made an arguably shady deal for their removal with the Ottoman sultan of the day. Their looting prompted outrage in Britain as well as Greece at the time and has remained an open wound for two centuries. Recently (May 2005), the British High Court ruled that the British Museum Act, which enforces the museum's claim to its holdings for posterity—British posterity that is—prohibits the return of the stolen marbles out of any "moral obligation"; so it seems that the New Acropolis Museum, if and when it opens, will be devoid of its *raison d'etre*, its core collection. That said, construction is nearing completion, and plans are underway for exhibits (most probably drawing heavily from those housed in the old Acropolis site museum) that should provide a grand introduction to anyone's exploration of the Acropolis and its monuments.

We have been given estimates for the likely opening date for the New Acropolis Museum, but it is safest to wait and see. Consequently no details regarding opening days and hours or entrance cost, much less the museum's collection, can be offered now. The museum building is located roughly across from the entrance to the Theater of Dionysos; so give its doors a knock and hope for a response; and in the meantime, if you happen to know a member of the British Parliament, bend his or her ear on behalf of the marbles. Like Odysseus, they long to come home.

The Sanctuary and Theater of Dionysos

As you turn in towards the Theater of Dionysos off of the pedestrian walkway, you will begin your exploration of the South Slope of the Acropolis, which in antiquity was virtually strewn with shrines and monuments. A new system of walkways, most following ancient lanes, leads from this spot to the grand entry-way, the Propylaia, of the Acropolis; and every notable site along the way is well marked and explained on panels in Greek and English, providing a guided tour taken at your own pace. The first major stop along this way is the sacred precinct of Dionysos, the birthplace of western drama.

Unlike later Roman theaters, frequently located next to the public toilets and brothels, the "theater district" of Athens, the precinct of Dionysos, was holy ground, marked off and surrounded by a wall, a fragment of which survives and is indicated on your left as your proceed. Within the *temenos* (sacred precinct), and behind or south of the orchestra and rectangular scene building, stood the (no longer visible) temple of Dionysos, where sacrifice was offered to the god prior to the performances with which he was celebrated here during his annual festival known as the Greater Dionysia. Preliminary to the performances, a sculpted figure of Dionysos, a cult image, was carried in procession into the choral area and placed there, probably on the *thumele*, a low altar or platform in the very center of the orchestra, so that the plays might be performed to him, for him. This was his house, the place of his revels and his revelation. Euripides reminded his audience of this in his great masterpiece *The Bakkhai*. When, at the opening of the play, Dionysos returns to Thebes, Euripides made it manifestly clear that he had in mind here the triumphant re-entry of Dionysos to his theater, the place of his birth as god of drama.

Next to the god, his priests enjoyed the best seats in the house, front and center in the amphitheater, which held well beyond ten thousand spectators. This was true public drama, civic drama, where the people of Athens, as well as visitors from across the Greek world, witnessed the enactment of their foundational myths, the disclosure of their collective consciousness, the pricking of their consciences, and the ridiculing of their fools and follies. This is where they laughed and wept together in comedy and tragedy and came together for personal and communal *katharsis* (purification or healing) after the year's battles and bloodshed; for the century in which Greek drama was developed—twenty-five centuries ago—was for Athens a century of war. It was at the *Pnyx*, in general assembly that the Athenians deliberated whether and when and how to wage their wars; but it was in the theater, more than anywhere else, that they discovered how and where best to recover from the traumas suffered and inflicted in those wars. When Athenian citizens went to the theater to see the tragedies, they anticipated unspeakable violence and suffering, as they did when they went to war. Neither was a matter of simple entertainment or diversion. The same men massed for both events. In the theater, playwrights, actors, and audience were soldiers, always either on their way to war or on their way home. Apart from the battlefield, the theater was where they gathered in force and found strength in each other. It may be argued, and sometimes is, that Athenian drama was developed as a form of civic group therapy, a ritual of catharsis and healing for a society saturated with violence, atrocity, and grief. What the ancients understood is that the process of healing from trauma lies fundamentally in communalizing it. In saying this, however, we must never confuse the "communalization" of violence with the publicizing, much less televising, of it. Communalization, in a theater or anywhere else, requires a live audience and live actors, all able to feel each other's presence and see each other's pain. This means mutual recognition and commitment, not the anonymity offered by the media. The same is true of the ancient theater, a sacred precinct, where fragile mortals are buffeted, broken, healed, and enlightened before our eyes. The ancient theater, more than any civic temple, was the house of truth. The audience, gathered in the theater of Dionysos, was no random collection of drama enthusiasts; rather, it was the citizenry of Athens, come together for one of the most sacred and consequential civic rituals of the liturgical year.

To acknowledge that ancient Athenian drama was ritual drama—civic and sacred—is not to deny that it was also art and entertainment. Anyone who has witnessed a Greek Easter or a traditional sacred dance drama in India or, for that matter, a Gospel revival in New Orleans will not need further persuading that sacred ritual can at the same time, for the same participants, be both ritual and romp, holy and entertaining, profound and playful. The ancient audience in the theater of Dionysos knew that they were on sacred ground and were there to be "enthused" or "high"—shot up with divinity—but they surely did not see themselves as going "to church" as we commonly understand and utter those words.

What you see before you today on this site is not, however, the theater as Aeschylos, Sophokles, Euripides, and Aristophanes—master playwrights of the 5th century—knew it. The theater in which their plays were performed was far more basic or, quite literally, down to earth. There may have been limited seating on wooden benches or bleachers, with stone seats for a handful of priests and judges, while the remaining thousands made themselves comfortable as best they might on the bare earth. The orchestra, a great circle in most extent Hellenistic and Roman theaters, may have been originally a rectangle. The scene building was more or less makeshift, made of wood with painted backdrops. The fact is that the architecture of the original Classical theater here at Athens is a matter of conjecture and dispute, in which no stone is left unthrown. Reconstructive drawings displayed at the site depict the likely evolution of this theater from its humble 5th-century origins to its more grand and elegant forms in the 4th and ensuing centuries. Today, an extensive restoration is underway to embody in stone some of what is sketched on these panels.

It seems fitting to include here one of the ecstatic choruses composed by Euripides to be sung in honor of Dionysos, also called Bromios, by his god-driven devotees, the *bakkhai*.

Entrance from the west, off of the new pedestrian walkway Dionysiou Areopagitou (30-210-322-4625). Open daily 08:00–19:30. €€ The Theater of Dionysos is included in the 4-day package ticket for the principal Archaeological Sites of Athens and is the entrance to the sites of the South Slope of the Acropolis.

God of merriment and festal crowns?
He lightens our feet and our hearts
To honor him in the dance.
The music of our laughter
And the wild piping of flutes
Are a portion of his largesse.
Sweetest of all... the oblivion he brings,
The respite from all care,
When the bright blood of the grape
Bursts over the table of the gods,
And ivy-crowned revelers
Lift and tip the brimming bowl
To drink warm, sweet sleep...

Take me, Bromios, lord of the dance.
Bromios, god of bliss,
Take me there,
Where the Graces dwell,
Where desire leaves its banks,
Where the very air
Sanctions our devotions and our dance
To you.

—*Euripides*, Bakkhai, *tr. Robert Emmet Meagher*

The Odeion of Herodes Atticus

The first question you might have at this point is "who was this Herodes Atticus"? Well, in a few words, Herodes was the fortunate son of a very lucky man. Herodes' Roman name was a mouthful: Lucius Vibullius Hipparchus Tiberius Claudius Atticus Herodes Marathonios. Born in Marathon in 101 C.E., he inherited the fortune that his father literally found in the ruins of a house, and then, under the emperor Hadrian, Herodes held the office of *archon* (ruler) in Athens. Later, he was appointed as tutor of Marcus Aurelius and eventually retired to Athens. Like his father he was known for his civic generosity in dispensing vast sums of money for public works throughout the Greek mainland, one of which was this odeion, raised in memory of his wife Regilla, who died in 160 C.E.

The Odeion of Herodes Atticus is not simply a restored relic of the past. It endures as a vital, working theater in the present, hosting a range of national and international dance, music, and theater performances, especially during the summer months. In July and August it is one of the principal venues for the annual Athens Festival, for information and tickets, go to www.hellenicfestival.gr or contact the festival office at 30-210-327-2000.

Located west of the Theater of Dionysos on the south slope of the Acropolis. As you follow the ancient peripatos (walkway) you will pass the remains of the Stoa of Eumenes, dating from the 2nd century B.C.E. The odeion is best viewed from above and is rarely open to the public apart from ticketed performances. After stopping to study the structure of the odeion or to watch a rehearsal in progress, proceed on past the odeion to the Acropolis entrance, further ahead and up to your right.

The Monuments of the Athenian Acropolis

In antiquity, the Athenian Acropolis, perched atop a dramatic crag five hundred feet above the city below, was at once the most strategic and the most sacred site in Athens. Today, it is the most visited. As a Mycenaean fortress, it somehow survived the systemic collapse of the Mycenaean world. It held firm against the fabled siege of the Amazons and the not-so-fabulous onslaught of the Dorians. Early in the 5th century B.C.E., however, it was razed by the Persians, and later in the same century fell to the Spartans. In the years between those two catastrophes, however, it shone as no Greek city had or ever again would. Since then, across twenty-four centuries, the Acropolis has endured a series of incursions, humiliations, and atrocities. The Byzantines, Franks, and Venetians refitted the Parthenon to their own purposes as a Christian church; later, the Turks, in turn, converted it to a mosque. While a Muslim house of prayer it doubled as a munitions arsenal, and blew apart in 1687, struck by an enemy mortar. More recently, in the name of benign preservation, learned foreigners with shovels and sketchbooks came to admire and acquire its

greatest treasures. Eventually, men with guns and black boots made of it a symbol of arrogant conquest. Thus, during the Nazi occupation in World War II the flag of the Third Reich waved infamously from the Acropolis, until an enraged Athenian, a mere boy, climbed up and tore it down in defiance. Today, the greatest threat to the Acropolis and its monuments is from the eroding pollution rising from the city below, and its only invaders are the millions of world tourists who arrive here on cultural pilgrimage to see if what they have been told can possibly be true.

"The whole acropolis is sheer, with strong walls," wrote Pausanias. "It has one way in; it offers no other." The same remains true today. Entrance is from the west, accessed either from the Plaka and agora or from the Pezothromos Dionysiou Areopagitou, the new pedestrian walkway parallel to the south slope of the Acropolis. The climb on foot to the Acropolis is steep and precarious, as the stone steps are worn so smooth as to be a genuine hazard. If you are handicapped or at special risk for a fall, you may wish to take advantage of a wheelchair-accessible lift operated by the 1st Ephorate of Antiquities. Once on the Acropolis, a network of specially surfaced paths and ramps makes it possible to explore the site in a wheelchair. Anyone wishing to use this lift would do best to make a reservation in advance (30-210-3214172 or protocol@aepka.culture.gr) and plan to visit during off-peak hours (08:00–10:00 and 13:00–17:00).

After an arduous ascent along the ancient processional way, broadened in the Archaic Period to accommodate the great Panathenaic Festival of Athena, you pass through the Beule Gate (added by the Romans for defensive purposes in the late 3rd century C.E.) and mount a zig-zagging ramp to the Propylaia, the grand gateway to the Acropolis and prelude to the Parthenon. Though a magnificent achievement, the Propylaia fell short of its original design by the architect Mnesikles. It is likely that the funds necessary for its full execution were diverted so as to complete the Parthenon and to help fund the conflict with Sparta and her allies in the Peloponnesian War. Presently, in a time of peace, it is being partially restored to its 5th-century grandeur. The north wing once contained the Pinakotheke (picture gallery), whose paintings, many by the famed Polygnotos, are long lost. The south wing stood incomplete in the 5th century and still does. Plutarch tells how Athena herself intervened in the construction of the Propyleia. It seems that a master craftsman at work on the Propylaia slipped and fell one day from a great height and lay in agony. The attending physicians determined his condition to be hopeless. That night, however, Athena appeared to Perikles in a dream and prescribed treatment for the injured workman. Soon the fellow was back at work, and Perikles erected on the Acropolis a new altar in honor of Athena Hygeia, Athena Goddess of Health.

But there was one measure above all which at once gave the greatest pleasure to the Athenians, adorned their city and created amazement among the rest of mankind, and which is today the sole testimony that the tales of the ancient power and glory of Greece are no mere fables. By this I mean his construction of temples and public buildings; and yet it was this, more than any other action of his, which his enemies slandered and misrepresented. They cried out in the Assembly that Athens had lost her good name and disgraced herself by transferring from Delos into her own keeping the funds that had been contributed by the rest of Greece, and that now the most plausible excuse for this action, namely, that the money had been removed for fear of the barbarians and was being guarded in a safe place, had been demolished by Pericles himself, "The Greeks must be outraged," they cried. "They must consider this an act of barefaced tyranny, when they see that with their own contributions, extorted from them by force for the war against the Persians, we are gilding and beautifying our city, as if it were some vain woman decking herself out with costly stones and statues and temples worth millions of money."

Pericles' answer, to the people was that the Athenians were not obliged to give the allies any account of how their money was spent, provided that they carried on the war for them and kept the Persians away. "They do not give us a single horse, nor a soldier, nor a ship. All they supply is money," he told the Athenians, "and this belongs not to the people who give it, but to those who receive it, so long as they provide the services they are paid for. It is no more than fair that after Athens has been equipped with all she needs to carry on the war, she should apply the surplus to public works, which, once completed, will bring her glory for all time, and while they are being built willconvert that surplus to immediate use. In this way all kinds of enterprises and demands will be created which will provide inspiration for every art, find employment for every hand, and transform the whole people into wage-earners, so that the city will decorate and maintain herself at the same time from her own resources." ...

So heboldly laid before the people proposals for immense public works andplans for buildings, which would involve many different arts and industries and require long periods to complete, his object being that those who stayed at home, no less than those serving in the fleet or the army or on garrison duty, should be enabled to enjoy a share of the national wealth.

—*Plutarch*, Perikles, *12.1–5, tr. Ian Scott-Kilvert*

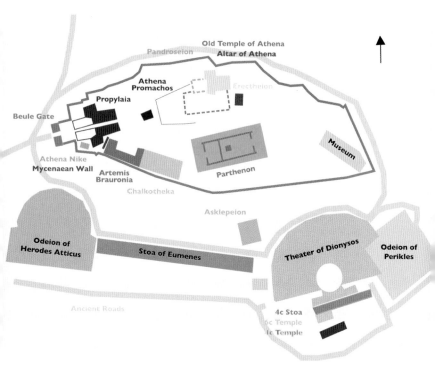

When Athens was embroiled in the longest and deadliest war in Greek history, the attenuated southwest wing of the Propylaia, to your right, became the site of a long-delayed Temple of Athena Nike, Athena Goddess of Victory. Already, in the 6th century, this site had been dedicated to the cult of Athena Nike—appropriately so, since the rocky spur on which the temple of victorious Athena stands had been, from Mycenaen times, the site of a bastion threatening the exposed right flank of any army making an assault on the Acropolis. In fact, in 1686 the Turkish army employed this very bastion as an artillery position, after dismantling the temple and using its stones to construct a gun emplacement further down the hill. The cult statue housed in the cella of the 5th-century temple was most likely a marble reproduction of a much earlier wooden image of the goddess, who held in her right hand a pomegranate and in her left a helmet, symbols of peace and war, fertility and ferocity.

It was on this same parapet that King Aegeus of Athens

was said to have stood and watched in desperation for the return of his son Theseus from Crete. What Aegeus finally saw—black sails mistakenly signaling his son's death—drove him over the edge of the Acropolis to his death on the rocks below. On a clear day the views from here of Cape Sounion, the island of Aegina, the bays of Phaleron and Salamis, and the peaks of the northern Peloponnese are quite splendid. Regrettably, days of such pristine clarity are rare today.

Passing through the Propylaia, you emerge within the walls of the Acropolis and at once your eyes fall inevitably on the north and west facades of the Parthenon. Sigmund Freud, seeing for the first time this same sight, said what comes to most everyone's lips: "So all this really *does* exist, just as we learnt in school!" A 5th-century visitor, however, would have seen from this perspective only the pediment of the Parthenon. Immediately ahead to the right, the southwest, was the sacred precinct of Artemis Brauronia, one of many cults imported and cloned from the Attic countryside, in this case from the nearby coastal sanctuary of Artemis, sister of

Athena, at Brauron or Vravrona, to be visited later this week.

Beyond the once spacious precinct of Artemis stands the Parthenon, the *naos* or temple of the virgin (*parthenos*) warrior-goddess Athena. Libraries of books have been written on this single structure, which some regard as the most perfect building

Pedimental sculpture, possibly Dionysos or Herakles, northeast corner of the Parthenon.

in the world, rivaled only by the Taj Mahal. At the very least it represents the flawless culmination of the Doric order, the oldest and simplest of the monumental architectural styles developed by the Greeks and emulated ever since. As much a matter of imperial self-assertion as of reverence for the goddess, the Parthenon is a supreme expression of piety and of power. In Periklean Athens, the two were not easily plied apart.

Unlike the truly huge temples of Egypt, Mesopotamia, and Asia Minor, the Parthenon—a mere miniature beside these—was thoughtfully scaled to human proportions by its master architect Iktinos, assisted by Kallikrates. Here the maxim that "man is the measure of all things" finds detailed embodiment and confirmation. Although the Parthenon is by design pervasively proportional, it is not relentlessly so. After all, precision can become tedious, and the unexpected can be more satisfying than anything else. Numerous intentional deviations from its otherwise mathematical regularity contribute to, rather than detract from, the Parthenon's compelling character.

What appear to be straight lines—horizontal and

vertical—are in fact often curved, forming overall a skewed trapezoid, and not a perfect rectangle. In part, the extra-ordinarily labor-intensive irregularities running through the Parthenon's structure may have been put there to counter the ways in which our own eyes deceive us. In other areas, it appears that the architects sought to amplify ordinary optical distortion so as to make this temple appear more vast than it actually was. What is manifestly clear throughout is that Iktinos and company kept the peculiarities of human vision in the forefront of their considerations as they designed this uniquely satisfying and surprising structure. Preoccupied with the elusive relationship between appearance and reality, and thus caught up in the struggle to reconcile what the mind knows with what the eye sees, the ancient Greeks must have found in this temple a monument not only to watchful Athena but to restless humanity.

What it is easy to overlook today, because it is no longer there, is the cella of the virgin, the inner sanctuary of the Parthenon, and the colossal cult figure of Athena which all but scraped the cella's walls and roof. Entering the Parthenon from the east, the ancient adorant would have passed through the six-columned porch into the inner chamber and confronted the massive chryselephantine (gold and ivory), statue of the goddess, created by Pheidias. The essential features of this colossus are known from Pausanias's description and from disappointing but surviving copies, one of which may be found in the National Archaeological Museum. This was, in gold and ivory, the same Athena sketched and celebrated by Aeschylus in his *Eumenides*. The fate of the original, when and how it disappeared, is unknown.

Three other famous statues of Athena once graced the Acropolis. The colossal bronze figure of Athena Promachos—Athena Warrior-champion of Athens—nearly thirty feet in height, created by Pheidias in the mid-5th century, stood approximately 40 yards directly in front of the Propylaia, on the western edge of the precinct once occupied by the palace of the Mycenaean kings, as well as a later archaic temple. The tip of Athena Promachos's spear and the crest of her helmet were said to glisten visibly as far as the coastal waters off of Sounion, welcoming home the Athenian fleet as they approached their base at Zea. Most sacred of all, however, was the archaic statue of Athena Polias, Athena Guardian of the City, believed to have fallen from the sky. Carved of olive wood, this holiest of Athenian icons was housed in the Erechtheion and displayed in the great city festival of Athena. Finally there was the modest and charming bronze figure of Athena Lemnia, commissioned from Pheidias and dedicated by the Athenian colonists of Lemnos. This Athena was both unarmed and disarming. Several ancient writers—Pausanias, Lucian, and Pliny—preferred this work to all of Pheidias's other more grand creations.

The Parthenon was, of course, adorned with magnificent relief sculptures, whose design and execution were at the very least supervised by Pheidias, while he focused his own energies on the statue of Athena, installed in her cella in 438 B.C.E. A year later the Parthenon was structurally complete and remained intact for nearly two thousand years. Work on the Parthenon's architectural sculptures—its pediments, metopes, and frieze—went on for six more years. These sculptures, ravaged by time and war, and mostly removed elsewhere by opportunists and conservators, depicted such mythical and historical moments as the birth of Athena and her contest with Poseidon; the wars of gods against giants, Lapiths against Centaurs, Athenians against Amazons, and Greeks against Trojans; and the liturgical splendor and excitement of the festive procession reenacted every four years in the Panathenaia, the Athenian "high holy days" in honor of Athena. As stated above, since its creation in the 5th century, the Parthenon has served as a Christian church, a Muslim mosque, a Turkish munitions dump, a Nazi command post, and is now, once again, a monument to the splendor that was Athens.

The last of the four more or less extant ancient structures on the Acropolis is the Erechtheion, whose remnants occupy the north side of the Acropolis. More ornate and complex than the Parthenon, the Erechtheion represents the highest refinement of the Ionic order in the 5th century. The Erechtheion overlays in part the site of the earliest Mycenaean

Porch of the Caryatids, Erechtheion

palace and of a later Doric temple, whose foundational outline is still quite clearly visible in the area adjacent to the Erechtheion on its north side. The structural history of this temple is a matter of some dispute. Clearly one of the temples occupying this site across time was destroyed by the Persians in 480 B.C.E and possibly restored. Beyond any dispute is the fact that this site is steeped in legend and history. The contest of Athena and Poseidon over possession of the Acropolis, Athena's gift of the first olive tree, the imprint of Poseidon's trident, the shared cult of Athena and Poseidon, the birth of serpentine Erecthonios, the reign of Erectheus, the tomb of Kekrops, and the miraculous re-sprouting of Athena's tree after the second Persian invasion are all identified with this site. This was, in short, ground hallowed by some of Athens's oldest and most sacred mysteries and cults.

The Erechtheion was begun around 421 B.C.E. and completed around 406 as part of the ambitious architectural program initiated by Perikles. Eccentric in its design and use, it accommodated the uneven contours of its site as well as the cults of diverse deities. The main body of the Erechtheion comprised multiple cult chambers with altars to Athena, Poseidon-Erectheus, Zeus, Hephaistos, and the hero Boutes. The Erechtheion housed, in addition, the statue of Athena Polias, before which burned a lamp filled with oil crushed from the olives of Athena's own tree, planted in the Pandroseion, the adjacent sacred precinct of Pandrosos, daughter of Kekrops. This was the tree said to have sprouted back to life after having been burned by the Persians, an omen of the city's own imminent rise from the ashes and ruins left smoldering by the invaders. Further to the south lay the Kekropion, the precinct and presumed burial site of Kekrops, founding king of Athens. The southern Porch of the Caryatids is today the most familiar face of the Erechtheion, presenting cast models of the original six pillar-maidens, whose surviving remnants are preserved in the old Acropolis museum, soon to be eclipsed by the new Acropolis museum.

The old Acropolis Museum lies inconspicuously below the surface level of the rock in the southeast corner of the Acropolis. It was founded in 1878 to hold all moveable objects found on the Acropolis; and, with the exception of certain ceramics and bronzes transferred to the National Archaeological Museum, it currently does just that. The general arrangement of its contents is chronological, particularly helpful in visualizing the development of Greek sculpture from the archaic to the Classical Period. Beyond the vestibule, the first three galleries contain pedimental sculptures from 6th-century buildings destroyed by the Persians. The fourth gallery offers an interesting group of *korai*, figures of young women, 6th-century votive offerings to Athena, also destroyed by the Persians in 480 and interred by the Athenians, only to be uncovered in the Acropolis excavations of 1882–86. These, as well as the pedimental sculptures, bear traces of the vivid colors with which they were originally painted. The fifth gallery offers pedimental scenes from the battle of the gods and the giants. These sculptures once graced the early 6th-century temple of Athena, whose foundations remain quite visible beside the Erechtheion. The sculptures of gallery six illustrate what is called the "Severe" style of Greek sculpture, transitional from the archaic to the Classical styles. In the seventh gallery are found a collection of badly damaged pedimental sculptures from the Parthenon. In gallery eight, quite effectively presented, are the only detached portions of the Parthenon frieze not removed by Lord Elgin, who understandably overlooked them, as they had been blasted away and buried before he began his removals. This gallery, in addition, contains several architectural sculptures from the temple of Athena Nike and the Erechtheion. In the ninth and last gallery are to be found the surviving caryatids from the southern porch of the Erechtheion, together with an assortment of other sculptural finds from later periods.

Before descending from the Acropolis to the agora, be sure to walk the circuit of the Acropolis and take advantage of the views of the city and its surrounds, ancient and contemporary below, as well as the vistas (on a clear day) to the Gulf of Corinth, Salamis, Aegina, and the mountains of the Argolid. From the south parapet, the vantage on the Theater of Dionysos is particularly striking.

Entrance from the west, off of the new pedestrian walkway Dionysiou Areopagitou (30-210-141-7232). Open daily 08:00–19:30. €€ The Acropolis and its site museum are included in package ticket for the Archaeological Sites of Athens. Free admission on Sundays November through March.

Athene

If it please you, men of Attica, hear my decree
now, on this first case of bloodletting I have judged.
For Aegeus' population, this forevermore
shall be the ground where justices deliberate.
Here is the Hill of Ares, here the Amazons
encamped and built their shelters when they came in arms
for spite of Theseus, here they piled their rival towers
to rise, new city, and dare his city long ago,
and slew their beasts for Ares. So this rock is named
from then the Hill of Ares. Here the reverence
of citizens, their fear and kindred do-no-wrong
shall hold by day and in the blessing of night alike
all while the people do not muddy their own laws
with foul infusions. But if bright water you stain
with mud, you nevermore will find it fit to drink.
No anarchy, no rule of a single master.
ThusI advise my citizens to govern and to grace,
and not to cast fear utterly from your city....
I establish this tribunal. It shall be untouched
by money-making, grave but quick to wrath, watchful
to protect those who sleep, a sentry on the land.
These words I have unreeled are for my citizens,
advice into the future. All must stand upright
now, take each man his ballot in his hand, think on
his oath, and make his judgment. For my word is said.

—*Aeschylus*, Eumenides, *685–710, tr. Richmond Lattimore*

The Areopagos

As you exit the Acropolis through the Propylaia, you will
see before you to the northwest (between the Acropolis
and the Pnyx) a bald rocky mound, polished and glistening in
the sun. This is the Hill of Ares—at once a revered ancient
site and a notorious contemporary hazard. It cries out to be
climbed—or so it would seem, given the innumerable tourists
who scramble up its slopes—but you should do so carefully
and at your peril. A stairway will take you part of the way.
After that, attend to your footing, as the Areopagos could not
be more slippery if it were molded of ice.

In antiquity, the Areopagos gave its name to the oldest and most powerful deliberative council in pre-democratic Athens. Under the aristocratic regimes of the Archaic Period, this was the seat of power, where the few and the best, or at least the wealthiest, made the city's rules and enforced them. The power and privileges of the Areopagos Council became a prime target of reform as power passed in stages to the people in the 5th century. By 461 B.C.E. the Areopagos had lost all of its political clout and survived only as a tribunal for judging certain types of offenses, such as deliberate homicide, arson, and sacrilege. It was here, in his *Eumenides,* that the playwright Aeschylus set the trial of Orestes for the crime of matricide, providing a unique glimpse of this court in action.

Here too, in the age of kings, Theseus, the great unifier of the Athenian state, is said to have battled the Amazons who had laid siege to the Acropolis. The crag of Ares was, it seems, their stronghold and the site of their last stand. In fierce and livid combat—the stuff of many later legends and reliefs—the two sides fought hand-to-hand, to the death, dying in each other's arms like confused lovers.

The Ancient Athenian Agora

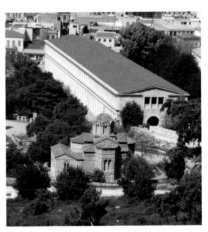

The heartbeat of any ancient Greek city was best taken at the Agora, the pulsing center of civic life. In the mid-5th century B.C.E., the Athenian Agora was the center not only of Athens and Attika, but also of the Athenian empire. Here the everyday as well as the extraordinary affairs of state were conducted. Whether you were shopping for something special, standing trial for theft or treason, seeking public services, serving jury duty, sitting in the City Council, meeting

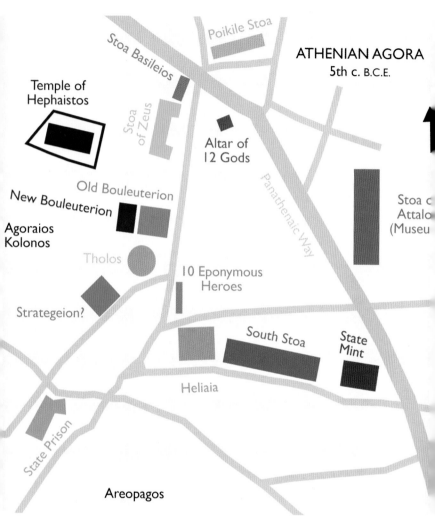

a friend, reading the news, or eavesdropping on your favorite philosophers, you would likely be doing it here in the Agora. It was at once a sacred precinct, a governmental complex, an open market, and *the* social scene. The monuments of the Classical Agora—temples, stoas, law-courts, government buildings, assembly places, and a prison—reflect the many dimensions of shared public life. Today, however, the buzz is understandably gone. It is a place of memory, mostly lost memory, a place crawling with tourists from every corner of the world whose only agenda is to connect with a past that for some reason seems crucial to them.

Excavations in the Agora have revealed its many layers: a Neolithic settlement, a Mycenaean cemetery, an archaic neighborhood, and eventually a dedicated public precinct or commons. This area of the city was not set aside exclusively for public use until approximately 600 B.C.E. and even then some private houses survived at its edges. The first public buildings—modest in scale and design—date from the early 6th century. Only after the 5th century did the Agora's governmental structures acquire grand or monumental proportions. In the 2nd century, thanks to the largesse of wealthy graecophiles far and near, it became an architectural showroom. Our focus here, however, will fall primarily on the Classical Agora, although relatively little remains from that period. Despite the fact that this is the best-preserved ancient agora in Greece, it mostly lies in ruins, apart from the magnificent 5th-century Temple of Hephaistos and the beautifully restored Hellenistic Stoa of Attalos, housing the Agora Museum.

We recommend launching your exploration of the agora with an ascent of the hill of Agoraios Kolonos and a visit to the Temple of Hephaistos (also known as the Hephaisteion or the Theseion), not only because this magnificent 5th-century (449–415) temple is clearly the site's surviving architectural gem but also because it occupies an elevated vantage-point from which you can take your bearings and survey the full span of the agora and its monuments below. Originally dedicated to Theseus and later to Hephaistos, this Doric masterpiece is the most fully preserved ancient temple in Greece. Its architect, whose name has not come down to us, was also responsible for the Temple of Poseidon at Sounion, the Temple of Nemesis at Rhamnous, and the Temple of Ares, moved stone by stone to Agora centuries after its erection elsewhere. The cella of this temple once held the cult statues of Hephaistos and Athena—the work of the sculptor Alkmenes. Hephaistos (patron god of smiths) and Athena (patron goddess of craftsmen) must have been at home here amidst the workshops and furnaces unearthed on the surrounding slopes and with the potters of Kerameikos as their neighbors. The Hephaisteion, an architectural cousin to

Temple of Hephaistos

the Parthenon, enjoys some of its refinements, as well as fine relief sculptures in its frieze, metopes, and pediment, depicting the mythical labors and battles of Theseus and Herakles. The gardens adjacent to the temple offer not only a delightful respite from the sun but an opportunity to sit in tranquility to admire this exceptionally intact temple at your own pace.

From the hill of Agoraios Kolonos and its Theseion, you look down over the Agora. Down to your left stood the Stoa of Zeus Eleutherios, the Stoa of Zeus of Freedom. The gift of freedom attributed here to Zeus is the freedom of Greece from Persian invasion and tyranny following the victory of the Greeks at Marathon, Salamis, and Plateia. It was after this last, decisive battle and victory, that this sacred monument was raised here in the Agora. Next to (north of) the Stoa of Zeus, stood the Stoa Basileios, the Stoa of the Archon Basileios, the "King" Archon, the second-ranking official in the Athenian state. This once housed the statues of Solon and Drako, and at its front stood a massive rectangular stone on which the city archons swore to uphold the Athenian constitution and all the laws of the state. It was very near here that the notorious assassination of Hipparchos occurred in 514 B.C.E. Across from the Stoa of Zeus and the Stoa of the King Archon was the Altar of the Twelve Gods, an ancient place of sanctuary and the umbilical center of the city of Athens, from which distances in every direction were measured. Further north across the ancient Panathenaic Way and today's Adrianou Street, stood the Poikile Stoa, the Painted Stoa, dating from roughly 460 B.C.E. and once a chosen meeting-place of philosophers. In the 5th century it was adorned with paintings of Athens' triumphs, such as the Battle of Marathon, and on its walls hung the bronze shields of dead and dishonored Spartans in memory of another great moment in Athenian military history when Spartiate warriors shocked the Greek world and surrendered to their Athenian opponents at Pylos in the Peloponnesian War.

Down to your right (south), near the entrance to the Agora from the Acropolis, stood the State Mint, where silver—mined by slaves at Laureion—was made into silver Athenian "owls" or four-drachma pieces, the dollar of the empire and beyond. Next to (west of) the Mint stood the South Stoa, constructed of mud brick early in the 5th century and used to prepare and serve meals to market officials. Just west of the South Stoa, in the southwest corner of the Agora, there remains the nearly square footprint of a structure thought to be the Heliaia, Athens' largest law-court, which would have been required to contain the many hundreds of jurors needed to decide a case. Intriguingly, to the southwest of the Heliaia, beyond today's fenced site, it seems that the State Prison has been unearthed. A long corridor with square rooms on either side, together with a supply of small clay bottles suitable for a dose of hemlock (the "lethal ingestion" used for Athenian state executions) are among the clues leading to the claim that this may indeed have been the next (and, for some, the last) stop for those found guilty in the nearby court.

ATHENIAN CIVICS 101

Direct Democracy in the Periklean Age

Ekklesia: Assembly of Citizens

The ultimate legislative body, open to all citizens of good standing, one man one vote. Dealt principally with war, peace, and foreign policy rather than everyday civil administration. Convened at the Pnyx four times a month and when necessity demanded.

Prytaneis: Executive Council

Fifty members of the Boule on call 24/7 to maintain the state, respond to state exigencies, and to call the Boule to full session. The composition of the Prytaneis rotated monthly according to tribal district. The acting chairman of the Prytaneis—chosen daily by lot—was also chairman of the Ekklesia. Resident in the Tholos.

Boule: Council of 500

State council—fifty citizens selected by lot from each of ten *phulai* (tribal) districts—charged with preparing legislation and fixing the agenda for the Assembly. The Boule served as a steering committee for the debates conducted by the Assembly and were responsible for the execution of the Assembly's decisions. Members of the Boule (*bouleutai*) were required to be 30 years of age or greater. Convened in the Bouleuterion.

Archons

Nine senior state officials selected annually by lot from citizens of good standing age 30 and above, subject to approval by the Boule. Their jurisdictions and responsibilities may be outlined as follows:

- Archon eponymous: state festivals and familial affairs
- Archon basileus: state religion, cult and ritual
- Archon polemarch: immigration (lawsuits involving resident aliens and foreigners)
- 6 Thesmothetai: judicial administration and citizen jury-courts

Strategoi

Ten "generals" elected annually, one from each district, to maintain the security of the state and empire, and to wage war when charged to do so by the Assembly.

Hendeka: "The Eleven"

Public servants charged with sentencing convicted criminals and administering the state prison.

Hellenotamiai

State treasurers overseeing the financial affairs of the empire, elected by those citizens of good standing over 30 who met a land-ownership requirement.

Areopagos

A council and court composed of ex-archons, charged with safeguarding the constitution, enforcing executive accountability, and hearing certain high-profile cases.

Just north of the Heliaia is thought to be the original site of the monument to the Ten Eponymous Heroes, which was later moved to its present location. This consisted of a marble platform topped by a row of ten bronze statues, each bearing the name of an ancient hero. When the reformer Kleisthenes, in 508/7 B.C.E., redrew the constituencies of Athenian democracy and replaced Athens' four traditional Ionian tribes with ten artificial tribes (*phylai*) or districts of his own devising, he needed a name for each of these new constituent units. His solution was to send the names of 100 ancient heroes to Delphi, asking the oracle to narrow the list to ten. Apart from commemorating and serving perhaps to legitimize constitutional reform, this monument was used to hang wooden plaques containing vital information for citizens, such as proposed legislation and conscription lists.

At the foot of the hill of Agoraios Kolonos and the western edge of the Agora, there were a series of government buildings central to the workings of the Athenian state. First there was the Strategeion, possibly located southwest of the Tholos. This was the Athenian War Department, the headquarters of the Athenian army, housing the offices of the ten *strategoi* (generals). Here Perikles, Sophokles, Nikias, Lamachos, Alkibiades, Demosthenes, Kleon, and other Athenian military leaders met to deliberate and map out the strategies of Athens at war; and Athens was indeed at war for much of the 5th century. The headquarters of the Athenian fleet were not here, but at the other end of the long walls at Piraeus.

IN THE STRATEGEION

Nicias... was a man of great dignity and importance, especially because of his wealth and reputation. It is said that once at the War Department, when his fellow commanders were deliberating on some matter of general moment, he bade Sophocles the poet state his opinion first, as being the senior general on the Board. Thereupon Sophocles said: "I am the oldest man, but you are the senior general."

—*Plutarch* Nikias, *15.2, tr. Bernadotte Perrin.*

A bit further north stood the Tholos, the administrative hub of the state. Here the 50 *prytaneis*, the on-duty core of the Council of 500 ate, slept, and stood ready to address the most pressing matters of state. Next door was the New Bouleuterion (Council Chamber), where the *Boule* (State Council) of 500, met to draw up legislative motions and working agenda for the full Assembly citizens on the near Pnyx. This structure was constructed between 465 and 470 B.C.E. to replace the Old Bouleuterion, which was used subsequently to store archives and possibly to house the shrine of the Mother of the Gods until the much later construction of the Metroon, in the 2nd century B.C.E.

It is now time to descend and explore the Agora in detail, on foot, picking your way through an admittedly complex and confusing site, composed of ruins from many different periods and strewn with myriad sculptural fragments, the preserved flotsam of centuries of tumultuous history.

Lastly, on the far east side of the Agora, stands the fully restored Stoa of Attalos (standing over the site of Mycenaean and Protogeometric graves as well as a Classical law-court). The original structure dates from the mid-2nd century B.C.E. and was the gift of Attalos II, then King of Pergamon. In its present reincarnation it is the handiwork and gift of the American School of Classical Studies at Athens. In antiquity an upscale shopping mall and meeting place, it now houses the Agora Museum. Not only its impressive collection of finds from the Agora but also its air-conditioning will come as deserved rewards for a long and exhausting day of exploration.

Located just northwest of the Acropolis (30-210-321-0185). Open daily 08:00–18:00. €€ The Athenian Agora is included in the package ticket for the Archaeological Sites of Athens and is the entrance to the sites of the South Slope of the Acropolis.

DAY TWO

Today is museum day, a day for kind shoes. If you bring your camera, keep in mind that no flash photos will be permitted in any of the museums on our itinerary. Also watch for signs, not always conspicuous, indicating which exhibits or items are simply not to be photographed under any condition. A first offense will bring down on you no more than an embarrassing public reprimand from a guard, ever vigilant and rarely soft-spoken. Oversights are forgiven. Repeated defiance is not. The museums on our list are all within a healthy trek of the Plaka or Syntagma. Taxis are always an option if you are feeling more generous than energetic; and the metro will save you a portion of the longest walk to the National Archaeological Museum.

First, before setting out, a few thoughts about museums, and archaeological museums in particular. They mostly house objects stripped for safe keeping from the temples, palaces, tombs, battlefields, bedrooms, and other sites that they once inhabited. Those sites, scattered across the Greek mainland and islands, now lie open to the elements as well as to visitors—unoccupied, unadorned, and unfurnished—their ancient inhabitants long gone to their destinies, their surviving appurtenances decommissioned and displayed elsewhere. Archaeologists, it seems, have accomplished what the ravages of time did not—the final separation of bones and belongings from what had been their first and presumably final resting places, the necessary cost of preserving them. As a result, archaeological sites inevitably resemble demolition areas, wrecked by ensuing centuries and their countless destructive accomplices. For the most part, mere footprints from the past remain *in situ*, with the occasional wall, pillar, gateway, or road to suggest the scale and splendor of what once stood there. Meanwhile, the orphaned objects extracted from those sites—objects of worship, of war, of adornment, of every life and death— dwell in museums, far from the soil, stones, and stories with which they make mutual sense. A common grave without its bones, burial gifts, and marker is just a hole, while trinkets, pots and pans, perhaps even a child's toy cart, and other grave goods are soulless ancient debris when removed from the corpse to whom they were given and from the dirt once soaked in tears.

Everyone knows that the artifacts housed in museums belong where they were found, which is why the provenance of each item, large or small, is clearly noted whenever it is known. It is up to the viewer, however, to restore each object to its proper home, to reunite it with its familiar surroundings, to bring it back to life or use in the imagination. This is why it is so important to spend days both in museums and on sites. Each is at a loss without the other. Recapturing the past, insofar as this is possible, only occurs in the mind's eye of those who gather up its scattered remnants and return them, one visit at a time, to their familiar haunts.

The National Archaeological Museum is unquestionably one of the great museums of the world. While most major Greek cities and many archaeological sites boast their own museums, displaying objects found in the adjacent or surrounding area, the National Archaeological Museum represents all of Greece and contains, for the most part, the pick of the archaeological crop, as it were. That said, some of the finest civic or site museums, such as those at the Athenian Acropolis, Delphi, Olympia, Iraklio, and Vergina, may be said to rival or even surpass the holdings of the National Museum within their own special focus. All of its museums combined, it must be noted, house only a fraction of Greece's ancient treasures. The rest remain in diaspora across the globe, housed in other national, civic, and private collections. In a sense, then, the National Archaeological Museum of Greece may be said to have international branches in London, New York, Los Angeles, Vatican City, Naples, Paris, Berlin, and Moscow, to mention a few of the more prominent.

PRINCIPAL SITES

The National Archaeological Museum

Prepare to be overwhelmed. The treasures of the National Archaeological Museum are numerous and stunning, and of course they grow in significance as you visit their places of origin on the Greek mainland and islands. A color-coded map of the museum will accompany your entrance ticket. In each gallery the wall panels and exhibit cards are in English as well as Greek; so at every turn your way will be expertly guided and many of your questions answered. There seems little point here in doing more than turning you loose. I rarely see the point of supplementary museum guides or commentaries; so I won't provide one here. It's easy to burn out in a museum of this scale and importance; so keep in mind that there is a café and sculpture garden on the basement level for recovery and nourishment as needed.

When to begin? At the time of opening, jet-lag permitting, to avoid tour groups and the tourist masses. If today is Monday, we would advise your visiting the Goulandris Museum (below) in the morning and the National Museum after lunch. Where to begin? The museum's collections are arranged chronologically; so you can chart your own course in accord with your focal interests. Our advice, regardless of your personal fixations, is to begin with the Prehistoric Collection (Rooms 3–6), found on the ground floor to the right of the ticket counter. Why not be dazzled right off? There's nothing quite so dazzling as Mycenaean gold, nor more sublime than Cycladic sculpture; and you'll found both in these rooms.

Located at 44 Leoforos 28 Oktobriou (also known as Patission), a short walk (10 min) from Metro stops Omonia or Biktoria (30-210-821-7724). Open Monday 13:00–19:30, Tues–Sun and holidays 08:30–15:00. Free admission on national holidays, all Sundays Nov–Mar, and 1st Sundays Apr–Jun and Sept–Oct. €€

The Goulandris Museum of Cycladic Art

This gem of a museum is as close to perfect as any architect and collector might reasonably hope to reach. Founded in 1986 by the Nicholas P. Goulandris Foundation to house the private collection of Nicholas and Aikaterini Goulandris, it represents one of the most exquisite collections of ancient Aegean art in the world, presented in a serene setting conducive to its contemplation. A visit here is likely to renew and uplift even the most museum-weary visitor. Like the Cycladic islands from which they come, these works delight the eye and are good for the soul.

The New Wing of the museum, located in the nearby neo-Classical Stathatos mansion, is used for special temporary exhibits; so be sure to note what is on offer there. Access to the Stathatos House is through a special passageway from the central courtyard of the main museum building. Regardless, the mansion itself is worth a visit, as is its own modest collection of antiquities.

Located at 4 Neophytou Douka Street (30-210-722-8321) www.cycladic-m.gr. The nearest Metro stop is Syntagma, from which the museum is a 10-minute walk. If you decide to walk directly from the National Museum, note on your map that a diagonal route through Kolonaki is preferable to retracing your steps to Syntagma and walking from there to N. Douka Street. Open Mon, Wed, Thurs, Fri 10:00–16:00 and Sun 10:00–15:00. Closed Tues and Sat. €

End-of-Day Outing

After spending most of your day indoors, reading wall panels and staring through glass at ancient remains, you may be up for some exposure to the sun and a splash in the sea. Athens and its surrounds have an array of beaches to offer, some free and some quite expensive. Since 2001 most are in private hands and charge admission. In summer, especially on weekends, the beaches near Athens can be so overrun that you might prefer a shower in your hotel room to the crush of the seashore; but weekdays at a private beach can be another matter.

Perhaps the easiest beach for a first-time visitor to find and reach is the Asteria Beach at Glyfada, a seaside resort town 32km southwest of Athens center. This is more for a dip than a serious swim, as the water is quite shallow, but the landscape is attractive. It is open 08:00–21:00. Just south of Glyfada, lie two other beaches, Voula Beach A and Voula Beach B, the former a teen hot-spot and the latter relatively tranquil. The new Athens coastal light-rail tram will take you south to Glyfada and Voula from Syntagma. Take Tram Line A from Syntagma to Edem, transferring to Tram Line B for Glyfada or Voula, currently the end of the line. After your swim, there are plenty of opportunities on the beach for a drink, snack, or dinner before returning by tram to Syntagma.

DAY THREE

Today you will make one of the oldest and most sacred pilgrimages of the ancient world—to Delphi, the navel of the earth (as many Greeks understood it to be) and the oracular site of the god Apollo. While you may choose to rent a car and drive the 178km yourself or book a one or two-day package tour, we recommend here that you take a public bus and make a long day of it, leaving in early morning and returning in the evening. The journey each way runs approximately three hours, so at least six hours of your day will be consumed en route. There are 5 or 6 buses daily from Athens to Delphi and back. Athens buses leave from the KTEL Bus Terminal B at 260 Liossion Street (30-210-831-7096). The roundtrip fare will run just over €25, a fraction of what an organized tour would cost; and, as they say, freedom is priceless. For first-time visitors, Bus Terminal B is not easy to find, so allow some time for getting lost. It's possible to walk from Plaka, though the walk is significantly shortened by taking the Metro (Red Line) from Syntagma to Larissis. From the station, walk north up Dheliyianni Street which soon intersects Liossion Street. Allow 10 to 15 minutes, depending on whether you've had your morning coffee. There should be an early bus leaving Athens around 7:30 and this is the one to catch, if you are to have adequate time in Delphi. Currently, there are buses leaving Delphi for Athens at 16:00 and 18:00, either of which gets you back in Athens at a good hour. To confirm bus times and for detailed directions to the KTEL Bus Terminal B, it would be wise to seek assistance from your hotelier. Otherwise, a taxi will relieve stress and assure your timely arrival at the terminal. When arriving in Delphi, get off the bus at the archaeological site; but to catch the return bus for Athens walk up through the town in the direction of Itea to the bus station (30-226-508-2317) on Vasileon Pavlou-Friderikis Street opposite Café Astra and the BP station.

PRINCIPAL SITES

The Sanctuary of Apollo at Delphi

Delphi is a compelling example of the fact that many or most ancient Greek temples mark rather than make the sacred sites that they occupy. The first *templum* at Delphi was not a building, however aged, but the site itself—sacred space if there is such anywhere. The first response of anyone coming to Delphi and gazing at the natural splendor above, below, and on every side is mute silence, as any words one might summon will invariably fail to convey the wonder of this place. It is unquestionably the most breathtaking location of any sanctuary or ruin in Greece. For the ancient Greeks this was the center of the world, the earth's navel, a belief more likely confirmed by your soul than by your GPS. That Delphi is also a World Heritage Site is obvious and an understatement.

The first spectacle, then, at Delphi is Delphi itself, the great cleft in the rock opening to the sky far above and the sea far below. This is more than the setting of the sanctuary, it *is* the sanctuary, so be sure to pause now and then and look beyond the hewn to the un-hewn grandeur of the place. Next, you will note that the steeply terraced sanctuary of Apollo is comprised of several essential elements: the Sacred Way ascending the steep temple slope and leading past what was once a vast sprawl of monuments, treasuries, altars, sculptures, stoas to the Temple of Apollo, seat of the most famed oracle of the East Mediterranean and Aegean world. Beyond and above the temple lay the theater and the stadium. We recommend that this precinct, in all its rich complexity, be your first destination; then, after exploring the sanctuary of Apollo, we suggest that you walk to the archaeological museum, where you can escape the sun, enjoy a light lunch or snack in the museum café, and take in the museum's treasures at your own pace. Finally, in whatever time remains before your return bus leaves for Athens, you will want to walk back past the sanctuary to the Kastalia Spring and the Sanctuary of Athena Pronaia.

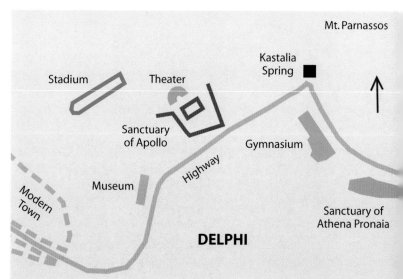

The pre-history of this site and its cult is largely lost, and not entirely by accident. Settled from the Mycenaean Period, the earliest cult here was goddess-centered. Gaia, the Goddess Earth and first Mother of all that lives, including the gods, was worshipped here, in association with her son Python, a great serpent. In myth, Apollo seized the precinct by force, slaying Python and usurping temple, oracle, and Pythian priestess, who served as a human conduit for divine revelation. This Olympian takeover occurred sometime in the late 9th century B.C.E. But this is but one strand in Delphi's mythic tapestry. In the course of its life, the sanctuary of Delphi, in addition to Gaia, Python, and Apollo, was associated with a long and distinguished roster of gods, demigods, and heroes, including Athena, Poseidon, Zeus, Dionysos, Herakles, Theseus, Jason, Oedipus, Orestes, and Neoptolemos.

In the centuries following its archaic Apollonian foundation, the sanctuary and its oracle grew from a regional shrine under local management to a panhellenic sanctuary presided over and protected by a federation of twelve tribes and the states of Athens and Sparta. In the early 6th century Delphi held its first panhellenic games. As one of four panhellenic sanctuaries, Delphi hosted its games once every four years. In the interim, however, the site was frequented by kings, state representatives, and individual pilgrims from throughout the Greek world and beyond, seeking divine answers to their all-too-human questions and quandaries. In nearly unbroken succession, then, ancient peoples from the Greek and East Mediterranean world made their way to Delphi from the 15th century B.C.E. until it was shut down by the Christian Emperor Theodosius in the late 4th century C.E. and became the site of a 5th-century Christian basilica.

Delphi's history was hardly one of undisturbed tranquility. A tempting prize for the taking, it fell victim to numerous rivalries, wars, and battles, to say nothing of natural disasters. Never immune to corruption, the shrine was held sometimes sacred and sometimes suspect, depending on whose voice and interests were believed to be issuing from the oracle's secret recesses. One of the most notorious attacks on the shrine was conducted by Persian invaders, who made a marauding detour to Delphi in 480 B.C.E. Instead of the easy plunder they anticipated, the Persians met with divine resistance and retribution (see below).

PERSIAN ASSAULT ON DELPHI · 480 B.C.E.

When the barbarians drew near in their invasion and were looking at the temple from outside, the prophet, whose name was Aceratus, saw the sacred arms, which no human hand might touch without impiety, brought out from inside the shrine and laid in front of the temple. So he went to tell the Delphians of the miracle. But when the barbarians in their haste to invade were near the temple of Athena Pronaia, there befell them miracles greater than the first one. For it was indeed a wonder that arms of war should stir of themselves and come to lie outside the temple; but what happened after that was the most marvelous of anything miraculous yet seen. For when the barbarians were, in the rush of their attack, near the temple of Athena Pronaia, at that moment there fell upon them bolts from heaven, and from Pamassus two chunks of cliff broke off and crashed upon them with a vast din and destroyed many of them, while from the temple of Athena there came a shout and a war cry. With the conjunction of all this, the barbarians were seized by panic. The Delphians seeing them in flight, descended on them and killed a large number. Those who survived fled straight for Boeotia....

—*Herodotus*, The History, *8.37–38, tr. David Grene*

Your ascent of the sanctuary hillside along the ancient Sacred Way is well-marked and accompanied by a series of markers and panels, pointing out and explaining the most notable monuments surviving in some form from the Classical, Hellenistic, and Roman Periods. Now mostly all that remains are traces, remnants, and reconstructions of what was once a plethora of sculptures, inscriptions, votives, and treasuries packed with trophies, booty, and memorabilia, from military battles or athletic contests won by states and individuals who wanted their achievements never to be forgotten. These displays were presumably a matter of gratitude, pride, and ongoing rivalry. Battles, wars, and games decided long ago were revived here as the states, kings, and celebrities of Greece reminded each other and posterity of the otherwise ephemeral moments when they shone bright and cast a long shadow on their competition—all in the name of honoring the gods ultimately responsible for what we mortals do and suffer. Here and on the accompanying map, we will point out only a few of the highlights on your way.

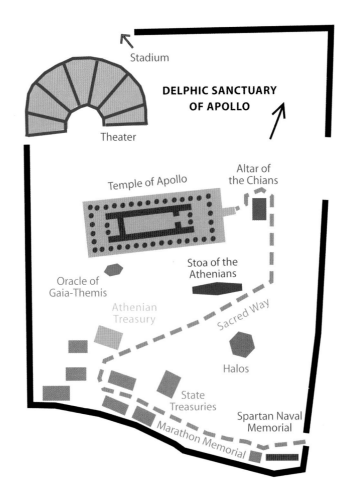

Stadium

**DELPHIC SANCTUARY
OF APOLLO**

Theater

Temple of Apollo

Altar of
the Chians

Stoa of the
Athenians

Oracle of
Gaia-Themis

Athenian
Treasury

Sacred Way

Halos

State
Treasuries

Spartan Naval
Memorial

Marathon Memorial

The first stretch of the Sacred Way comprised in large part a number of war monuments. Two of the most significant were: firstly, the Spartan Naval Memorial commemorating their devastating defeat of the Athenians at Aegospotami, a sea battle that effectively brought the 27-year Peloponnesian War to an end; and, secondly, the Marathon Memorial dedicated by Athens to their leader Miltiades who led them to victory of the Persians in 490 B.C.E. Next, we come to a clustering of State Treasuries once erected and stocked by various Classical states—Sikyon, Siphnos, Thebes, Boetia, Megara, and others—culminating in the only such treasury to be restored, the Doric style Athenian Treasury. Originally built of marble and funded (according to Pausanias) from the spoils of Marathon, the city of Athens saw to its reconstruction in 1903–1906. Many of its original ornamental sculptures and inscriptions can be seen in the site museum. Next, little trace remains of two intriguing nearby sites: the site of an early Oracle of Gaia-Themis, reputedly guarded by the serpent Python; and the Halos, a circular site where every eight years, in a ritual drama known as the Septeria, an adolescent boy reenacted the torching of Python's palace, by setting fire to a miniature wooden model. Today, only the stairs leading to the Halos are evident. Across from (northwest of) these stairs, stands what remains of the Stoa of the Athenians, with its portico of eight Ionic columns of Parian marble. Constructed after the Persian Wars, an extant inscription indicates that it once contained, as votive offerings, prows from the defeated Persian fleet and bits of cable used by the Persian invaders to hold together their pontoon bridge across the Hellespont.

A bit further up the hillside en route to the Temple of Apollo, we come to the Altar of the Chians, a massive monument of Chian black marble erected by the people of the island of Chios in the 5th century B.C.E. in grateful recognition of their deliverance from the Persians.

Finally we stand before the Temple of Apollo, of which six restored Doric columns still stand, though only one to its full height. These date from the 4th century B.C.E. The temple remnants before us mark a site with a long architectural history.

The first stone temple constructed here in the 7th century burned to the ground in the 6th, soon replaced by another, which was destroyed by an earthquake and reconstructed in the 4th century. It is this latter temple whose remains we witness today. The legendary oracle is thought to have been located in a subterranean *adyton* (inner shrine) behind the cella. It was to this inner sanctum that the Pythian priestess withdrew nine times a year, after purifying herself in the Kastalia Spring. Within, at the omphalos, seated on a tripod, and (it is surmised) breathing mind-altering gases released from fissures beneath the temple, she waited entranced for the god Apollo to speak to her in response to the queries brought by anxious states and individuals. Her often raving utterances were invariably obscure, requiring the interpretive services of the oracle's priest before delivery to waiting petitioners. Beyond the specific prophesy and counsel issuing from the *adyton*, the temple offered free bits of general advice to all who came, in the form of inscriptions quoting the Seven Sages. Two of them are so widely familiar as to be universal proverbs: "Know yourself" and "Nothing in excess."

Look, now the sun's burning chariot comes
Casting his light on the earth.
Banned by his flame, the stars flee
To the awful darkness of space.
The untrodden peaks of Parnassus,
Kindling to flame, receive for mankind
The disk of the day.
The smoke of unwatered myrrh drifts
To the top of the temple.
The Delphian priestess sits on the
Sacred tripod chanting to the Greeks
Echoes of Apollo's voice.

You Delphians, attendants of Phoebus,
Go down to Castalia's silvery eddies:
When you have bathed in its holy dews,
Return to the temple.
Let your lips utter no words
Of ill-omen, may your tongues
Be gracious and gentle to those who
Come to the oracle.

—*Euripides,* Ion, *82–101, tr. Ronald Frederick Willetts*

Ascending a flight of steps above the temple, you will come to the Theater, completed in the 2nd century B.C.E. and serving both as a place of civic assembly and as a venue for music and poetry contests. Its stone platforms will seat an audience of roughly 5,000, depending as always on each person's actual mass and sense of personal space. Be sure to take this opportunity to extend your gaze well past the orchestra to the panorama below, perhaps the most spectacular vista in all of Greece.

Still further up the hill, behind the theater, you will find the Roman Stadium, constructed in the 2nd century C.E. to seat 6,000–7,000 spectators. Throughout the Archaic and Classical Periods, the Pythian Games were held not here but in the grassy plain far below. It was not until the 3rd century B.C.E. that the games were moved to this site. Today, the roar of the crowds is replaced by the roaring of surrounding woodland bees, which gives to this eventless venue a new buzz.

Located 178 km northwest of Athens on the road from Livadia to Itea (30-226-508-2312). Open in summer daily 07:30–19:30, winter daily 08:30–15:00. €€ A combined ticket for site and museum is available and advisable at reduced cost.

After retracing your steps back along the Sacred Way to the entrance of the Sanctuary of Apollo, turn right at the Livadia-Itea road and walk several minutes in the direction of town to intersect the walkway to the archaeological museum up the hillside up to your right.

The Archaeological Museum of Delphi

This is one of the finest museums in Greece. As a premier panhellenic sanctuary and the most renowned oracle of the Classical world, Delphi was all about display and largesse. States strove to outdo each other in their treasuries, dedications, and offerings, as did kings and other individuals tall of stature and deep of pocket. All of this means that ancient Delphi was and is a treasure house, no matter how many notable and rapacious plunderers have made an appearance here over the centuries.

You will be able to find your way through the museum collection quite fruitfully with the expert direction and illumination provided you at every turn. It is particularly rich in sculpture, free-standing and relief. Perhaps the most famed sculpture here is known simply as "The Charioteer" and is one of the few surviving bronze statues from the Greek Classical Period.

Located adjacent to the Sanctuary of Apollo (30-226-508-2312). Open in summer Monday 12:00–18:30, Tues–Sun 07:30–19:30, winter daily 08:30–15:00. €€ A combined ticket for site and museum is available and advisable at reduced cost.

After completing your tour of the museum, if time and energy remain for one last exploration before catching your return bus to Athens, return to the main public highway and this time turn left, walking past the entrance to the Sanctuary of Apollo another 1.5 km to the Sanctuary of Athena Pronaia. On your way you will come to the Kastalia Spring, from which flow the sacral waters in which the Pythia would purify herself before ascending to the Temple of Apollo and entering the adyton for the oracular mysteries. The sanctuary's priest and officials, as well as visiting pilgrims and suppliants, would also bathe here to prepare themselves to enter the sacred precinct of Apollo. The hewn fountain visible today dates from the Hellenistic and Roman Periods. Now, proceed further down the road in the direction of Arachova/Livadia until you see the Sanctuary of Athena Pronaia across the road on your right.

The Sanctuary of Athena Pronaia

The site of the Sanctuary of Athena Pronaia, also known as Marmaria ("the Marbles"), inhabited since the Neolithic, has yielded evidence of cult activity from as early as the Mycenaean Period (14–11th century B.C.E.), when Gaia was the principal deity worshipped here. A number of the figurines and sculptures unearthed on this site are on display in the Delphi archaeological museum.

The lesser monuments within the present sanctuary include: a shrine to the hero Phylakos, who helped fight off the Persians from here in 480 B.C.E.; numerous altars dedicated to Athena (in her various roles as Goddess of Health, Goddess of Childbirth, etc.) and one to Zeus; and two ruined marble treasuries.

The earliest known temple on this site was constructed in the mid-7th century. Presumably destroyed, it was replaced by a later Doric Temple of Athena, dating from c.500 B.C.E. This second temple was damaged in the "god-sent" rockslide on the occasion of the Persian assault and finally succumbed to an earthquake a century later. Still another, third temple of Athena was erected c.360 B.C.E. 50 meters west of this site, beyond the Tholos.

The semi-surviving gem of the sanctuary is its early 4th-century B.C.E. Tholos, or rotunda, designed by the architect Theodoros and constructed of fine Pentelic marble and dark Eleusinian limestone. Of its original 20 Doric columns, only three stand today. The dedication and purpose of this exquisite monument are sadly unknown.

Located 1.5 km east of the Sanctuary of Apollo on the Livadia–Itea public highway. Open site. No admission fee.

Northwest of the Sanctuary of Athena Pronaia lay the ruins of the ancient gymnasium. Once densely wooded, this area was, according to legend, where the youthful Odysseus was gored by a wild boar, leaving the notorious scar by which he was many years later identified by his nurse when he returned incognito from the great war and his wanderings. What remains of the gymnasium complex, first constructed in the 4th century B.C.E. and later rebuilt by the Romans—running tracks, practice rooms for wrestlers and boxers, baths, etc.— can be surveyed from far above at the theater and probably doesn't warrant closer inspection now, on your initial visit to Delphi, when the focus is on Classical Greece.

DAY FOUR

Today will take you first to Piraeus, the ancient port of
Athens, and from there by hydrofoil (Flying Dolphin) to the
nearby island of Aigina in the Saronic Gulf. If the weather is
on your side, the excursion to Aigina—a most welcoming and
delightful destination—and the exploration of the Temple of
Aphaia will likely prove to be especially memorable. In
summer, as always prepare for heat, as well as for a swim; and,
if you are inclined to rent a moped or motorcycle on the
island, bring an appropriate operator's license. Otherwise
public transportation or taxi will suffice. Due to limited public
transport on the island, with quite restricted timetables, it's
best to arrive on Aigina by the late morning; so you will want
to plan on a reasonably early start to the day.

Before heading out—preferably the day before—inquire
at the tourist office or your hotel or online—whether the
Piraeus Archaeological Museum is open to visitors. At the
time of publication it is closed indefinitely for renovation,
which means that it could reopen in three months or in three
years. For walking directions from the Piraeus Metro Station
see below; but carrying your own map of Athens (with a
detailed inset of Piraeus) will lessen the risk of getting lost as
you shuttle between the Piraeus Metro Station, archaeological
museum, and Flying Dolphin docks. If the Piraeus
Archaeological Museum is closed, then walk straight to the
Flying Dolphin docks (see directions below) to depart for
Aigina. There are multiple competing carriers whose kiosks
are all proximate to each other; so you ought to encounter no
difficulty booking a departure within the hour. In high season,
you may wish to consult in advance the Greek National
Tourist Office at 26a Amalias (30-210-331-0392) for schedules
and assistance.

The first stop of the day is Piraeus. Take the Metro (#1,
Green Line) south to the end of the line. When you exit the
station you will be stepping out into one of the most
congested, frenetic scenes in Greece. Precious little of the
ancient port survives apart from its energy. Then as now,
Piraeus is where worlds meet. Once the chief port of the East
Mediterranean, Piraeus was the headquarters of the Athenian

fleet and the commercial center of the Athenian empire. A 9km corridor of fortified walls linked the port to its mother city, creating a self-contained civic molecule able to sustain itself and administer its far-flung empire by means of its commercial and military fleet. Its ancient population, resident and transient, were notably international, radically democratic, and culturally syncretistic. Today, together with its suburbs, Piraeus is the third most populous city in Greece; and after an hour of navigating its streets, you may imagine you have bumped into most of its residents.

Piraeus, then and now, comprises three harbors, not one. The principal harbor, Kantharos, lies before you as you exit the metro station. Most domestic and international ships arrive and depart from here. To the east, there are two smaller harbors: Zea (or Pasalimani) and Mounychia (or Mikrolimano).

Whether or not you plan to visit the archaeological museum prior to departing for Aigina, we recommend that you walk directly from the metro station to the Flying Dolphin port and purchase your ticket to Aigina now, either to depart as soon as possible or later in the morning after visiting the museum. To reach the departure point and ticket kiosks for Flying Dolphins to Aigina and the other Saronic Islands, turn left on the street immediately in front of the metro station, following that street for 5–10 minutes until you come to signs for Flying Dolphins to Aigina. More specifically, turn left (south) onto Akti Kalimassiati, crossing briefly onto Akti Poseidonos and then bearing right onto Akti Miaouli. The Flying Dolphin port will be on your right.

To find your way from the Flying Dolphin port to the Piraeus Archaeological Museum, continue south/southwest along Akti Miaouli roughly six blocks, turning left onto Sachtouri and taking the first left onto Charilaou Trikoupi (which intersects Sachtouri at a 30° angle. The museum will be on your left at 31, Charilaou Trikoupi, just shy of Zea Harbor. After visiting the museum, if you have a keen interest in Classical Athens and, in particular the Peloponnesian War, you may want to explore briefly Zea harbor, where you will find some remains of the walls of Piraeus and of the trireme sheds where the Athenian war fleet would winter or return to dry dock. In antiquity, there were said to be roughly 200 slipways here for the Athenian fleet.

PRINCIPAL SITES

The Archaeological Museum of Piraeus

This museum, currently under major renovation, boasts an exceptional collection of finds from Piraeus, Athens, Attika, Kythera, and the Saronic area, spanning several millennia, from the Minoan to the Roman Periods. Classical Piraeus was once a center of Asiatic religions and mystery cults, in addition to being the commercial and naval hub of the empire, and the museum reflects its rich, diverse, even exotic history. The museum's bronze Apollo, dating most likely from the end of the 6th century B.C.E., is held to be the oldest extant full-length bronze statue in Greece. In addition, the museum has a fine collection of 5th and 4th century bronzes. The Piraeus Archaeological Museum is an important museum, and we recommend highly that you make room for it early in your day before leaving for Aigina, provided of course that it has reopened by the time of your visit.

Located at 31, Charilaou Trikoupi, just off of Zea Harbor (30-210-452-1598). Days and hours of opening are unknown at this time. €

The Archaeological Museum of Aigina

Aigina, legendary birthplace of Peleus, lies 17 nautical miles (30km) southwest of Piraeus at the mouth of the Saronic Gulf. The journey from Piraeus to Aigina town takes roughly (or, to be more hopeful, smoothly) 35 minutes. When you arrive at the modern port of Aigina, the ancient site of Kolonna will be on your left, at the northern end of the harbor, marked by a lone column (all that remains of a late 6th-century temple of Apollo, the third to stand here). Watch for signs to the archaeological site and the museum as you exit the quay.

Port of Aigina

Founded in 1829, this was the first archaeological museum established by the modern Greek state. It stands on the archaeological site known as ancient "Kolonna"—a modern nickname inspired by the one visible column (*colonna* in Italian) here. First occupied in the 4th millennium B.C.E. and by the late 3rd millennium a major fortified settlement, Aigina was a prosperous trading hub in the Middle and Late Bronze Age and went on to play a major role in the historical period, first as an independent power and eventually as a victim and pawn of greater powers and their rivalries. The 6th-century "turtles" of Aigina were the first silver coins struck in Greece. Like so many of the proud and free states of Greece contributing to the defeat of the Persian invaders of the early 5th century, Aigina became first an ally and then an enemy of Athens, in time absorbed into the Athenian empire and later colonized. These days, Aigina is known mostly as a favored weekend getaway for Athenians and as the premier source of Greek pistachios (*phistíki*).

Museum and site located on Cape Kolonna, just outside (north) of modern Aigina (30-229-702-2248). Open Tues–Sun 08:30–15:00. €

The museum and site of Kolonna are of only modest interest, so we would recommend that, before taking time out to explore them, you first walk to the town bus station at Plateia Ethatneyersias and determine the next best departure time for the east of the island and the Temple of Aphaia, which is the true archaeological gem of the island. These buses run infrequently, so catching one should be your first concern. At the same time, be sure to look ahead to your return. Otherwise, your next best alternative is a taxi, which involves paying the driver not only for transport but also for the time he will spend waiting for you at the site of the temple. This will be costly. How costly depends on your bargaining skills and the driver's need for your business. If you have in hand a license to operate motorbikes or motorcycles, these can be rented in the town, as can mountain bikes. Before deciding to pedal your way across the island, however, bear in mind that the island is quite hilly and the round-trip to and from the Temple of Aphaia is nearly 25km. In planning out your day, you'll want to allow ample time to explore the town, enjoy a meal at one of Aigina's alluringly delightful waterfront fish tavernas (on your left as you first face the town), and perhaps take a dip in the sea. While the island's prime beach is at distant Agia Marina (visible from the Temple of Aphaia), there is also swimming on offer at the town beach and off the far side of Cape Kolonna.

The Temple of Aphaia

This is one of the best-preserved ancient temples in Greece, and its location, perched high atop a pine-covered mountain (300m) overlooking Agia Marina and the Saronic Gulf, is itself inspiring. Aigina's Bronze Age Cretan connections are a matter of record, and the cult of Aphaia rooted in this site since at least the Geometric Period and perhaps since Mycenaean times provides one more evidential layer of Minoan influence. Since antiquity, Aphaia has been identified with Britomartis or Diktynna, the Minoan Artemis, and her name may be derived from the Greek verb *phaino* ("to appear" or "to shine forth") which would make this place and

> In Aigina, as you approach the mountain of Panhellenic Zeus, there is a Sanctuary of Aphaia to whom Pindar composed a song for the Aiginetans. Her story is a local matter in Crete, where they say Euboulos was, the son of Karmanor, who purified Apollo from the murder of the Python, and his daughter Karme bore a child to Zeuswhose name was Britoniartis. Her pleasure was running and hunting and she was a particular friend of Artemis. Running away from Minos, who fell in love with her, she flung herself into a net let down for fishing. Artemis made her a goddess,and not only the Cretans worship her, but also the Aiginetans,who say Britomartis appears to them on their island. Her title in Aigina is Aphaia and in Crete Diktynna.
>
> —Pausanias, *Guide to Greece*, II.30.3, tr. Peter Levi.

the goddess resident here a site of revelation. The sanctuary of Aphaia has been the locus of a series of monumental structures, culminating in the late Archaic Doric gem, completed in the late 6th or early 5th century B.C.E. and remarkably intact to this day. Of the original 32 poros stone columns in the peristyle, 24 still stand.

Before exploring the precinct on your own, a preliminary visit to the small on-site museum is advised. Here you will learn more fully what is known of the history of the Aphaia cult and sanctuary and, after studying the museum's scale model of the sanctuary, you will be more able to envision the original structures and so to appreciate and place into context their remains. Apart from its marble roof and pediments, the temple was made of local limestone, most of which would have been stuccoed and painted. The marble pediments, preserved in the Munich Glyptothek, presented sculpted scenes from the Trojan campaigns of Herakles and Agamemnon and were vividly painted. Within the temple, in the cella—protected by railings in the pronaos and the opisthdomos—there once stood the chryselephantine image of the goddess Aphaia, a small fragment of which is preserved in the National Archaeological Museum.

Located 12km east of Aigina town (30-229-703-2398). Open Mon–Fri 08:30–19:00 and Sat–Sun 08:30–15:00. €

DAY FIVE

Today you have at least one decision to make, as we have multiple suggestions for the day from which you will need to choose the one that best suits your interests and your daring. The first involves your renting a car and driving to several nearby archaeological destinations: Vravrona, Marathon, and Rhamnous, all three on the eastern coastline of Attika. The furthest of these is roughly 50km from central Athens. There is no public transport to all three. In fact, public transport is problematic to any of these challenging but rewarding sites, and a private taxi for the day will be prohibitively expensive. One-day auto rental, on the other hand, is quite convenient and affordable, but of course entails navigating Greek roads, which is not everyone's idea of a holiday. We leave the decision with you. An alternative would be to book a one-day coach tour either to the Argolid (Mycenae and Epidauros) or to ancient Corinth. A third option would be to move on to Day Six in the itinerary and reduce your stay in Athens accordingly. On weekends in the summer months, Athenians avidly take to the hills and coasts of Attika, as well as to nearby islands, in unfathomable numbers, so we do not recommend your attempting such excursions between Friday and Sunday. These, in outline, are your options, and for each, we will now offer some detailed suggestions and tips. Our fullest treatment below will be of the first option, the exploration of Vravrona, Marathon, and Rhamnous.

Bus tours to the Peloponnese—whether to Corinth or to the Argolid—will need to be booked in advance. We especially recommend your visiting Mycenae and Epidavros, as they are extraordinary sites; and tours of the Argolid also frequently include a stop in Nafplion, one of the very most attractive small cities in Greece. On any of these tours, you will of course be guided to and through each site; but you may also want to consult what we have to say about these Peloponnesian destinations in Itinerary #2. For booking a tour, you may consult the EOT (Greek National Tourist Organization) office at 26a Amalias (30-210-331-0392) or go directly to either of these tour companies: Key Tours at 4, Kallirrois Street (30-210-923-3166 www.keytours.gr) or Ivis

Travel at 3, Mitropoleos Street (30-210-324-3543). Key Tours is located very near the Temple of Olympian Zeus, and Ivis Travel is just off of Syntagma.

If you decide to take the wheel, the first order of business will be to reserve a one-day rental car. This can, of course, be done on the spot at a car rental agency in central Athens or at the Athens airport. Hertz, Avis, Budget, Dollar, Alamo, Thrifty, and other internationals all have desks at the airport arrivals hall and most have city-center offices. For last-minute rentals, one reasonable and convenient local agency is Kosmos at 9, Syngrou (30-210-923-4695). You will likely get the best value, however, by reserving your car in advance from outside of Greece. This can be done, of course, even if you yourself are already physically in Greece. An overseas phone call or a visit to the internet offers all of the distance that you may need to secure good value on a rental car. Our long-time favorite source is Auto Europe (www.autoeurope.com), at least until they let us down, which they have not done as yet. Regardless of your car source, however, we recommend that you arrange to pick up your car at and return it to the Eleftherios Venezelos International Airport. Think Theseus. Without Ariadne and her string, he never would have made it out of the labyrinth; so too, without an installed GPS system and either iron nerves or yogic serenity, you may as well just surrender without a struggle to the Minotaur. That would be the nearest taxi driver.

The Eleftherios Venezelos International Airport, as you already know from your arrival there days ago, is linked by the metro to the city center. Take the airport Blue Line from the Monastiriaki metro station. It leaves roughly every twenty minutes and takes about an hour to reach the airport. Groups of two or more may travel at a discount. At the time of publication, the individual one-way fare was €6 and the rate for two was €10. The airport offers easy access to the new Attiki Odos (E94), the central artery of Greater Athens as well as a strategic staring point for today's explorations, for which we will offer general but not turn by turn directions here. You will want and need your own detailed map of Attika. Again we will recommend *Road Editions* as the map source of choice. Their travel bookstore in central Athens is located at 39, Ippokratous (30-210-361-3242) perhaps a 20-minute walk from Syntagma. For a free general map of Attika, all but useless on the ground but helpful in picturing today's routes, go to www.eot.gr, click on "Downloads," then "Maps," then "Attika."

The first of today's three principal sites is Vravrona, a little under 40km from central Athens. It's roughly 5km from the airport as the crow flies, but alas we are not crows. From the airport, take E94 (which soon becomes 61) south towards Markopoulo. On the northern edge of Markopoulo, take the road east signposted for Porto Rafti. Not surprisingly it is called Porto Rafti Avenue. Once in Porto Rafti, follow signs to Vravrona (5km northwest of Porto Rafti) and Artemida or Loutsa.

PRINCIPAL SITES

The Sanctuary of Artemis at Brauron

Brauron (Vravrona) is one of the nearly forgotten archaeo-logical treasures of Attika, and today suffers from this neglect. Its defiant tranquility— nearly devoured by urban sprawl and transgressed by over-head flight lanes— ironically echoes the bold words of the young priestess said to be buried here: "I have imagined my death, and all is well." This priestess is the famed Iphigenia, the daughter of Agamemnon, whom he was willing to slaughter in sacrifice to Artemis as the price for fair winds to fill the sails of his thousand ships aimed at Troy. Whether or not his blade slit her throat or that of a deer substituted by the goddess to spare the life of the girl has remained an open question in myth and legend ever since.

Here at Brauron the canonical version is that the deer indeed died on the altar, while Iphigenia was wafted away to serve as priestess in the temple of Artemis among the wild and wooly Taurians until she was rescued by her brother Orestes and brought here to live out her days as priestess of this sanctuary. In her exodus from Taurica, she is said to have taken with her a sacred wooden cult image of Artemis, fallen from the sky. Enshrined here, this image was worshipped for centuries until the Persian invasion of the early 5th century when it became a spoil of war borne back to Susa by defeated Persians.

The Sanctuary of Brauronian Artemis, one of the oldest, most revered, and best preserved sanctuaries of Attika, occupies a site settled since the Neolithic Period. When the cult of Artemis—goddess of the wild, mistress of animals, protector of women, infants, young girls, and childbirth—was established here is not known with any precision; and whether this was ever the site of human sacrifice remains a matter of conjecture. Assuredly, in the Classical Period the rites and mysteries practiced here were more tame. There is said to be in nature no more fiercely protective a parent than the she-bear, and so the rites of Artemis at Brauron involved at times the initiation of young girl "cubs" likely clad and masked as bears. Young girls who died in childbirth—exhausting their lives at the border of girlhood and womanhood—were seen as victims to Artemis and the bloody sheets off their beds were hung here as offerings on the walls of Artemis' shrine. In the Brauronia, an Attic festival celebrated here every four years, it is said that young girls re-enacted the legendary killing of a bear sacred to Artemis by Athenian youths and the vicarious sacrifice of girl-cubs (*arktoi*) in atonement for the sacrilege. This narrative is echoed in the legend of Iphigenia whose sacrifice was demanded by Artemis to compensate for the death of her sacred stag, slain by Agamemnon in the sacred grove of the goddess.

This, then, is the shrine both of Artemis and her avatar, Iphigenia, whose relationship to the goddess resembles the relationship of Helen to Aphrodite. Both Artemis and Iphigenia, in tradition, are mistresses of cruel sacrifice, while at the same time embodying the ferociously tender

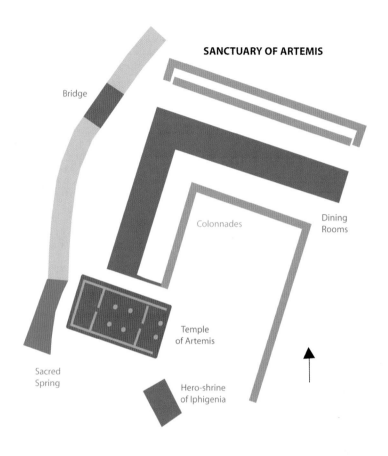

SANCTUARY OF ARTEMIS

Bridge

Colonnades

Dining Rooms

Temple of Artemis

Sacred Spring

Hero-shrine of Iphigenia

You, Iphigenia, shall preside over the temple of the goddess
        on the terraces of Brauron,
    and keep her holy keys again.
There you shall die and be laid to rest.
And as tokens on your honor,
    women shall drape your tomb with lovely gowns,
        woven of the finest threads,
    and left behind by women in their beds,
        who gave their lives in giving life,
    exhausted in their labor.

—*Euripides,* Iphigenia in Tauris, *1462–1467,*
tr. Robert Emmet Meagher

protectiveness of mother bear over her cub. The stories, rituals, and realities celebrated here surely resonated and reflected the joys, the fears, the risks, and the griefs that made up the lives of young girls and women in ancient Attika.

The principals elements of the sanctuary evident today are the bridge which would have been crossed every four years by the procession of women walking from Athens to celebrate the Brauronia; the never completed late 5th-century stoa which included multiple colonnades and eleven dining rooms; the early 5th-century Doric Temple of Artemis, built over an early archaic temple; and the Hero-shrine of Iphigenia marking the site of the collapsed sacred cave associated with her burial and earliest cult here.

Located 38km from central Athens and 5km northwest of Porto Rafti on the eastern Attika coast (30-229-902-7020). Open Tues–Sun 08:30–15:00. €

Exiting the archaeological site and facing the road, the Brauron Archaeological Museum is down a short distance to your left.

The Brauron Archaeological Museum

A brief visit to this small but fine museum will undoubtedly inform and enhance your understanding and appreciation of the site that you have just explored. The scale models of the ancient sanctuary in the museum vestibule will help you picture the ancient site as it once stood and drew devotees to its rites. The museum collection includes finds not only from the Brauron sanctuary but also from a variety of sites in the region (Mesogeia), dating from the Mycenaean to the Classical Periods. Especially intriguing are the sculptures of *arktoi* (young girls as she-bears) and the sculpted heads of young girls presented as votives to the goddess. The many votive reliefs and plaques of Artemis, her sacred deer, her fellow deities, and her pilgrims provide a crack, if not a window, into the beliefs and devotions of the ancient sanctuary.

Located 38km from central Athens and 5km northwest of Porto Rafti on the eastern Attika coast (30-229-902-7920). Open Tues–Sun 08:30–15:00. €

Leaving Vravrona bound for Marathon, retrace your route to the Attiki Odos (E94) and now take it north in the direction of Athens until exit 15 (Marathonas Avenue). Take Marathonas east just over 22km through Nea Makri until you see signs on your right for the Tomb, or Tumulus, of the Athenians, which is roughly 3 km south of the town of Marathona. A short distance after turning right you will signs for the archaeological area and the car park on your left. If before or after visiting Marathon you experience hunger pangs or just want to take a break from ruins and roads, you are at this point little more than a stone's throw from the surprisingly peaceful seaside village of Marathon Beach, which true to its name offers a beach but also a handful of appealing waterfront tavernas. If you wish to go straight on to the Marathon Archaeological Museum, go back to Marathonas Avenue, turn right and then start looking for signs on your left to the Tumulus of the Plateians and the Marathon Museum. The Museum is well set back and not visible from the Marathon Avenue. If you reach the modern town of Marathon, you have gone too far and missed the turn.

The Tumulus of the Athenians at Marathon

The Athenians of 490 B.C.E., together with an infantry contingent from the city-state of Plataia, may have won a decisive victory here over the Persians, but more recently they have clearly lost the battle against seaside development on the coastal plain of Marathon. To visit the battlefield of Marathon today, you would do best to close your eyes to all that surrounds you and conjure the rest in your imagination. That said, it is possible and fitting to pay your respects at the tumulus, or funeral mound, of the Athenian dead, known as the *Soros*. It is said that the cremated remains of the Athenian dead—192 warriors killed by the invading Persians—lie beneath this dramatically simple earthen monument, raised soon after the battle. The tumulus of the Plataian dead stands not far off, but has not been identified with any certainty and is not open to the public. The Athenian tumulus, like countless other

The country district of Marathon, halfway between Athens and Karystos in Euboia, is where the barbarians landed in Attica, were beaten in battle, and lost some ships as they retreated. The grave on the plain is that of the Athenians; there are stones on it carved with the names of the dead in their tribes… Here every night you can hear the noise of whinnying horses and of men fighting. It has never done any man good to wait there and observe this closely, but if it happens against a man's will the anger of the daemonic spirits will not follow him. The people of Marathon worship as divine heroes those killed in the battle, and Marathon from whom the place gets its name, and Herakles; they claim to have been the first Greeks to believe Herakles was a god. They say there was a man in the battle with a country look about him and country equipment; he killed numbers of barbarians with a ploughshare, and vanished when the fighting was over. When the Athenians asked about him they got no reply from the god except the command to pay honours to the hero Echetlaos. There is a trophy made of white marble. The Athenians say they buried the Persians because under all circumstances religion demands the covering of a dead body with earth; but I was unable to find any grave and there was no mound or any other sign: they must have carried them to a pit and thrown them in anyhow.

—*Pausanias*, Guide to Greece, *I.32.3, tr. Peter Levi*

suburban cemeteries here and elsewhere, is mercifully sealed off from further incursion in a small park, which allows visitors some respite from the traffic and trivia around them to consider one of the most moving and momentous episodes in western history. The battle fought here ascended from mayhem to myth in a matter of hours. Like an engraving from which many future prints would be made, it was cut deep in the imaginations of the Greeks and of all who came to admire and imitate them. Against outrageous odds, free citizen soldiers defied the greatest empire and the most invincible army of the 5th century and made them run for their lives. The lessons and consequences of that day, for Athens, for Greece, and for the world, are still being studied, celebrated, and suffered.

Next to the brilliant strategist of the Athenian forces, Miltiades, the most renowned hero of the day was Pheidippides, who ran with news of the Greek victory from the battlefield to the Athenian agora, a distance of 42km, or 26

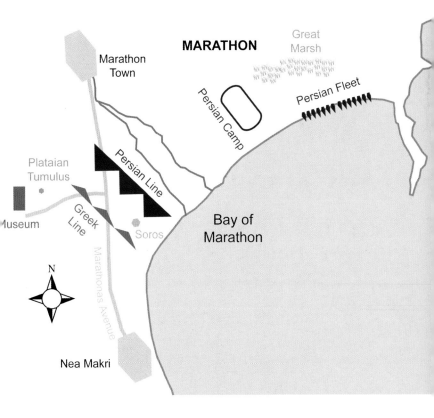

miles. As the story goes he reached the agora, shouted "We are victorious" and dropped dead. This, of course, is the origin of the marathons run to this day in cities across the globe. Pheidippides was one of under 200 Athenian casualties, which included the brother of the playwright Aeschylos, while the Persian dead are thought to have numbered roughly 6,000. The ancient battlefield, the plain of Marathon, was 10km long and 5km wide and is not preserved. In fact, a portion now lies underwater, as it was flooded to form the rowing venue for the 2004 Summer Olympics. The map below may be helpful in envisioning the plain as it was in 490 B.C.E. and the great battle as it unfolded then.

Located off (east) of Marathonas Avenue between the towns of Nea Makri and Marathona (30-229-405-5462). Open Tues–Sun 08:30–15:00. (Joint ticket for monument and museum.) €

The Marathon Archaeological Museum

This small, excellent museum—enhanced for the 2004 Olympics—is well worth a visit. Its excellent collection of finds from the Marathon battlefield as well as from the nearby environs will help to articulate the silent testimony of the Athenian tumulus and to appreciate the long and rich history of the area, which was the birthplace of Herodes Atticus. Adjacent to the museum is an excavated and covered prehistoric (Middle Helladic 2000–1600 B.C.E.) cemetery in use through the Late Helladic Period until 1200 B.C.E.

Located off (west) of Marathonas Avenue, just north of the Athenian Tumulus and just south of the town of Marathona (30-229-405-5155). Open Tues–Sun 08:30–15:00. € (Joint ticket for monument and museum.)

As you leave the museum and drive towards Marathonas Avenue, you will note on your left a covered site housing an Early Helladic Cemetery (3200–2100 B.C.E.) It has been closed since the Olympic summer of 2004 but the graves are quite visible through glass and are impressive. There are plaques describing and explaining the site.

The next and last site on today's itinerary is Rhamnous, and it is not to be missed, so however weary you might feel at this point, we urge you to carry on. Return to Marathonas Avenue and turn left in the direction of Marathon town. As you find your way to Rhamnous, retain a clear memory of your route as you will be retracing it at the end of the day. Before reaching Marathon town, take the first major road to your right in the direction of Lofos and Schinias. After passing through Lofos you will see signs pointing right to Schinias, but continue on instead to Kato Souli and Avra. Past Avra, ignore the right turn to Aghia Marina and carry on, following signs to Rhamnous. From your initial right turn off of Marathonas Avenue to Rhamnous is roughly 12km.

Rhamnous

Rhamnous is perhaps the most pristine archaeological site in Attika, and surely one of the most scenic in all of Greece. You should allow at least a couple of hours for its exploration, as it is complex and rewarding. It unfolds in stages down a steeply terraced hillside towards the sea—and just when you imagine you've seen it all, there's more. Apart from the striking ruins, there are spectacular natural vistas of the Southern Evian Gulf.

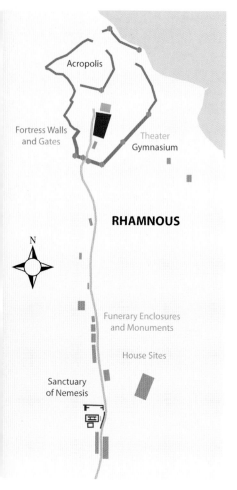

In myth, this is the spot where Zeus, taking the form of a swan, either wooed or raped the goddess Nemesis (in the form of a goose) after which she is said to have laid a magic egg. The egg, bestowed upon Leda, Queen of Sparta, eventually cracked open and produced Helen and her twin brothers Kastor and Pollux, all of whom Leda more or less passed off as her own offspring.

The ancient deme (miniature polis or subdivision of Attika) of Rhamnous comprises two principal complexes: the Sanctuary of Nemesis and the fortress town. The former stands above the latter and is encountered first as you proceed from the parking lot, through the entrance gate, and into the site. The Sanctuary of Nemesis comprises two temples and represented in antiquity the most important cult site in Greece to the implacable goddess of measure and retribution, who was counted on to take the arrogant and prideful down to size. The fortress was built by Athens during the Peloponnesian War to help her to protect the northeast coastal border of Attika and to watch over and control shipping in the Euboian (Evian) Gulf. Rhamnous, then, was at the same time a sacred site of profound religious significance and a military site of crucial strategic importance to Athens and her empire.

Ancient Rhamnous and the Southern Evian Gulf

Although the sanctuary dates from the Archaic Period, the ruins visible here today are from the 5th century. There are two temples: a smaller, early 5th-century temple dedicated to Themis, goddess of right order and fairness; and a more grand mid- or late 5th-century temple (the Nemesion) dedicated to Nemesis, whose famed cult statue was carved by a pupil of the incomparable Pheidias, creator of the colossal cult statues of Athena (in the Parthenon) and of Zeus (at Olympia). This temple, regarded in antiquity as a memorial to the Athenian victory at Marathon, is thought to have been the work of the remarkable architect responsible for two of the finest temples of the Classical Period: the Temple of Poseidon at Sounion and the Temples of Hephaistos (the Theseion) and Ares in the Athenian Agora. An earlier temple, dating from the early 6th century was destroyed by the Persians in their second invasion of the Greek mainland (480–479 B.C.E.,) when they were able to wreak substantial havoc in Attika and elsewhere before being defeated (most decisively at Salamis and Plataea) and dispatched.

Nine towers of the 5th-century fortress are visible today. The outer circuit walls once measured 800m or a half-mile in length, and their main gate was flanked by two towers. This outer circuit encompassed a number of public spaces and structures, including the theater, the agora, and a gymnasium. Further north and nearer the sea, on elevated ground, stood the acropolis, the military core and summit of the fortress, enclosed by its own inner circuit of fortifications. From 336/335 B.C.E. (i.e., throughout the Peloponnesian War), the fortress of Rhamnous was patrolled by Athenian ephebes ("scouts"), Athenian youths in training for full military service, from which we may conclude that the fortress was regarded as secure and unlikely to come under attack.

Today's walkway to the sanctuary and down the slope to the fortress follows the ancient road to Rhamnous from Marathon. The principal monuments along the road, south to north, are the Sanctuary of Nemesis, with its two temples, and the fortress. All along the route from the sanctuary to the fortress, to the right and left of the road, you will see the remains of numerous funerary enclosures as well as house sites, some dating to the Mycenaean Period.

Located on a remote promontory 12km northeast of Marathon (30-229-406-3477). Open Tues–Sun 08:30–15:00. € Extended hours in summer.

END-OF-DAY SWIM AT SCHINIAS

Before retracing your way back to Marathonas Avenue and from there to the E94 south to the auto rental return area at the Eleftherios Venezelos International Airport, you may want to take a swim at one of Attika's most attractive beaches. Well before reaching the town of Marathon, follow signs directing you to the Schinias Olympic Rowing and Canoeing Center and Karavi Beach. Soon you will come to a long, sandy, pine-fringed Blue Flag beach, mobbed on weekends but more manageable mid-week and off-season. It was on this stretch of beach that the Persians first assaulted Attica, landed their warships, and prepared for battle. Today, of course, you are more likely to see the sails of local windsurfers than the prows of Persian invaders.

Day Six

The focus and culmination of today's explorations is the Sanctuary of Poseidon at Sounion. Since the best time to visit Sounion is in the late afternoon so as to avoid the crush of bus tours and to witness the often spectacular sunset at the Cape, it will be up to you to have one eye on your watch during the day. It's best to decide on your desired arrival time at Cape Sounion and work backwards. Cape Sounion, the drop-dead stunning site of the Temple of Poseidon, is the southernmost tip of the Attika peninsula, roughly 70km southeast of Athens. The journey by bus from the city center will take approximately two hours. If you wish, you can book a half-day bus tour with Key Tours at 4, Kallirrois Street (30-210-923-3166 www.keytours.gr) or with CHAT Tours at 9, Xenofontos Street (30-210-323-1200 www.chatours.gr). Taking a tour has only one advantage—convenience. Otherwise, tours are costly, crowded, rushed, and likely to return to the city well before sunset. As this book is called an explorer's guide for a reason, we strongly recommend that you set off on your own by public transport and control your own destiny, at least for an afternoon. To confirm the latest bus and site schedules, consult the EOT office, several minutes' walk from Syntagma, at 26a Amalias (30-210-331-0392) open Mon–Fri 09:00–19:00, Sat–Sun 10:00–16:00. At present the preferred bus to Sounion via the coast road runs every hour beginning at 6:30 am from Filellinon Street just off (south) of Syntagma. Buses to Sounion also leave from the Mavromateon Terminal (30-210-880-8000) on the south-western edge of Areos Park, roughly 250m north of the National Archaeological Museum. More specifically, the bus stop is at 14, Mavromateon along the west side of the park off the western end of Alexandras. Round-trip or return fare will run well under 10 euros, less than a third the cost of a tour bus. Keep in mind as you plan and pack for the day that just beneath the temple at Sounion (on the west, or Saronic, side of the strip of land on which the temple stands) is a small harbor, with fish tavernas and a beach. Meals at land's end are predictably overpriced, so if you don't mind the extra weight, you may want to bring your own.

Depending when you rise for the day and when you have decided to leave for Sounion, you should have at least several hours to explore several significant archaeological sites that until now we have overlooked, all clustered west of the Acropolis: the Hill of the Muses; the Pnyx, or Athenian Assembly; the alleged prison cell of Sokrates; and Kerameikos, the ancient state cemetery of Athens. To begin today's excursion, find your way to the pedestrian walkway Dionysiou Areopagitou south of the Acropolis. Follow this walkway west past the Odeion of Herodes Atticus on your right. Then, as the walkway bends left to intersect Apostolou Pavlou, enter the pine-wooded park area before you and follow signs to the 15th-century chapel of Aghios Demetrios Loubardiaris, which after a brief walk you will see on your right. Just beyond the church, take the first paved road to your right, which will take you a fenced site. Take the third gate for entrance to the Pnyx.

PRINCIPAL SITES

The Pnyx

Although this site affords unsurpassed views of the Acropolis and the city below, there is not much to see but a great deal to imagine. This is one of the most significant sites in Athens; for this is the epicenter of Athenian democracy, where the *ekklesia* (assembly) of Athenian citizens convened to debate and decide everything from its most commonplace to its most grave affairs. Every citizen, in theory, had the right to speak for a fixed amount of time from the raised platform, or bema, still extant before you. Time, of course, always runs out, and Greeks like everyone else played favorites, so some voices were heard more often than others from the now silent bema. Thanks to Thucydides, we can still listen, with a degree of confidence, to many of the most momentous speeches given here in the latter half of the 5th century.

In the Classical Period, attending citizens would have gathered around the platform on what was then bare rock.

This open area would have accommodated no more than 6,000 men, though it is thought that rarely, if ever, was that number approached. The Boule (or Council of 500) was provided with wooden seats. Despite the predictably frequent contributions from acknowledged leaders and demagogues such as Perikles, Kleon, Hyperbolos, Nikias, Alkibiades and others, and notwithstanding the clout of political clubs and cliques, this was radical democracy in action as the world has rarely witnessed it. It was one citizen, one vote, deciding whether to wage war or make peace, to grant mercy or exact revenge, even to dissolve the democracy itself or restore it. A seismic crack, of course, in direct democracy Athenian style was the exclusion of women from citizenship, a gap not lost on women as well as on many men. One of these was Aristophanes, the comic playwright, who gave them their voice, not here but not far away either, in the theater of Dionysos, visible if not audible from here at the foot of the Acropolis. In one of his plays—*The Congresswomen* (*Ekklesiazusai*)—he had the women of Athens hiding their husbands' clothes so as to confine them to their homes, and

PRAXAGORA *(impersonating a man)*:
Therefore, gentlemen, why waste time in debate?
Why deliberate possible courses of action?
Simply hand over the City and let the women
rule. You need convincing? Reflect: Mothers
all, their first desire will be to preserve
their soldier sons.
      Provisions? Who quicker than
the hand that rocks the cradle at filling the mouth?
Finances? Nothing more wily than women at scrounging
a budget—and rest assured that, once in power.
They won't allow embezzlement of public funds;
by dint of training, they themselves are Athens'
finest embezzlers.
      I say no more. Give me
your support, and vote yourselves a life of bliss.

—*Aristophanes*, The Congresswomen, *tr. Douglas Parker*

convening at the Pnyx, dressed and bearded as men. With a swift efficiency not characteristic of the Assembly's deliberations, the women of Athens suspend the constitution, grant themselves supreme authority, and create a utopian civic commune in which love is made more freely than war and men are relieved of all political duties, duties which the women have watched their men bungle for a century.

You needn't be reminded to take in the magnificent Athenian vistas available from the mound of the Pnyx. The nearby Hill of the Muses (also known as Philopappos Hill), if you climb to its top, also offers rare views of Athens, provided the skies are reasonably clear. This pine-shaded park, once the site of an ancient sanctuary of the Muses, is also a very pleasant place to stroll, away from the day's heat and the city's stress.

Located on the Hill of the Pnyx (109m), south of the Areopagos. Open daily 08:00–17:00. No entrance fee.

As you leave the Pnyx, retrace your steps back to the road on which you entered the park and turn left. Almost at once you will walk past, on your left, the chapel of Aghios Demetrios Loubardiaris. At this point begin looking for signs on your right pointing to the alleged Prison Cell of Sokrates.

The Prison Cell of Sokrates

What you will come upon looks at first to be several primitive caves cut from a rocky ledge. Metal bars, surely not ancient, secure the doors. In fact, this surprisingly complex structure, cut from bedrock, seems to have once comprised multiple rooms, two or possibly three floors, and a cistern at the rear. A popular tradition has designated this to be the prison cell of the martyr-philosopher Sokrates, a tradition that can be neither confirmed nor denied with any certainty. During World War II these chambers were used to conceal and protect antiquities from the Acropolis and the National Archaeological Museum. At this point in time the caves are used to reveal and protect the memory of Sokrates,

and with an eye on that goal it matters little for the moment whether Sokrates ever occupied this space, much less died within it. Greece is littered with ancient hero-shrines and, in most cases, it is anyone's guess whose remains lie within or nearby. The tholos tomb of Agamemnon, as well as his death mask, are known misnomers, and they neither top nor complete the list. If visitors, enjoying the Hill of the Muses, pause here and recall arguably the greatest pride of Classical Greece, there is no harm done. Sokrates asked as many questions as he could think of, refused to violate his conscience, chose his words carefully, gave his life to educating the next generation, spoke truth to power, kept his sense of humor in dark times, and lived as if there were worse fears than death.

Located on the Hill of the Muses, south of the Areopagos. Open site. No entrance fee.

When you exit the Hill of the Muses, turn left onto Apostolou Pavlou and proceed in the direction of the Thiseio tram

THE LAST HOURS OF SOCRATES

"Evidently you think that I have less insight into the future than a swan; because when these birds feel that the time has come for them to die, they sing more loudly and sweetly than they have sung in all their lives before, for joy that they are going away into the presence of the god whose servants they are. It is quite wrong for human beings to make out that the swans sing their last song as an expression of grief at their approaching end; people who say this are misled by their own fear of death, and fail to reflect that no bird sings when it is hungry or cold or distressed in any other way; not even the nightingale or swallow or hoopoe, whose song is supposed to be a lament. In my opinion neither they nor the swans sing because they are sad. I believe that the swans, belonging as they do to Apollo, have prophetic powers and sing because they know the good things that await them in the unseen world; and they are happier on that day than they have ever been before. Now I consider that I am in the same service as the swans, and dedicated to the same god; and that I am no worse endowed with prophetic powers by my master than they are, and no more disconsolate at leaving this life..."

The executioner gives the hemlock to Socrates, and Socrates drinks it.

Up till this time most of us had been fairly successful in keeping back our tears; but when we saw that he was drinking, that he had actually drunk it, we could do so no longer; in spite of myself the tears came pouring out, so that I covered my face and wept broken-heartedly— not for him, but for my own calamity in losing such a friend....

"Really, my friends, what a way to behave! ... Calm yourselves and try to be brave." This made us feel ashamed, and we controlled our tears. Socrates walked about, and presently, saying that his legs were heavy, lay, down on his back—that was what the man recommended. The man (he was the same one who had administered the poison) kept his hand upon Socrates, and after a little while examined his feet and legs; then pinched his foot hard and asked if he felt it. Socrates said no. Then he did the same to his legs; and moving gradually upwards in this way let us see that he was getting cold and numb. Presently he felt him again and said that when it reached the heart, Socrates would be gone.... Such, Echecrates, was the end of our comrade, who was, we may fairly say, of all those whom we knew in our time, the bravest and also the wisest and most upright man.

—*Plato*, Phaedo, *tr. Hugh Tredennick*

station. On your way, to right and left, you will notice various lesser archaeological sites of interest, such as the Sanctuary of Pan. After ten minutes or so, when you reach the tram station, cross to the far side of the tracks and turn left on Ermou, with the tram tracks on your left, until you see the entrance to Kerameikos, the state cemetery of Athens, which in antiquity lay just outside the city walls and just west of two ceremonial gates to the city: the Dipylon Gate and the Sacred Gate. The Panathenaic procession passed through the Dipylon Gate on its way, via the Agora, to the Acropolis; and the procession of initiates to the Mysteries passed through the Sacred Gate en route to the Sanctuary of Demeter at Eleusis.

The Athenian Cemetery and Archaeological Museum of Kerameikos

The area known as Kerameikos (or Cerameicos, which reads "ceramics" after dropping a couple of vowels) took its name in antiquity from the hero Keramos (son of Dionysos and Ariadne) and from the community of potters who established their workshops and made their homes here on the banks of the River Eridanos. The city walls of Themistokles, constructed in 478 B.C.E., divided Kerameikos in two, one side for the living and the other for the dead. Those working in clay were inside the walls, and those returning to clay were outside. Just northwest of the cemetery, portions of the Themistoklean wall, the Dipylon Gate, and the Sacred Gate all survive and can be examined close-up.

Visiting the Kerameikos cemetery is like exploring any cemetery in which one has no loved ones or friends interred. It is partly a matter of snooping and partly a matter of paying one's respects. There is no fixed route. It's a matter of strolling randomly and getting lost. Parts of the cemetery are overgrown; so you can never be sure what you will find. One inhabitant sure to cross your path is a tortoise. The cemetery is all but overrun with tortoises, some of whom nearly qualify as ancient.

The small but very interesting on-site archaeological museum should not be missed, as it will substantially enhance your appreciation of the cemetery, its history, its finds, and its losses.

The state cemetery of Athens once, of course, occupied an area considerably larger than the space currently excavated and designated an archaeological site. This fact was made dramatically clear in 1997 when, quite by accident, the *Demosion Sema* (or "People's Grave") of Classical Athens was uncovered on either side of the road to the Academy, the sanctuary of the hero Akademos and the site of an olive grove sacred to Athena. Here, if we are to believe Pausanias, were buried many of the most famed men of Athens who, named and unnamed, fill the pages of Herodotus and Thucydides: Solon, Kleisthenes, Harmodios and Aristogeiton, Perikles, Thrasyboulos, Konon, and Phormion, as well as a host of Athenian warriors and seamen who died in various hoplite or trireme battles before and during the Peloponnesian War. Here was where men who had deserved the honor were buried or memorialized at state expense. The full plot is thought to extend 1,500m in length and, at least at its beginning, 40m in width, which would calculate to a maximum area of just under 15 acres. Excavations so far have revealed four mass grave memorials from the 5th century, thought to correspond closely with the description of communal warrior graves in Thucydides. Quite likely then it was here that the fallen Athenian dead from the first year of the Peloponnesian War were laid to rest and here that Perikles delivered one of the most famous eulogies of all time in 431 B.C.E.

Kerameikos is located on Ermou just north and west of the Thiseio tram station (30-210-346-3552). Open daily 08:00– 18:00. € (Admission is included in the 4-day package ticket to the principal Archaeological Sites of Athens; but by now your ticket, purchased on "Day One" will have expired.) The site of the Demosion Sema is an on-going excavation, which began with 35, Salaminos and will be extended as additional adjacent lots can be expropriated by the Greek Ministry of Culture as part of a master plan entitled "The Unification of the Archaeological Sites of Athens."

In this winter, following their traditional custom, the Athenians held burial rites at public expense for the first to die in this war, in the following manner. They lay out the bones of the dead two days beforehand, after setting up a tent, and each person brings whatever offerings he wishes to his own relatives. When the procession takes place, wagons carry cypress coffins, one for each tribe, and within are the bones of each man, according to tribe. One empty bier, fully decorated, is brought for the missing, all who were not found and recovered. Any man who wishes, citizen or foreigner, joins the procession, and female relatives are present at the grave as mourners. They bury them in the public tomb, which is in the most beautiful suburb of the city and in which they always bury those killed in war, except of course for the men who fought at Marathon; judging their virtue outstanding, they gave them burial right there. After they cover them with earth, a man chosen by the state, known for wise judgment and of high reputation, makes an appropriate speech of praise, and after this they depart. This is their burial practice, and throughout the whole war, whenever there was occasion, they followed the custom. Now for these first casualties, Perikles son of Xanthippos was chosen to speak....

It seems to me that this conclusion of these men's lives is what reveals a man's virtue, whether as the first indication or final confirmation. Even for those who were worse in other ways it is right that first place be given to valor against enemies on behalf of country; by effacing evil with good, they became public benefactors rather than individual male factors. None of these men turned coward from preferring the further enjoyment of wealth, nor did any, from the poor man's hope that he might still escape poverty and grow rich, contrive a way to postpone the danger. Thinking defeat of the enemy more desirable than prosperity, just as they considered this the fairest of risks, they were willing to vanquish him at that risk and long for the rest, leaving to hope the uncertainty of prospering in the future but resolving to rely on their own actions in what confronted them now, and recognizing that it meant resisting and dying rather than surviving by submission, they fled disgrace in word but stood up to the deed with their lives and through the fortune of the briefest critical moment, at the height of glory rather than fear, departed....

So fared these men, worthy of their city... in giving their lives in common cause, they individually gained imperishable praise and the most distinctive tomb, not the one where they are buried but the one where on every occasion for word and deed their glory is left after them eternally. The whole earth is the tomb of famous men, and not only inscriptions set up in their own country mark it but even in foreign lands an unwritten memorial, present not in monument but in mind, abides within each man."

—*Thucydides*, Peloponnesian War, *II.34, 42–43, tr. Steven Lattimore*

After visiting Kerameikos and before setting out for Cape Sounion, you may want to have lunch. As you will have already noticed, the café district just south of the Thiseio tram station is very pleasant and convenient, or you may wish to head east on Ermou to Monastiraki, where there are many cafes and lunch spots, as well as street food aplenty.

When you begin your journey to Sounion, your first challenge will be to get to your bus. From here we recommend taking the tram/metro (Line #1) in the direction of Kifisia but getting off at the Vikoria (often spelled Biktoria) station. From there, walk two blocks west to the edge of Areos Park and turn right (south), walking two blocks south to the Mavromateon bus station. Alternatively, you may walk to the Monastiraki metro station, take Line #3 one stop to Syntagma, and from there walk several minutes to Filellinon to meet your bus. This latter option can be tricky, however, as you will need to flag down the Sounion bus, whose moment of appearance can be sudden and unpredictable. Lastly, when you arrive at Sounion, be sure to check the return bus schedule and, most importantly, the time of the last bus. You can get this information from the bus driver, if he speaks English, or else from the cashier in the confection/souvenir shop adjacent to the large open-air taverna, which you can't miss. If the worst case happens and you miss the last bus—a highly unlikely event for which you would likely bear sole responsibility—just remember that you needn't take a taxi all the way back to Athens and declare bankruptcy upon arrival. A middle ground would be to take a taxi along the coast road to the nearest tram station at Voula or Glyfada and take Tram Line B north to Edem, changing to Tram Line A bound for Syntagma.

The Sanctuary of Poseidon at Sounion

The earliest mention of this site in Greek literature can be found in Homer's *Odyssey*. He cites this promontory as the place where the steersman of Menealos' ship was targeted by Apollo, an archer not known to miss. Dropped at the tiller by a cluster of divine arrows, he died a swift and, we are told, painless death and buried with appropriate rites on this holy ground. Why Homer called this site holy is unknown, as there

is no clear evidence of cult activity here earlier than the beginning of the 7th century B.C.E. All the same, the burial of the named Trojan war veteran, and thus hero, Phrontis was later commemorated at Sounion with a sacred precinct and hero shrine dedicated to this man of whom nothing else is known than that he died softly at the king's helm, a victim of Apollo's wrath. The Archaic hero precinct of Phrontis intersects and occupies a portion of the west side of the Sanctuary of Athena Sounias.

Once again it's a matter of location. Needless to say the siting of Greek temples was not a matter of throwing a dart at a map. If there is truth in the saying that who you are is where you are, then we needn't wonder why the sanctuary and temple that we see before us here, commanding the Aegean on three sides, belong to Poseidon, divine lord of the sea. This was a sacred site at least as early as 700 B.C.E., when four colossal marble kouroi stood atop the headland. These Archaic votives survived until the early 5th century when they fell afoul of invading Persians prior to the battle of Salamis. The extant temple stands over the site of an earlier unfinished temple also destroyed by the Persians in 480 B.C.E. Its original Doric peristyle comprised 34 Doric columns (13x6), and 15 stand today. The continuous frieze of the temple

Menelaus and I were sailing then
On our way back from Troy, the best of friends.
But when we came to holy Sunium,
The cape of Athens, Phoebus Apollo
Shot Menelaus' pilot with his arrows,
Killing him softly as he held the tiller
Of the speeding ship—Phrontis his name,
The best rough-weather pilot in all the world.
So Menelaus stopped, eager though he was
To press on, and gave his comrade a funeral.

—Homer, Odyssey, *iii.278–285*, tr. Stanley Lombardo

displayed the legendary wars of Gods vs. Giants and Centaurs vs. Lapiths, as well as the heroic feats of Theseus.

The full site actually contains two sacred precincts, one dedicated to Poseidon and the other to Athena Sounias. Little remains of the sanctuary of Athena (situated on a hillock 500m north of the temple of Poseidon) apart from the foundations of two small Classical temples, the larger of the two dating from the second half of the 5th century. The date and dedication of the smaller temple are uncertain and remain matters of debate. In the late 5th century (412 B.C.E.), the promontory was walled by the Athenians and the sanctuary of Poseidon became a fortress; for this site was as strategic as it was sacred. Indeed, Athenian piety and politics frequently commingled in the 5th century. At the end of the day, then, it was not only Poseidon's claim to lordship of the seas that was maintained here. Athens had her own maritime hegemony to assert and defend. Fortress and sanctuary, towers and temples all played their part in the partnership of Athens, Athena, and Poseidon, proclaiming a united power over the Aegean, on earth as it was on Olympus.

The imperial fleet of Athens patrolled the Aegean and the regional waters of the East Mediterranean at least eight months out of every year, from March through October, for much of the second half of the 5th century B.C.E. They entered the Peloponnesian War with roughly 300 triremes

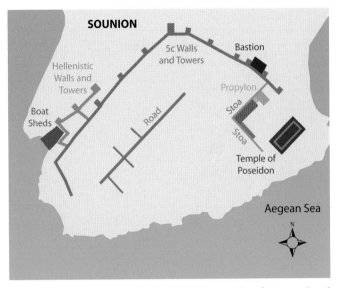

(literally cutting-edge battleships), a number that fluctuated and in time greatly diminished, as the changing tides of the 27-year war finally turned against them. Whether rowing to victory or defeat, this was land's end for Athenian sailors as they went to war, their last glimpse of the motherland ever or until their homecoming. To Athenians this jagged promontory and its towering temple were a welcome and reassuring sight, and for enemies a formidable reminder of Athenian might.

The 5th-century fortification walls—300m long, with 10 rectangular towers—enclosed an area of roughly 8.6 acres. The Sanctuary of Poseidon occupied the southwest corner of this fortified space. The principal structures within the sanctuary's temenos, or precinct walls, were the Propylon, two stoas, and the temple. Some evidence of the enclosed settlement's roads and houses has also survived. In the Hellenistic Period, the fortification walls were extended, a bastion was constructed at the southern extremity of the 5th-century fortifications, and ship sheds were built at the sea's edge to the northwest of the site. The path to the sea to the ship sheds lies across the road from the Sanctuary of Athena, and this is also a nice place for a swim.

Located 70km southeast of Athens (30-229-203-9363). Open daily 10:00–sunset. €

ITINERARY FOUR

AEGEAN CIVILIZATION:
THE CYCLADES 3000–336 B.C.E.

PRINCIPAL SITES

"Essential Athens"

Temple of Olympian Zeus, Acropolis Museum,
Theater of Dionysos, Odeion of Herodes Atticus,
Acropolis, Agora, National Archaeological Museum,
Goulandris Museum of Cycladic Art

SANTORINI

Archaeological Museum of Ancient Thera
Museum of Prehistoric Thera
Prehistoric Settlement of Akrotiri
Ancient Thera

NAXOS

Apollo Gate
Mitropolis Site Museum
Archaeological Museum of Naxos
Dionysian Sanctuary of Iria
Sanctuary of Demeter and Kore and
Archaeological Museum at Yiroulas, Sangri
Archaic Kouroi of Apollonas and Flerio

DELOS

Sanctuary of Delian Apollo and Archaeological Museum

ARRIVAL IN ATHENS

This itinerary, like the three others in this guide, begins in Athens, with arrival in Athens' new Eleftherios Venezelos International Airport. Unlike its predecessor, "Venezilos" or "Spata" (as it is commonly known) is well designed, easily negotiated, and linked directly to the city center by both Metro and rail lines, as well as by taxi and bus. Before leaving the airport, you will do well to stop by the EOT (Greek National Tourist Organization) office in the arrivals hall and pick up free copies of their Athens map, cultural events guide, and other free hand-outs, such as up-to-date lists (for Athens and Greece) of current openings and closings at every state archaeological site and museum. Also ask for a free "Athens Public Transport Pocket Map"; and, if they don't have one for you, try the ticket counter at the Syntagma Metro station. If you miss or take a pass on the airport tourist organization office, there is another very helpful EOT office, several minutes' walk from Syntagma, at 26a Amalias (30-210-331-0392), open Mon–Fri 09:00–19:00, Sat–Sun 10:00–16:00.

Since all of the Athenian hotels recommended here are located in or near the traditional, in fact ancient, district known as the Plaka, we will assume that you will be seeking a bus or Metro to Syntagma or Constitution Square, which adjoins the Plaka. The airport bus to Syntagma runs roughly every twenty minutes, takes about an hour, and costs just over €3 per person, while the Metro leaves every thirty minutes, takes a half hour, and costs €10 for two persons. In general we avoid Athenian taxis whenever possible and we are not alone in this. They have a dire and mostly well-deserved reputation for unarmed theft. I have heard the view expressed more than once that Athenian taxi drivers ought to be required to wear masks to alert the unsuspecting visitor to the true nature of their profession.

DAYS ONE AND TWO

Days One and Two in this itinerary correspond directly to the first two days in "Itinerary Three • Classical Civilization" found on pages 223 through 258. In case you are already familiar with Athens and its treasures or for some other reason prefer to skip or reduce your time in Athens, simply make your way to Santorini and proceed to Day Three. Depending on which form of transport you choose for your journey to Santorini, you may need to cut short your second day in Athens and visit the sites you missed when you return from the islands. Remember that Day One for this itinerary is assumed to be a Saturday. This is important because at present the only excursions from Naxos to Delos run on Sundays, Tuesdays, and Thursdays. This fact, combined with the Monday closing of most archaeological sites and museums, necessarily exercises considerable control over the shape of Itinerary #4.

BED AND BOARD

Our recommendations for lodging and eateries in Athens may be found in "Itinerary Three" on pages 212 through 215. At this point you will be spending between one and three nights here, as determined by the particulars of your arrival in Athens and of departure for Santorini.

TRAVEL TO SANTORINI (THERA)

As Santorini is an island, there are only two ways to reach it—in the air or across the sea. The latter, of course, will consume more of your time and the former more of your money. The choice is yours; but for our purposes, keeping count of the days in this itinerary, we will assume that you have reached Santorini and checked into your lodging there either by the night of Day Two or by the early afternoon of Day Three. Either a night ferry from Piraeus or a 50-minute flight from Athens will keep you on this schedule. By air you can choose between Olympic (30-210-966-6666 www.olympic-airways.gr) and Aegean (30-210-998-2888 www.aegeanair.com). Sea travel is more complicated and, depending on the season and the seas, can fall prey to long, uncertain delays or cancellations. Take note that most every ferry or hydrofoil will deliver you to Santorini indirectly, after stopping at several other islands. To begin exploring your options for sea transport to Santorini, consult the Greek National Tourist Organization (30-210-870-0000 www.gnto.org) or a ticket agent in Athens or Piraeus, where they abound. You can also book passage online at www.greek-islands-ferries.gr with most credit cards. If airfare is not a painful financial burden, we recommend that you begin this itinerary with a flight from Athens to Santorini and complete it with a return flight (or voyage) from Naxos to Athens (or Piraeus).

CYCLADIC CIVILIZATION

In Greece, the encircling primacy and preponderance of water are undeniable—shaping myth, history, and daily life. Most Greeks, ancient and modern, have made their lives near the sea, if not at water's edge. Nowhere is this more true than on the islands, numbering in the thousands and comprising over 20% of the land mass of the modern Greek state. Another inescapable presence in Greek imagination and life is the sun, which saves for Greece its most entrancing brilliance. The islands—set like jewels in the encircling sea and bathed in the light above—are where sky and sea, light and water, touch as nowhere else. Their lure has lost nothing over the millennia.

Individual Greeks all have their own favorite islands to which they are drawn, traditionally for Easter, otherwise for personal renewal or collective revelry. Among these, the cluster of over 200 islands known as the Cyclades—"the Encirclers"—have few peers. What they encircle is Delos, an island sanctuary dedicated to Apollo—for centuries the most sacred cult center in the Aegean. The encirclement of Delos is all but tangible from that island, with Mykonos only 3km to the east, Tenos to the north, Syros to the west, and Naxos and Paros to the south. Most of the Cyclades are uninhabited crags, but there are twenty with sizeable populations. Among these Santorini (Thera) and Naxos, our two bases in this itinerary, represent two extremes—the one a barren volcanic masterpiece and the other a green oasis rimmed with sandy beaches. Both are soaked in a unique Aegean island civilization whose origins reach back at least 5,000 years.

The building of the Poseidonianists, Delos

Surprisingly little is known of the lives and communities of the early Cycladic islanders. The first settlers arrived on a number of these islands by 5000 B.C.E.; and by the Early Bronze Age (3000 B.C.E.) a unique Cycladic civilization was flourishing. Cycladic prosperity—rooted in a demanding and fruitful life of farming, animal husbandry, fishing, and hunting—grew as the islanders became increasingly skilled craftsmen, artists, and seafarers. While gifted in pottery and metal work, they were inspired sculptors, whose achievements have transcended time and stunned modern artists and art lovers with their sublime simplicity. The Cycladic sculptors worked in marble, for which they had only to bend over. Most of these islands are literally made of marble, some grey and some luminously white. Parian marble has indeed been legendary for thousands of years. The creative focus of the Cycladic sculptors was on figurines or idols, mostly female in form and miniature. Seemingly all of these were destined to accompany the dead. The truth is that whatever we know of the lives of these people has so far come mostly from their graves. No clearly identifiable sanctuaries have been found, and relatively few settlements have been excavated and explored.

Island life in the Early Cycladic Period seems to have been peaceful though precarious. While the farmers, fishers, artists, and traders of these islands displayed no recognizable need for thick walls or other defenses, the sea around them could be, then as now, unpredictable and lethal. The Aegean is notorious for its sudden, violent storms; and, even when the sea sleeps, the region's fault lines and volcanoes can and do awaken with little or no warning. Throughout this period of independence and remarkable prosperity, early Cycladic seamen explored and traded throughout the Aegean, the East Mediterranean, and beyond. The rise of the Minoan thalassocracy, however, soon overshadowed the splendor of Cycladic civilization and came to dominate much of the southern Aegean. This marked a decline from which the unique and independent civilization of the Cyclades never fully recovered, as the cultural hegemony of Crete was eventually replaced by that of the mainland. Rediscovered in the 20th century, however, the wonder that was Early Cycladic Civilization is once again recognized and celebrated.

DAY THREE

By our calculation today is Monday, which means that virtually all of Santorini's archaeological sites and museums are closed. Of necessity, then, it is a day set aside for travel, settling in, and exploring the rare spectacle that is Santorini. You will also need to book passage to Naxos for the day after tomorrow if you have not already done so. It will be a very full day. You will be tempted, no doubt, to spend a few extra days on Santorini, if not longer, and we urge you to succumb if your schedule and finances permit. Just keep in mind the excursion schedule from Naxos to Delos so as to assure your visit to one of the most important archaeological sites in the Aegean.

No number of postcards or second-hand accounts can prepare you for your first sight of the great *caldera* (Italian for "cauldron") of Thera (a.k.a. Santorini). Only an "act of god," or a long chaotic series of them could possibly have resulted in the exquisite visual catastrophe that is Santorini. It is a landscape defined and perfected by disaster. Apart from a few surviving geologic souvenirs of the island's pre-catastrophic past (e.g., Mt. Profitis Elias and Monolithos) the entire island is comprised of volcanic rock. In fact, it is more accurate today to describe Santorini as an island group rather than as a single island. First, there are the three islands that make up the broken ring encircling the caldera: Thera, Therasia, and Aspronisi. Then, afloat as it were in the waters of the caldera, are two charred and still active volcanic crags—Palia Kameni and Nea Kameni—whose names might be translated "Old Crispy" and "New Crispy" (*kameni* means "burnt"). At one time all these bits and more formed a single intact island, home to multiple volcanoes whose successive eruptions have torn the island apart. Like the shredded flesh and severed limbs of Pentheus in the *Bakkhai*, the body of Kalliste ("Loveliest of all" as Thera was called in antiquity) was hurled in every direction—into the sky as well as into the sea's depths. Recent studies indicate that the most notorious of Thera's convulsions, the Bronze Age eruption of c.1650 B.C.E., was nearly twice as powerful as was previously thought, spewing more than six times the amount of volcanic ash and molten rock produced by the 1883 Krakatoa eruption. In this regard Santorini's past is never entirely past, as the island remains at risk for future volcanic eruptions and earthquakes—once and future disasters that dare not diminish the sublime light in which this island is bathed.

When you first set foot on Santorini, whether you've arrived by sea or air—your first order of business will be to find and check in to your lodgings. With luggage in tow and without your own bearings on the island, we recommend that you hail a taxi to take you directly from the harbor or airport to your hotel.

Bed and Board

Of all the possible spots to settle in on Santorini, our decided preference is for Oia. While the bus hub is in Fira (making it a convenient base), so are the greatest number of tourists. Oia, for all of its hotels, tavernas, and tourist shops, retains charming shreds of its traditional character as a lived-in Cycladic village, especially in early morning and after sunset. And the panoramic vistas of the caldera from Oia are without equal. That said, we have also included some reliable recommendations for lodging in Fira, both because Oia is often booked solid and because to some the central location of Fira and its high energy—day and night—may have special appeal.

The following hotels in bustling central Fira all have dramatic caldera views available, so inquire when you book to avoid disappointment if that is important to you. All are signposted in front of the Orthodox Cathedral and require some stair climbing. The pleasing Scirocco Apartments (30-228-602-2855) www.scirocco.gr €€ are decorated in the island style with a palette of fresh white and Cycladic blue. The pool and shared terraces are especially welcome after a day of exploring. Helpful, friendly service is a highlight in this unpretentious lodging. The nearby Keti Hotel (30-228-602-2324) www.hotelketi.gr € offers simple rooms with a village feel, many with domed traditional ceilings, and shared terraces. The Theoxenia Hotel (30-228-602-2740) www.theoxenia.net €€ is a welcoming small hotel with ample contemporary rooms, a refined atmosphere, and a hot tub on the roof where you can bubble at your leisure.

From among the dizzying array of dining choices in Fira we recommend two extremes, according to your mood. Inside the unassuming and always popular Nikolas Taverna € on Erythros Stavros St. you will find exceptional home cooked food that is worth the wait. For a stunning caldera view on a romantic terrace where you can dine in fine style inside or out we suggest the Sphinx Restaurant €€ directly in front of the Orthodox Cathedral. The wait staff is gracious and the menu includes local as well as continental specialties.

Our very favorite lodging in Oia is the Chelidonia Traditional Villas (30-228-607-1287) www.chelidonia.com €€ where one can stay in superbly reconstructed and tastefully decorated traditional "cave dwellings" built by the native master craftsman Triantaphyllos Pitsikali and his artistic and talented wife, Erika Moechel. Each villa is roomy, peaceful, and has its own terrace opening onto a jaw-dropping vista of the caldera. The Pitsikalis have built their villas with special attention to safety in the unlikely event of an earthquake. A more modest lodging in Oia with a pool, but without a caldera view, is the hospitable Flower Pension (phone & fax 30-228-607-1130) www.pensiontheflower.com € with comfortable, unpretentious rooms set in a bright garden. It is located across from Cava Jama on the main road into Oia. For deluxe accommodation, the Canaves Oia Hotel (30-228-607-1453) www.canaves.com €€ has all the bells and whistles.

When your eyes have taken in enough and you require gastronomic restoration, we encourage you to explore the fine eateries Oia has to offer. For topnotch fresh seafood and mezedes go straight to the Sunset Taverna €/€€ on Amoudi Harbor. On the main road through Oia, the Restaurant Papagalos €€ puts a delicious twist on Greek traditional food and international dishes amid appealing minimalist decor. Also found on the main road is the elegant, award-winning 1800 Restaurant €€, considered by many as one of the finest on the island, and the intimate Ambrosia Restaurant €€ off the church square features fresh Mediterranean dishes. At the steps to Armeni Port, the Skala Restaurant € offers good, simple food and a commanding view of the caldera.

SUGGESTED OUTINGS

It is unlikely that you will be at any loss for things to fascinate and exhaust you during your first day on Santorini. Exploring Oia and Fira will consume hours. Buses run regularly between the two, and from Fira's central bus station you can catch a bus to most any other destination on the island. Bus routes and timetables are posted at each station, but you may also request your own copy, which we highly recommend that you do. If you want to escape the tourist crush and stroll through some intriguing Cycladic neighborhoods, the village of Finikia, a 10-minute walk east of Oia along the main road, will offer you a less complicated glimpse of everyday life on the island. Another appealing and remarkably unspoiled getaway is the traditional hilltop village of Pyrgos, easily reached by bus from Fira. Once in Pyrgos, you can't go wrong for lunch at the Taverna Kallisi € in the main square.

If you want to spend the day or a part of it on the beach, the chances are good that you will have lots of company, as the beaches of Santorini are no secret. From Fira, you can get a bus to Perissa or Kamari, two of the most popular beaches on the island; and, if you want to try out both, a water taxi ferries bathers back and forth from the one to the other. On the north end of the island, there are two smaller, less frequented beaches—Baxedes and Koloumbos—accessible by bus or a healthy trek from Oia.

It's always possible, given the diversity of the human species, that you will be more drawn to tread on an active volcano than to step foot into the sea. If so, there are multiple daily explorations of the caldera and Nea Kameni leaving from Fira Scala. There are also water taxis running regularly between Oia's port of Ammoudi and the comparatively remote and tranquil island of Thirasia. Should you decide to drop anchor on Santorini for a number of days, rest assured that the island offers a rich array of adventures and diversions from sea kayaking and scuba diving to submarine dives and horseback riding.

DAY FOUR

Today is a full day replete with antiquities, but also not without a deserved soak in the sea. We begin in Fira's Museum of Prehistoric Thera and then, after a brief visit to the Archaeological Museum of Thera, catch a bus to Akrotiri (provided that the excavations have reopened by the time of your visit). After exploring the archaeological site of Akrotiri, you must decide whether you have had your fill of ruins for the day. If so, then we suggest that you walk from Akrotiri to Red Beach, arguably Santorini's most scenic strand. After-wards, a short stroll east along the shore, you can also enjoy an excellent taverna lunch before returning by bus to Fira. If your exploratory needs for the day have not been met, however, or if you have an extra day at your disposal, catch a bus to Kamari and from the town center climb to the acropolis of Ancient Thera, after which you can descend the south slope of the peak to the town and beach of Perissa.

PRINCIPAL SITES

The Museum of Prehistoric Thera

While the principal holdings here are from the excavations at Akrotiri, the museum's exhibits and text panels provide a richly illuminating introduction to the prehistory of the island from the Late Neolithic to the Late Cycladic I Period (17th century B.C.E.), when the island blew apart. The panels tracing the geologic evolution of Thera are particularly informative and helpful. Everything you see and read here will substantively enhance your understanding and appreciation of the excavations at Akrotiri which you will soon be visiting. The numerous exhibits documenting and depicting life in the flourishing prehistoric port of Akrotiri help to restore color and motion to the still, monochrome mud brick walls of the long-buried city.

Located in Fira, across from the central bus terminal and behind the Orthodox Cathedral (30-228-602-3217). Open

Tues–Sun 8:30–15:00. €€ (Combined ticket provides access to the Museum of Prehistoric Thera, the Archaeological Museum of Thera, the archaeological site of Akrotiri, and the archaeological site of Ancient Thera.)

The Archaeological Museum of Thera

The focus of this modest museum is on the sculpture, pottery, and clay figurines of Thera from the Archaic through the Roman Periods. Many of the finds are from the cemetery and acropolis of Ancient Thera. If you are running late or wish to concentrate your energy on Thera's most dramatic treasures, you may want to take a pass on this museum. In any event, a brief visit will suffice to take note of its more remarkable items. Surely the most eccentric holding is the 480kg volcanic boulder whose inscription reads: "Eumastas, son of Kritobolos, lifted me off the earth." Kritobolos was an athlete, and this rock is apparently his enduring claim to fame.

Located in central Fira, on M. Nomikos, just up from the cable car station and just south of the Catholic Cathedral (30-228-602-2217). Open Tues–Sun 8:30–15:00. €€ (Combined ticket provides access to the Museum of Prehistoric Thera, the Archaeological Museum of Thera, the archaeological site of Akrotiri, and the archaeological site of Ancient Thera.)

The Prehistoric Settlement of Akrotiri

Without assistance from an active imagination, Akrotiri may fail to impress. Apart from a few pots, floor tiles, and grinding stones left in place, it is the deserted, ruined shell of a neighborhood: narrow streets, haphazard house blocks, independent villas, some preserved up to three floors, gaping doorways, stone stairs that no longer lead anywhere. The vivid frescos—so full of Aegean *vie*—discovered here have been removed and preserved elsewhere. Left to itself, Akrotiri may present itself drained of life; but not if you remind

yourself of what you are seeing. This is the best-preserved Bronze Age settlement in the Aegean—an open window into a period and a people whose art—so full of celebration—still resonates with us today. Bear in mind too that only a tiny slice of ancient Akrotiri has been unearthed. Roughly 95% of the settlement remains hidden and presumably intact beneath the volcanic ash that buried it from sight thirty-six centuries ago.

Unlike Pompei—another thriving ancient city eclipsed by a volcano—Thera was abandoned before disaster struck. It boasts no victims caught forever in postures of panic or despair. The people who made their lives here fled the island in time, perhaps in response to a series of earthquakes that preceded the catastrophic eruption of the mid-17th century B.C.E. Akrotiri at its most prosperous was a key urban center and port in the Minoan commercial empire that dominated trade in the southern Aegean. The profound Minoan influence on Akrotiri is undeniable, but that fact is not enough to support the claim that Akrotiri was a Minoan colony or subject. The status of Akrotiri at the time of its destruction is a matter of debate. This site has revealed evidence of habitation from the Late Neolithic and was already a sizeable community in the Early Cycladic Period, well before the emergence of Minoan hegemony in the southern Aegean. Akrotiri's trade connections were not limited to Crete but extended more widely to the Greek Mainland, the Dodecanese, Cyprus, Syria, and Egypt.

Ongoing excavation, as well as the installation of a new bioclimatic canopy over the site, has left public access to the Akrotiri site an uncertain matter. The reopening of the site to the public was predicted for 2006. Be sure to inquire into the latest periods and times of opening when you visit the Museum of Prehistoric Thera, so as to save yourself a fruitless bus trip to the site.

Located 12km south of Fira (30-228-608-1366). Open Tues–Sun 8:30–15:00. €€ (Combined ticket provides access to the Museum of Prehistoric Thera, the Archaeological Museum of Thera, the archaeological site of Akrotiri, and the archaeological site of Ancient Thera.)

If you decide to balance your exploration of Akrotiri with a dip in the sea, you are little more than a stone's throw from Red Beach (Paralia Kokkini). With the entrance to Akrotiri to your back, cross the road before you and walk straight along a gravel road for roughly five minutes until you see a beach path descending on your left. Red Beach is much sought out, so you will likely be able to ask directions on the spot or else just follow the foot traffic.

If you decide to make your way to Ancient Thera, return to Fira and catch the next bus to Kamini, asking the driver to let you off at Ancient Thera. In fact, this is wishful thinking, because the bus goes nowhere near Ancient Thera. It can and will, however, drop you off at the foot of a steep road ascending to Mt. Selladha and the ancient city of Thera. The narrow, saddle-back road before you represents a 4km climb. You are fully within your rights to do this on your own, but you will be under some pressure either to take the available minivan or to mount one of the rental donkeys. Whatever you decide, be sure to bring plenty of water and a hat, as Ancient Thera is nothing if not a skillet on midsummer days. After exploring the summit, you may descend either the north side of the slope to Kamari or the south side to Perissa. Both have appealing beaches and both are linked to Fira by regular bus service. If you choose the descent to Kamari, rather than retrace your steps along the main road, take the trekking trail that after several minutes veers off to your left. This trail, en route to Kamari, will take you to a sacred cave and spring, as well as a small chapel.

Ancient Thera

Within the historical contours of this book, the mountaintop city of ancient Thera is of interest primarily for the stunning views it gives of the island and sea below. Although there was a Dorian colony here already in the 9th century, the preserved ruins date from the Hellenistic, Roman, and early Byzantine Periods. The full site is quite vast, comprising nearly 28 acres, with a central agora, a theater, a gymnasium, a stoa, and numerous sanctuaries. Most of these have been reduced to little more than their foundational footprints. Cemeteries, with graves dating back to the 9th century, spill down the slopes towards the modern towns of Kamari and Perissa.

Located 10km southeast of Fira, above the town of Kamari, the ancient Theran port of Oea. Open Tues–Sun 8:30–15:00. €€ (Combined ticket provides access to the Museum of Prehistoric Thera, the Archaeological Museum of Thera, the archaeological site of Akrotiri, and the archaeological site of Ancient Thera.)

Day Five

A good part of today will be spent in transit, sailing the Aegean from Santorini to Naxos (87km). Although both Santorini and Naxos have airports, to fly from one to the other it is necessary to return to Athens, which makes flying rather pointless so long as the seas are relatively calm. Besides, you really should not leave Greece without at least one experience of island hopping, which I must warn you can easily flower into an addiction. By now you will have booked your passage to Naxos through one of the many travel agents in Fira or Oia. Your choices are between high-speed hydrofoils and ferries of varying swiftness, all leaving from the port of Athinios, which can be reached either by taxi or by bus from Fira. The boat will take you past Nea Kameni, north to Ammoudi Bay and provide a marvelous opportunity to reverse perspective and to gaze up at the cliffs of Oia and Fira from the caldera.

Upon arrival on Naxos, you will want to book at once, if you have not already done so, your Thursday (Day Five) cruise to Delos and Mykonos aboard the Naxos Star. Your hotelier should be able to accomplish this for you. Otherwise you can contact a local travel agent in the port or ring the Naxos Star line at 30-228-502-2356. It would be wise at the same time to arrange an auto rental for Day Seven; your hotelier is likely to be a willing and reliable guide in this transaction.

The remainder of the day may be spent getting settled and exploring the port town of Khora, whose narrow laneways and handsome Venetian and Frankish architecture will afford a number of unexpected discoveries and adventures. Our advice in a new place is always to get yourself thoroughly lost, for that is often how you find what you didn't know enough to look for.

Naxos—the largest, greenest and, many say, the most beautiful of the Cyclades—was an important center of Early Cycladic civilization. Like nearby Paros, Naxos was a favorite source of fine marble, and at the same time was (and is) blessed with fertile soil, shaded orchards, and an abundant water supply. Numerous post-WWII excavations on the island, some on-going, have revealed the rich archaeological interest and wealth of the island. Only a handful of these, however, have produced sites open to the public. The open field just south of the Grotta Hotel, for example, has been the focus of recent archaeological exploration, where at least one Mycenaean tomb was uncovered. The northwestern neighborhoods of the modern town of Khora, known as Grotta and the Hill of Aplomata, mark the location of the principal Mycenaean settlement of Naxos in the Bronze Age. In recent years, Metropolis Square, the plateia in front of the Metropolis Cathedral, has been transformed into an archaeological park, whose focus is the new Mitropolis Site Museum. This, we are told, was the ancestral hearth of the city, the site of the tumulus (or burial monument) where the ancient Naxians honored their founding fathers, preserved in the agora of the Classical Period, which also occupied this site. Here too you will find traces of the city's ancient fortification walls. If you want a closer, direct look at the ancient city, you can purchase a mask and snorkel in a local shop and dive off of the Grotta beach. There beneath you lie portions of the ancient agora, long engulfed by the ever-encroaching sea, the most relentless and irresistible of the island's invaders.

If time permits, this afternoon might be a convenient time to visit two of Khora's excellent museums, which we have otherwise scheduled below for the morning of Day Seven. Another less ambitious option would be, after checking into your hotel, to succumb at once to the sand and surf of St. George's Beach, one of many exceptional beaches on the island. It's only a short walk from central Khora. To find it, stroll the waterfront away from the ferry port and keep going until you see sand and beach umbrellas and hopefully not half the population of the island. Actually, there is a series of still more attractive beaches further south, to which we will direct you on Day Seven, when you have a car at your disposal. No matter how you have spent the day, however, be sure to save sunset for the Apollo Gate, the eye-riveting sole remnant of the spectacular would-be temple of Apollo Delios.

Apollo Gate

Towering over a narrow spit of land known as the islet of Palatia, the Apollo Gate (known locally as the Portara) is all that remains of the archaic Temple of Apollo Delios, constructed in the mid-6th century. It was clearly vast in conception, judging from its surviving gate and foundations. Perhaps too vast, for it is thought never to have been completed. Construction apparently ceased here when Naxos went to war with Samos and may not have resumed until a thousand years passed and a Christian church was erected atop the remains of the never-finished temple. Centuries later, another vision altogether prevailed when Venetian conquerors mined the site for building materials for their Kastro in the Khora. Today, the Portara serves, true to its name, as a dramatic gateway to Naxos, past and present.

Located on the islet of Palatia, east of the harbor. Open site.

BED AND BOARD

A few minutes walk from Khora and north of the port is our local favorite, the Grotta Hotel at 7 Kampanelli St. (30-228-502-2215) www.hotelgrotta.gr €, with its immaculate, tasteful rooms and warm hospitality from the Lianos family. Ask for a room with sea view and enjoy the balcony, the hotel jacuzzi, and the generous breakfast buffet. For lodging in the quaint old town, the Chateau Zevgoli Hotel (30-228-502-6123, fax 30-228-502-5200) €€ at the lower end of the Kastro next to the Glezou Tower has picturesque, though smallish, rooms decorated with antiques, and offers a fine view from the rooftop sitting area. The family-run Panorama Hotel (phone & fax 30-228-502-4404) €, well signed in Kastro, offers very basic, comfortable rooms, and a truly breathtaking view from some of the balconies and the roof garden. On the edge of Naxos town, just past the bend of the harbor, south of the port, on popular Saint George's Beach, you will find the fresh Hotel Glaros (30-228-502-3101) www.hotelglaros.com € set in the midst of the beach umbrella and cabana scene, if that appeals. It is at most a ten-minute walk into Khora from Hotel Glaros.

EVENING ENTERTAINMENT TIP

The Domus Venetian Museum, located at the north entry to the Kastro, is home to an on-going series of evening garden concerts under the stars. Musical genres range from jazz to classical to traditional Cycladic folk music, and often include local wine tastings, which is no small opportunity, as Naxos has been famed for its wine since ancient times. For information, call the Venetian Museum (30-228-502-2387) or the Naxos Tourist Information Center (30-228-502-5201). These events, however, are well postered, so chances are you will be visually reminded at every turn of the latest concert.

Be sure to alert your hosts of your travel plans so they can arrange to meet you at the port or help you with your bags.

Now to dining. We suggest the courtyard O Apostolis € in the Old Town behind the Pan Co. Market (good local delicacies for picnics found here) for excellent grilled squid and other Greek specialties. Restaurant Irini € on the seafront has tasty, fresh local dishes and pasta, and Elli's € overlooking the arch of the Temple of Apollo from the pebble beach north of the port serves light fare in a most stylish contemporary setting. Just outside Kastro's south gate in the taverna-laden but charming Braduna Square, the Taverna O Kastro € offers more unusual regional cuisine and a sunset view over the town. For fresh fish, the popular O Nikos €/€€ above the Commercial Bank on the waterfront is a standout.

DAY SIX

Today the Captain of the Naxos Star has the wheel; and, given his nearly 40 years of experience on the Aegean, that's a good thing. Rest assured he knows the way. Your route will take you first to the sacred island of Delos, where you will explore the Sanctuary of Apollo, and then to Mykonos, because everyone has heard of Mykonos and is at least curious. The return route to Naxos will include a pause in the harbor of Paros, which

TRYSTING MAIDENS BEWARE

While we have no recent data on this matter, mythical precedents are dismissed always at one's own risk. In antiquity, Naxos enjoyed less than auspicious associations for love-stricken maidens. First there was Semele, princess of Thebes, whose amorous companion was none other than Zeus. In consideration of the gap between them, not only in age but also in what might be called general potency, the King of the Gods had made it his practice to take human form (no doubt dashing human form) when cavorting with young Semele. But in young love there is no such thing as enough, so Semele begged him relentlessly to come to her in all his divinity, unveiled and undiluted. Worn out by her pleading and finally unable to deny his lover what she longed for most, Zeus, Lord of Lightning-blasts, came to her as pure celestial fire and incinerated her in one last climactic embrace. From her smoldering corpse, however, he rescued his fetal son Dionysos, who after completing his gestation in the makeshift womb of his father's fatty thigh, was born from his father here on Naxos and reared by local nymphs. Dionysos, who had only fond feelings for Naxos, was waiting when Theseus arrived here years later with his newly beloved and desperately loyal Ariadne, princess of Knossos, who had betrayed her father and her homeland to rescue and run off with the daring and desirable young prince of Athens. Naxos was a stopover for the two fleeing lovers on their route to Athens; and all that is known is that while Ariadne slept on the shore, Theseus, under some strange compulsion, set sail without her, never looking back. Variants of the myth sought to explain the seeming wretched behavior of Theseus toward the young girl who had so completely surrendered her heart and life to him. One version proposed that Dionysos had spoken to him in a dream and commanded him to abandon Ariadne; modern skeptics might suspect committment phobia. Regardless, as the story goes, Dionysos either raped or won over (a thin line in Greek myth) the stricken Ariadne and made her his bride, crowning her with a golden wreath of laurel, and leaving her with four children.

turns out to be a tease because you will not be allowed to disembark. If you decide on a longer stay in the islands, however, you would do well to consider a day trip at least to Paros. Be warned, though, that so many tourists swarm onto Paros in high season that it's a wonder it doesn't sink.

PRINCIPAL SITE

The Sanctuary of Delian Apollo

Delos, the focal center of the Cyclades, is the most sacred of all of the Greek islands. Before becoming a major tourist destination and a World Heritage Site, it was a sanctuary, nothing more and nothing less. After the second Athenian purification of the island in 426 B.C.E., neither birth (apart from Apollo's) nor death were allowed on the island. Those approaching either had to go elsewhere to begin or end their lives.

The event that first sanctified this tiny (5sq.km.), barren island was the birth of Apollo. Some ancient authors also cite this as the birthplace of Apollo's twin sister Artemis, while others locate her birth on the nearby island of Reneia. Either way Artemis was duly and greatly honored here on Delos along with her slightly younger womb-mate Apollo. Their births were complicated by the fact that Hera, Queen Mother of the Gods, had hounded their pregnant mother (one of her philandering husband's many "lovers") threatening to curse any people or place that would offer her safe haven. It was the otherwise inhospitable crag of Delos that finally welcomed Leto; and in return the island became for many centuries a place of pilgrimage for all Greeks, far and wide.

An Ionic religious center already in the 7th century

B.C.E., Delos came under increasing Athenian influence and eventual domination from the mid-6th century, until it gained its independence in the late 4th century. Under Roman control it became an international port and a center of tax-free trade; and with prosperity came the perils of war and plunder. With the rise of Christianity, Delos like other pagan shrines lost more than its luster. It fell into neglect and ruin, and its monuments became a convenient source of recycled building materials. It rediscovery in the modern era by archaeologists led to further plunder, this time by museums; so that today very little remains of its ancient splendor, apart from its vast scale.

> ...Leto suffered
> for nine days and nine nights
> she was subjected to unimaginable pain.
> And all the goddesses were there...
> Only Eilithyia hadn't heard,
> who is herself in charge of a woman's pain...
> Hera kept her away
> through envy,
> because Leto, with her beautiful hair,
> was about to give birth to
> a perfect and powerful son.
> And when Eilithyia,
> who is in charge of a woman's pain,
> reached Delos,
> the labor pain seized Leto
> and she yearned to deliver.
> She threw her arms around the palm tree
> and knelt on the soft meadow.
> The earth laughed underneath her
> and the child jumped out
> towards the light.
> All the goddesses started cheering.

> —*The Hymn to Delian Apollo*, tr. Charles Boer.

Like other Pan-Hellenic Sanctuaries, such as Delphi and Olympia, Delos accumulated across the many centuries of its development a dazzling array of monumental structures and dedicated spaces: temples, agoras, stoas, shrines, treasuries, altars, sacred precincts, processional ways, a theater, a gymnasium, a stadium, and of course countless standing sculptures strewn throughout the complex. in all, there were three temples dedicated to Apollo, the grandest being the last and ultimately unfinished Temple of the Delians. Artemis too had her own temple here, as did Zeus and Athena, the Egyptian goddess Isis and even the thwarted but ever-feared Hera. The large green area in the far northeast portion of the complex was once a sacred lake, home to the swans and geese of Apollo and a focus of his cult. Banish the fantasy, of course, that the palm tree standing there today is a distant relation to the palm to which Leto clung when giving birth to her illustrious son (not to suggest that the authenticity of the tree is the weakest link in the story). One nearby landmark to look for is the Terrace of the Lions, a gift of the People of Naxos. Once, it is thought, nine of these reverently poised lions, exquisitely carved of fine Naxian marble, faced the Sacred Lake. They are signature icons of Delos; but the ones you see before you *in situ* are copies. Some of the weary and badly eroded originals can be seen in the on-site museum.

The less than inspiring truth about Delos today is that it is extremely complex, mostly reduced to ruin, and very poorly signed. Unless you take on a local guide, you are left to your own devices with very little illumination from on-site markers or panels, especially since nearly all are in Greek or French. The unavailability of any practically useful maps or printed guides on the island is inexplicable apart from the suspicion that visitors at a loss to find their own way are more likely to enlist the services of an on-site guide, for an additional fee, of course. We can hope that the situation has improved since our last visit, as Delos is a site that no one should fail to see or to appreciate. You will make your own best decision whether to take on a guide, but we will try to be as helpful as possible here to enable you to orient yourself within the site and to make some initial sense of it. The tiny site map provided with your entrance ticket will also likely be of some limited assistance.

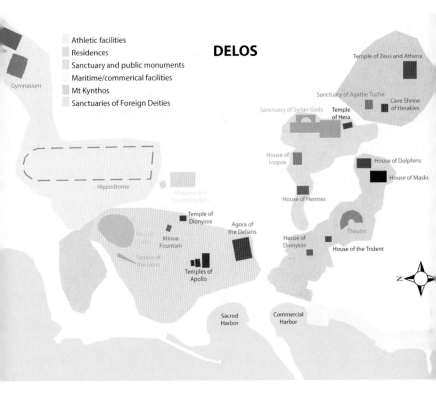

There are two principal opportunities to take your bearings and gain a perspective on the site as a whole. The first is when you step off the ship. This initial view of the sanctuary from the dock reveals certain landmarks that will become immediately more obscure or elusive once you enter the complexity of the site. In particular take note (at 2'clock as it were) of Mount Kynthos, on whose modest summit (112m) once stood the Temple of Zeus Kynthios and Athena Kynthia. Now, part way down the western slope of Mt. Kynthos you may discern a natural fissure or cave with a pitched roof formed by two massive granite slabs. This is the cave shrine of Herakles, which was also associated with the cult of Apollo. It is quite fascinating and is rarely ever visited, perhaps because it is invisible from just about every other point on the island except where you are presently standing. Mark its location now and your chances of reaching it will be greatly improved. In fact, we recommend, contrary to just about every other advice or direction you may be given, that you proceed first toward Mt. Kynthos, through the residential and theater district and up the ridge in the direction of the Temple of Hera. At that point in your climb when the path to the Temple of Hera and the Terrace of Foreign Gods leads off to the left, keep going straight up the stone steps a short distance until you come to an overgrown path on your right. You will notice a barely visible wall perhaps forty feet up and off to your right. Head towards that wall and you will find the cave shrine, which we at least consider quite intriguing. After exploring the cave shrine or abandoning the search for it, keep climbing to the summit where you will gain a second and even more privileged perspective on the entire Delos complex. From here you can decide on your own preferred plan for exploring the different precincts below. When you need a cool respite from the sun, the museum and adjacent tourist pavilion await you; and now is a good time to see exactly where they are, northwest of where you stand.

Our recommendation is to confine your explorations to the principal areas west of Mount Kynthos in the south and west of the museum in the north, and so to put aside any thoughts of visiting the ancient athletic facilities. Your time on Delos is limited to several hours and it's best to focus your attention on the areas of greatest density and importance. In the highly simplified plan provided here we highlight some of the monuments that we consider to be of greatest significance and interest. The division of the site into zones is not so precise as to suggest hermetically sealed units, but is rather to designate areas within which certain types of monuments or structures are concentrated.

Located 3km west of Mykonos (30-228-902-2259). Time and duration of visit to site and museum determined by boat captain; entrance costs included in excursion fee.

The Delos Archaeological Museum

The on-site museum collection includes items dating from the Mycenaean through the Roman Periods. Although many of the outstanding finds from the island have long since been removed to the National Archaeological Museum or to other world museums outside of Greece, there are a number of extraordinary items on view here, including five or six of the original marble lions from Naxian Terrace, worse for wear but still inspiring admiration if not awe. The torso of a kouros and two marble sphinxes, all from nearby Paros, are also quite impressive. You may also find interesting the collection of murals, household ornaments, and personal items from the Historic Period.

After leaving Delos you will be taken ferried to nearby Mykonos and left off for several hours before the return voyage to Naxos via Paros. Your time on Mykonos will be so limited that it is likely that the last door on which you will be inclined to knock is that of the Mykonos Archaeological Museum, located on Aghios Stefanos at the end of the harbor beyond the Leto Hotel. The museum was constructed to house, in particular, the finds from the "Purification Pit" in the necropolis of Reneia, remnants of the 426 B.C.E. Athenian purification of Delos. The museum's exceptional collection of vases includes a large 7th-century relief pithos with scenes depicting the Trojan horse and the fall of Troy. (30-228-902-2325) Open Tues–Sun 8:30–15:00 €.

DAY SEVEN

Today begins in museums and ends on beaches, with an exciting exploration of the island in between. That means an early rising and an ambitious pace until you call it a day and hit the sand. We assume that you noted our earlier mention that you would need a car (or motorcycle, if you are licensed and experienced) for today's excursion. Rental arrangements are best made well in advance; but last minute deals are not impossible except in times of greatest demand. Rental agencies tend to appear and disappear like mushrooms; so we recommend that you shop around and consult your hotelier. Keep in mind that not every road on Naxos is paved; so signing a contract restricting you to paved surfaces puts you at some financial risk, usually for nicks or dings from loose stones. Discussing this frankly with the agent should allow you to reach a resolution. The closest we will come to a personal recommendation is to say that we have been pleased with the service offered by Auto Tour Rent-a-Car in the Port of Knora (30-228-502-5480).

Our route directions for today's excursion will not replace the need for a map of the island. Free maps of the island are available from your hotel, the tourist office, and from auto rental agencies; but you would do far better to purchase the Road Editions (#111) 1:50 000 Map of Naxos. Otherwise, along with your free map you would do well to bring a pair of dice, which you will need to throw most every time you come to a crossing or fork in the road.

Unless you already explored one or both of them on Day Five, today's first stops will be the Mitropolis Site Museum and the Naxos Archaeological Museum. From there you will set out on a circuit of the island that will take you to two ancient sanctuaries—one dedicated to Dionysos and the other to Demeter—and to several sites where you can see ancient marble kouroi (male statues, often life-size or even colossal in scale) that never made it into temples, much less museums. The day's outing will involve, beyond ruins, a scenic tour of this most beautiful island, including a visit to the charming mountain village of Apiranthos, high on everyone's list of best-known Naxian secrets. Lastly, we will direct you to a string of expansive sandy beaches where you will be left to your own devices.

PRINCIPAL SITES

Mitropolis Site Museum

A few steps into this remarkable gem of a museum take you thousands of years into Naxian history and prehistory. Along ramps suspended above the excavations below, and with explanatory diagrams and at every turn, visitors are guided on a tour of Bronze Age Naxos. Unearthed, preserved, and open to view is the heart of the ancient Mycenaean city—hero-graves of its founders linking them to their past, fortification walls defending them from their enemies, pottery workshops, private dwellings, and family enclosures for the cult of ancestors. Every artifact here is left as and where it was found, allowing the visitor a rare sense of immediate discovery. The trades and rituals practiced on this spot are vividly described and explained, so that everything that is seen makes sense and reclaims its original context.

If we were entitled to bestow design awards on archaeological sites and museums, this would surely be among the recipients. Don't miss it. Outside the museum too, in Mitropolis Square, there are a number of panels enabling the visitor to imagine the fuller expanse of ancient Naxos, in its many stages of development across millennia. The museum represents, as it were, the surgically exposed open heart of the ancient city lying unseen but not forgotten beneath Aplomata, Grotta, and the sea.

Located in Metropolis Square, Khora (30-228-502-4151). €
Open Tues–Sun 8:30–15:00.

The Archaeological Museum of Naxos

While this fine museum's extensive collection spans the Late Neolithic through the Early Christian Period (5300 B.C.E. – 5th century C.E.), it is exceptionally rich in finds from the Early Cycladic (3200–2300 B.C.E.) and 12th-century Late Mycenaean Periods. The number and diversity of its Cycladic figurines, vases, and beaded jewelry rank it among the most important museums in Greece and beyond for the study of this period. Included in its Cycladic collection are a large number of figurines exceptional in their dimensions, proportions, and/or postures. One unusual type of Cycladic figurine, of which this museum has a surprising number, is that of a seated female. Most of these women are seated on benches, though one sits in an intricately detailed chair. In some the painted eyes are well

The Apollo Gate, Temple of Apollo Delios, Naxos

preserved, and some are looking backwards. The key here is not to be overwhelmed or discouraged by the sheer number of pots, and to focus instead on this museum's extraordinary Early Cycladic collection, regarded by many as second only to that of the National Archaeological Museum and containing some truly unique pieces.

Located in the Kastro (30-228-502-2725). Open Tues–Sun 8:30–15:00.

BEHIND THE WHEEL:

Once you have visited Khora's two fine archaeological museums, you will be ready to set out in search of today's first site destination, the Iria Sanctuary of Dionysos. From Khora take the road south towards the airport and Aghia Anna Beach and follow the signs that will appear for the temple, leading you along a rural road to the site. The crucial fork in your road will occur less than 2km from the port. At that point you bear left and proceed just under 2km until you see a sign to the site indicating a right turn.

The Dionysian Sanctuary of Iria

The recent (1982) discovery and on-going excavation of this pre-historic sanctuary of Dionysos have raised considerable interest and excitement among archaeologists. The communal worship of Dionysos here appears to have been an open-air cult from its Mycenaean beginnings to its Middle-Geometric II stage (1300–750 B.C.E.), when the first of four successive, superimposed houses of worship was constructed. This consisted of a one-room wood-and-brick structure, whose roof was supported by a row of central pillars. After only twenty years or so, this was replaced with a larger hall of mysteries, divided into four sections by three rows of columns running the length of the building. Along the outer walls of the structure, there were benches for worshippers. In roughly 680 B.C.E., still another hall replaced the second one. Again, this was a one-room structure, but with three aisles and a four-pillared portico. By the end of the 7th century, however, the cult had for some reason moved outdoors again and was focused on a four-sided clay hearth. Finally, early in the 6th century work was underway on an Ionic temple designed for the celebration of Dionysian mysteries. It is the remains of this temple that are still visible today.

The four successive phases of the temple hall at Iria are of extraordinary importance, as they document for the first time the first evolutionary stages of monumental temple architecture in Greece; and the fourth temple hall represents the earliest known Ionic prostyle marble temple in Greece. For architectural historians and archaeologists generally, as well as for historians of early Greek religion, Iria is no minor site.

The evolution of the temple of Dionysos here at Iria, as well as the even more recent discovery of an early archaic (7th-century) ritual dining hall are all presented and explained with vivid clarity on the site. This is a very accessible and well-designed archaeological park, where the emphasis is on instructing the visitor to appreciate the significance and import of the on-going discoveries here. It is not, however, a complex or extensive site; so your visit here is unlikely to a be prolonged.

Located under 4km south of Naxos town in Livadi (30-228-502-2725). € Open Tues–Sun 8:30–15:00.

BEHIND THE WHEEL:

The next destination is roughly 10km to the southwest. Return to the north-south road off of which you turned only a short distance to reach the Iria sanctuary. Turn right in the direction of Aghios Arsenios and Vivios. 2km south of Vivios, turn left (east) to Kato Sangri and Ano Sangri. From Ano Sangri follow signs to Dimitra's Temple and Museum.

The Sanctuary of Demeter and Kore and Archaeological Museum

Graciously situated in the island's central fertile plateau, this rural sanctuary, dedicated to the earth goddess Demeter and her daughter Kore, is a site of great significance. Fortunately, it is so well presented and explained to the visitor that none of that significance is lost on anyone who follows, panel by panel, the on-site self-guided tour. The entire site has been so beautifully landscaped and presented that to explore this sanctuary is as aesthetically delightful as it is deeply informative.

The original outdoor cult of Demeter and Kore was focused on the hilltop and dated from at least as early as the 8th century B.C.E. For even this early period the cult of Apollo was introduced here as an accompaniment to the mysteries of the Great Mother, perhaps in explicit acknowledgement of the contemporaneous creation of the polis or city-state of Naxos under the protection and patronage of Apollo. Evidence of the early open-air cult, such as twin offering pits, is preserved and presented to document the development of ritual here.

The sanctuary's partially restored temple of Demeter and Kore is rare in that over half of the structure's original marble has been preserved from antiquity. Like the earlier temples at Iria, this structure, dating from roughly 530 B.C.E., provides invaluable clues to the early evolution of marble temple architecture in Greece and, in particular, to the development of the Ionic order. A number of the ingenious curves and optical corrections later employed in the design of the Athenian Parthenon are already in evidence a century earlier here at Yiroulas, Sangri.

The Temple of Demeter and Kore, in form and function, is a *telesterion*, a sacred space designed for the celebration of the mysteries, in this case the mysteries of Demeter and Kore, for which the pan-Hellenic sanctuary and *telesterion* at Eleusis are more famed. Here, the roof of the hypostyle hall was supported by a central line of pillars. (See footprint of the temple structure below.) As this inner hall had no flat, interior ceiling, the supporting pillars were of varying height so as to extend to the pitched roof overhead. The roughly square temple was built entirely of marble, including the roof.

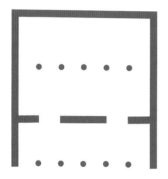

The elegantly simple and classy on-site museum here is an essential component of the sanctuary as it is experienced today. The preserved sculptural fragments and architectural elements from the temple serve to clarify and complete the visitor's comprehension of the design and construction of the temple, as well as its later conversion into a Christian basilica.

Located in the central valley of Naxos at Yiroulas, Sangri (30-285-502-2725). Open Tues–Sun 8:30–15:00.

The Archaic Kouroi of Appolonas and Flerio

BEHIND THE WHEEL:
The remainder of today's excursion is a combination of sightseeing and treasure hunt. The sightseeing component will take you along the mountainous spine of the island past Mt. Zas (Zeus), at 1,004m the highest peak in the Cyclades. We suggest that you stop for a stroll back through time in the marble mountain village of Apiranthos. Whether you find it in your heart to stop into the village's miniature archaeological museum is up to you. I'm sure visitors help to keep it

open and viable. In either event, Apiranthos is a fine place to stop for a late lunch, though it can become quite congested in high season. The treasures you are hunting for are several unfinished marble statues left to lie unfinished and abandoned for thousands of years as "seconds," rejected as broken or flawed. We will point you to a few of these and you can decide when you have had your fill. The first we will see is the most spectacular, measuring 11m in length.

Resuming our directions, from the Sanctuary of Demeter and Kore, return to Ano Sangri and proceed northeast just under 13km to Halkio, where you will join the main road from Naxos town. Turn right in the direction of Akadimi, Keramio, and Filotio, and proceed just over 10km to Apiranthos. After exploring Apiranthos, turn left back onto the main road, this time heading north in the direction of Koronos and Koronida. This road will treat you to spectacular mountain vistas that are not to be missed unless you are paralyzingly acrophobic. As Greek mountain roads go, this one is only modestly harrowing and offers far more in beauty than it exacts in fear. The journey north from Apiranthos to Apollonas, our next destination, is 26km. En route, in Skado, you will come to a confusing unsigned fork in the road. Either way will take you north. The lower road (right fork via Mesi) is a good deal less steep and winding and represents a reasonable shortcut if you find yourself short on time or nerves at this point. When you reach Apollonas, you may want to drive to the village and beach for a gaze at the northeast coast of the island. The first of our kouroi, and one that you should not pass by, is signposted on the left along the main road. It speaks for itself, though it could not be more silent. Now in an everlasting coma, this 11m marble colossus was once nearly chiseled into life and then abandoned in the 7th century B.C.E. It's feet alone stand taller than the average adult. Erect and complete it clearly would have taken the breath away.

Leaving Apollonas along the main road, in the direction of Aghia and Hilia Vrisi, proceed roughly 27km south along the west coastline of Naxos to Egares. Less than a kilometer south of Egares turn left (south) off the main road in the direction of Melanes, but follow signs to Kourounochori and

Myli, and eventually brown archaeological signs to the kouroi. Park in the lot by the road and go the rest of the way on foot so as to enjoy the lush green walkway to the kouroi, past the "Paradise Garden" of a local farmer, where he sells his own homemade citron, honey, and other local treats. The first kouros here, measuring a mere 6.4m lies in repose in the neighboring glade. This statue, thought to be of Apollo, is missing his left foot and a portion of his right leg. If you return to the green walkway, turn right, and continue on, you will come to a rocky slope on your right. A short uphill climb will bring you to two more stone figures. With these today's treasure hunt is complete, and all that remains is to choose your beach of choice along the west coast, south of Naxos town.

Naxos town

Retrace your route in the direction of Egares, turning left to rejoin the main road. This will take you in a matter of minutes back to Khora, where you should take the main south coastal road in the direction of the airport but following the coastline. The first beach that you will come to is St. George's (Aghios Georgios), followed by Aghios Prokopios, and Aghia Anna, from which you can walk to Plaka Beach. Its 5km carpet of white

WHAT BE THIS CITRON?

Citron is a buzz word on Naxos. You will see it on menus, in store windows, on shop signs, and if you are fortunate, you will be offered a taste. Citron or *Citrus Medica* was in the pre-Christian era the only citrus fruit cultivated in Europe. It was said to be brought to Greece by Alexander the Great, though he receives personal credit for far too many imports from the east. Just how spacious can one conqueror's shopping cart really be? Regardless, it has many uses. The fruit is quite acidic and is often used as a sort of vinegar for dressing fruit salads or marinating meat, though it can also be sweetened to make spoon-fed desserts and toothsome candies. The power of the plant, however, resides in its leaves to make a form of Greek "white lightning," not so potent as to be disabling but not so harmless as to disgrace the island of Dionysos. It is the signature liquor of Naxos, a matter of insular pride, so pretend to love it even if you don't. It is unlikely, however, that much pretense will be required.

sand along a nearly uninhabited and all but flawless coastline leaves it with no serious rival among the beaches of Naxos. The next beach south, Kastraki, has the reputation of being the cleanest in the Aegean. In general, the further south a beach is from Khora, the less crowded and more secluded it will be. Aghios Georgos, for instance, is in town and is often paved with beach mats. By the time you reach Plaka, however, some privacy is usually a clear option. Keep in mind, at the same time, that the farther you go from town the fewer swimsuits you will see in use. Nudity is never an obligation on Greek beaches but in some locations full swimsuits may seem as eccentric as raincoats. Explore the beaches of Naxos and you will easily and gladly find your place. Once you do, don't be surprised, as you drift off on the sand, if you entertain thoughts of staying longer, much longer or even forever, here in the Cyclades. In time, you may lose some of your initial sympathy for Ariadne, abandoned here to become the bride of Dionysos. You may even come to envy her.

SOURCES

Some Pre-exploration Suggestions

Since the seas and stones, palaces, temples, theaters, agoras and stadia of Greece are no longer resonant with relevant sounds and voices, it's important to bring those voices with you or rather within you as you go. Here are a handful of our favorite sources, intended for the general reader:

HISTORY

Minoans: Life in Bronze Age Crete, Rodney Castleden (Routledge)
Peoples of the Past: Minoans, J. Lesley Fitton (British Museum)
The Mycenaean World, John Chadwick (Cambridge)
The Mycenaeans, Lord William Taylor (Thames and Hudson)
A History of Greece to 322 B.C., N.G.L. Hammond (Oxford)
A Traveller's History of Greece, Timothy Boatswain and Colin Nicolson (Interlink)
Salt and Olives: Morality and Custom in Ancient Greece, John M. Dillon (Edinburgh)

ARCHAEOLOGY

Blue Guide: Crete, Pat Cameron (Norton)
Blue Guide Greece: The Mainland, Sherry Marker, James Pettifer (Norton)
Greece: An Oxford Archaeological Guide, Christopher Mee and Antony Spawforth (Oxford)
The Earth, The Temple, and the Gods, Vincent Scully (Yale)

ANCIENT LITERATURE

Works & Days and Theogony, Hesiod, tr. Stanley Lombardo (Hackett)
The *Iliad* and the *Odyssey*, Homer, tr. Stanley Lombardo (Hackett)
Also available on CD, read by the translator (Parmenides)
As a companion to Homer: *Celebrating Homer's Landscapes*, J.V. Luce (Yale)
The History, Herodotus, tr. David Green (Chicago)
The Peloponnesian War, Thucydides, tr. Rex Warner, (Penguin)

THE DRAMAS OF AESCHYLUS, SOPHOCLES, AND EURIPIDES

Specific recommedations:
Oresteia, Aeschylus, tr. Richmond Lattimore; *Theban Plays*, Sophocles, tr. Peter Meineck and Paul Woodruff (Hackett);
The Essential Euripides, tr. Robert Emmet Meagher (Bolchazy-Carducci)

ATHENS

Athens: A Cultural & Literary Companion, Michael Llewellen Smith
    (Interlink)

The Stones of Athens, R.E. Wycherley (Princeton)

Pericles of Athens and the Birth of Democracy, Donald Kagan
    (Simon & Schuster)

A Traveller's History of Athens, Richard Stoneman (Interlink)

FOR CHILDREN OR THE INNER CHILD

The many classic historical novels of Mary Renault, all available from
    Knopf: *King Must Die, Bull from the Sea, Fire From Heaven, Last
    of the Wine, Mask of Apollo*

Ancient Greece, Anne Pearson (DK)

Ancient Greece and the Olympics, Mary Pope Osborne and Natalie Pope
    Osborne (Random House)

Curious Kids Guides: Ancient Greece, Fiona Macdonald (Kingfisher)

D'Aulaires Book of Greek Myths, Ingri D'Aulaire and Edgar Parin
    D'Aulaire (Delacorte)

The Ancient Greece of Odysseus, Peter Connolly (Oxford)

A Greek Theater, Peter Chrisp (Raintree)

Lost in the Labyrinth, Patrice Kindl (Houghton Mifflin)

Island of the Minotaur, Sheldon Oberman (Interlink)

FOOD

Flavors of Greece, Rosemary Barron (Interlink)

Culinaria Greece: Greek Specialities, Editor Marianthi Milona
    (Konemann)

INDEX